Creative COMMUNICATION

PROJECTS IN ACTING, SPEAKING, AND ORAL READING

BY FRAN AVERETT TANNER

Author's Dedication

To My Father
Byron Lamont Averett
1907-1971

Fifth Revised Edition

Cover and Design by Todd Ricardo Kinney
Layout by Todd Ricardo Kinney and Elizabeth Peck

Photo and Illustration credits can be found on page 315, which constitutes a continuation of this copyright page.

Perfection Learning® Corporation
1000 North Second Avenue, P.O. Box 500
Logan, Iowa 51546-0500
Phone: 1-800-831-4190 • Fax: 1-800-543-2745
perfectionlearning.com
Printed in the U.S.A.

2 3 4 5 6 LO 06 05 04 03 02

ISBN 0931054-40-0 Papercover

Creativity is not just for the artistic or the gifted. It is for all people. It is a way of working, a way of thinking, a way of living.

Preface

To The Fifth Edition

While on the phone to a large company, one has only to try to get through to the correct department, while being besieged with numerous recorded messages and directions, before one ends up demanding of the computers, "Please let me talk to a human!"

Our "high tech" society with its increasing use of computers now seems to need more than ever before a reconnection on the human level. Schools are sensing the frustrated societal demands to train students in communication. Educators are being called upon to provide students the opportunity to explore the creative imagination and to think critically in the sharing of ideas and feelings.

Teenagers particularly must learn communication skills that will provide them with the expertise and confidence necessary for productive, happy adult lives. This book was written to provide such opportunity for today's teenage students. The assignments—all in the form of practical activities—help them to gain an understanding of the communication process and help them to function confidently in many verbal and nonverbal situations. Creative drama, speech, listening, and oral interpretation materials provide them with a wide range of communication experiences through which they can learn to interact successfully with others.

In addition, this text has been written for the teacher of speech and drama who believes that students learn best by getting on their feet and doing, but who finds it demanding to constantly activate students with imaginative material that stimulates creativity. Such claims on the teacher's resources are great. Yet class loads are frequently full and preparation periods shockingly short. This text will assist the busy teacher by providing numerous activities for student involvement. Each chapter features one major project plus many additional suggestions for further work. The assignments are basic and presented in detail. Everything the student needs to know in preparing and presenting the activity is given in easy-to-follow steps. The teacher need not be harassed by students asking questions about the assignment. The students need not be confused by lack of necessary information. When they read each chapter, they know what is expected of them.

All projects require careful student preparation. The requirements are not easy. At first, many students may grumble because they must think out their project in advance, organize it on the activity sheet provided in the teacher's manual, and—except for improvisations—rehearse it. They will learn, however, that only through such preparation can they be successful; and they will succeed if they meet the assignments, which have been used in schools around the nation and in other English speaking locales.

With this book the teacher is released from spending precious time on activity details. Therefore, the teacher is free to provide the special attention that students need if they are to become resourceful, self-confident, and responsible individuals in their role as communicators!

This fifth edition includes updated classroom videos, updated source material and addresses for theatre, speech, and interpretation needs, and a current bibliography. There are also contemporary suggestions for speech topics, some additional project items, and new outline samples for the speeches. The feature "What's In a Word?" has been expanded and applicable cartoons have been used. The Word Bank has a new icon to help draw students' attention to key words.

ACKNOWLEDGEMENTS

This text is a compilation of my experiences as a student and teacher of speech, drama, and oral interpretation. Some of the projects are of my own invention; others I have borrowed from numerous teachers in the field who in turn, no doubt, have at times borrowed from their teachers. For example, the "mirror" improvisation is believed to be original with Stanislavski, but that exercise now appears in the books of Rapoport, Spolin, Benedetti, Held, Hansen and Contrucci. Some of the drama activities that I have used in this text I observed while studying theatre in England, both in professional schools (Royal Academy of Dramatic Art, London Academy of Music & Dramatic Art, and Central), in child drama (Peter Slade and his colleagues), and in community theatre (British Drama League). Other exercises I have adapted from Viola Spolin's *Improvisations for the Theatre* and from the numerous classes and workshops in which I have participated.

To all these people and the many other unnamed influences I give my thanks and acknowledge my indebtedness. Specifically, I wish to acknowledge Karl Robinson and Charlotte Lee, *Speech in Action*, for the information in the debate chapter; Irene Coger, *Readers Theatre Handbook*, for the term "theatre of the mind" used in Chapter 48; and Kay Jensen Nubel for the radio program format idea in Chapter 43.

For reprint rights I wish to thank Wayland Maxfield Parrish and John Wiley and Sons for the verse in Chapter 45, Tim Bryson for the script that begins Chapter 48, Kathleen Ramonda and the Speech Communication Association for the Listening Quiz, and United Feature Syndicate for the "Peanuts" cartoons.

It is with warm appreciation that I acknowledge my indebtedness to Clark and Flora Carlile.

I am especially grateful and give my heartfelt thanks to my late husband, Marion, and to my mother, Lois Averett Fisher, for their constant encouragement, assistance, and kindness.

Fran Averett Tanner
Twin Falls, Idaho

Dr. Fran Averett Tanner

ABOUT THE AUTHOR

Fran Tanner is professor of speech and drama at the College of Southern Idaho and chairman of that department. She has an M.A. in speech and a Ph.D. in theatre. Dr. Tanner teaches in both areas, directs conventional and Readers Theatre, and coaches forensics. Dr. Tanner has been a Fulbright scholar to England, received the national Woman of Achievement award, was named an Idaho Distinguished Citizen, is listed in the Outstanding Educators of America Index, and served as a U.S. delegate to the International Amateur Theatre Congress in Austria. She has been named recipient of the Teaching Excellence Award at the College of Southern Idaho and was given a Professional Achievement Award from Idaho State University. She has conducted workshops in the U.S. and abroad. At the College of Southern Idaho she has directed more than 60 drama productions, and her speech students have been national forensics winners.

Table

Contents

◆ UNIT 2: SPEECH ◆

◆ UNIT 3: ORAL INTERPRETATION ◆

◆ APPENDIXES ◆

Student

Introduction

Imagine yourself standing at one end of a living room. At the other end sits a person whom you like very much. Maybe that person is someone you want to date, or a good friend who is feeling sad, or your elderly relative who is ill. You have an intense desire to indicate to that person your affection towards him or her. How do you respond? What are the ways you have of transferring the feelings and ideas inside you to the outside world, where they can be shared with people? In other words, how do you *communicate*?

In this class you are going to study communication, the interaction or sharing of ideas and feelings between you and the people around you. There are numerous ways to communicate.

1 You communicate by ***symbols*** that "stand for" something you have experienced. You use both audible and visual symbols. Words, whistles, laughter, grunts are audible symbols, the ones that ears pick up and translate. For example, if you hear the audible symbol "chalk," you translate that to mean the object your teacher uses to write on the board. Visual symbols are picked up by your eyes. Turn off the sound on your television set and you are receiving only the visual symbol. Pictures, paintings, statues, books are all visual symbols.

2 You communicate by ***movement and gestures*** of your body. You nod your head, point your finger, smile, wink, shrug your shoulders, and frown, and by so doing you transfer meaning. The old adage "actions speak louder than words" is often true.

3 You communicate by physical ***touch***. When you pat someone on the back, shake hands, put an elbow in someone's ribs, or tap a shoulder, you make yourself understood.

4 You communicate by ***silence***. If your teacher asks you a question and you fail to respond, your silence tells much.

5 You communicate in the way you use ***space***. The distance you place yourself from others transfers meaning. You move toward people you like. You separate yourself from strangers, from those of higher rank, or from those you dislike.

6 You communicate with your use of ***time***. In our culture if you are early for an appointment, you transfer one meaning. If you are late for an appointment or fail to arrive at all, you express something entirely different.

7 You communicate with the silent language of ***color***. Scientists say the dominant color of our environment affects the communication that takes place. "Cool" colors of green, blue, and gray encourage meditation and quietness, thus lessening the degree of communication. "Warm" colors such as red, orange, and yellow stimulate creativity and make people feel more responsive to each other.

8 You communicate with your ***choice of clothes***. If you show up at a formal dinner in shorts and a sweat shirt, you are communicating not only something about yourself, but your attitude toward the occasion, your host, and the other guests.

So you see, there are numerous ways for humans to transfer meaning. In this class you will explore the basic communicative areas and learn how to use them effectively. Unit 1 stresses Creative Theatre and focuses primarily on physical and nonverbal communication. Units 2 and 3 stress Speech and Oral Interpretation, primarily focusing on intellectual and verbal communication. In all of these areas you will learn how to respond to yourself and your environment—to make you an effective communicator.

UNIT I

Creative Theatre

Chapter 1

Breaking the Ice

evaluate
improvisation
creative
side coaching
focal point
simultaneous
"freeze"
spontaneous

Watch for these valuable words wherever you see the word bank icon. 

BRAIN TEASERS

(1) What is the difference between existing and living?
(2) What are the eight rules for the acting games?

CUE SHEET

You are breathing and moving. But are you *alive*? Are you alive to the world inside of you? The world around you? The world beyond you? Or do you fit the category of those who feel they are a breathing corpse, a dull robot secluded in a self-made coffin?

Living is quite different from existing. Really to live during your life, to be really happy and successful requires two qualities:

(1) An ability to respond creatively—to yourself and your environment.
(2) An ability to communicate with others—to share ideas and feelings.

The exercises, games, and improvisations in this drama section will help you achieve the above two qualities of total awareness and response, developing a *creative* and communicative You. The assignments will mainly be *improvisations* where you make up action and words on the spur-of-the-moment in order to achieve the game's goal. As in any game, there are certain ground rules that the participants—you, your classmates, and your teacher—must accept. Here they are:

(1) **Work toward the focal point.** In each improvisation you will have a specific *focal point* or goal on which to concentrate, allowing you to be successful at one thing at a time. All of your powers and energy must be directed toward that focal point. Your whole being should be absorbed by it. In so doing, you will solve the problem or achieve the goal.

(2) **Do anything you wish within the focal point and the rules.** Complete freedom is yours as long as you stay within these rules and the specific goal of your activity. Don't worry about "making a fool" of yourself. Anything goes. There is no right or wrong way to solve the acting problem. What you must strive for is an effective way—and there may be many of those. So you will want to respect what your classmates are doing, even if it is different from what you are doing. In turn, they will respect your activity. Remember, everyone has his or her own special way. Do your own thing; do not copy others. If what you are doing works well within the rules, continue. If not, change it.

(3) **Believe what you are doing—and do it in a believable way.** Even if you are seeing imaginary things, believe them. Work toward truth in every situation.

(4) **Create a spirit of working together.** Most of the improvisations must be done as a group, working in harmony. You are not competing with each other, but contributing in a stimulating way to the solution of the problem. Even the audience is part of the experience, for you must share with them if communication is to take place. Accept your responsibility as a valuable group member. If you make wisecracks or clown or manipulate others, you are hindering, not helping the group. Remember, these activities are not "kid stuff." These same games and improvisations are used in professional acting courses.

(5) **Respond to *side coaching*.** Your teacher will serve as a guide or director, sometimes being part of the acting group and sometimes being part of the audience. When seeing your needs or those of the scene, your teacher will "side coach" you with a voice command that you are to obey. When you hear side coaching, don't stop what you are doing. Just listen to what is being said and keep on with the scene, adjusting to the command.

In side coaching, your teacher is not suggesting that you are doing something good or bad, but rather is helping you to develop and communicate the specific thing you are doing. Side coaching is completely *spontaneous*, arising from what is going on at that moment. Examples are, "Really see the apple tree. Feel the bark, its roughness. Touch the smooth leaves. Reach high for the fruit." "Share your voice with us." "Feel with your knees, your toes, your whole body." "Concentrate on your focal point." "Talk to each other. Pursue that point."

(6) **Limit pre-planning.** In all of these exercises you will be given a problem to solve through a focal point. The only plans you need to make involve structure:

(a) Where the scene takes place.
(b) When it takes place.
(c) Who is there.
(d) What is happening.

You do not plan *how* the problem is solved. That develops out of what you do on the spur-of the-moment as you play the scene. It is similar to a game of basketball; you know the structure, but the game develops only as you play it.

(7) ***Evaluate* yourself throughout these drama sessions**. Are you truly focusing on the goal? Are you really believing? Are you contributing to the group? Are you creating in your own special way?

Your teacher and classmates will help you evaluate as the scenes progress, and there will be questions and checklists on your creative growth. Accept these suggestions and build from them. They will help you to keep alert as to your accomplishments and your needs.

ACTIVITIES

To break the ice your first exercises will be involved with movement in a group, attuning your body to respond to your imagination. If it is possible to work in a large empty room, each class member can participate *simultaneously*. If you must work in smaller spaces or at the front of the room and down the aisles, count off into groups of 10 to 15. Groups will take turns participating and observing.

Read the exercises below so you can respond to side coaching when your teacher selects which ones you are to do. All class members should work apart and simultaneously, using all available space. Participate without talking or giggling. Concentrate on what you are doing and on the side coaching. Exercises demand total concentration and use of imagination.

Wake-up
Show us one thing that might wake you up in the morning if there were no alarm clocks.

Play Day
Close your eyes and concentrate on a beautiful summer day. See the blue sky and the fluffy clouds. Feel the faint warm breeze. Open your eyes and show us in your own special way an activity—other than lying down—that you would like to do on such a day.

Brushes

(1) Show us how you used one brush this morning as you got ready for school.
(2) Show us how to use a cleaning brush.
(3) Show us how to use one household brush.
(4) Show us how to use a brush associated with certain occupations.

Magic Pin

See the imaginary straight pin in front of you on the floor. Pick it up and use it for something. Now the pin changes. Use it according to the suggestions of your teacher. It may become a conductor's baton, broom, fishing rod, tennis racket, shovel.

Balloon Blowup

(1) Concentrate on the color, the shape, and the feel of a limp balloon. You are to become that balloon, starting from an empty state and filling completely up with air on the last of three blows your teacher makes. When you are filled to capacity, *"freeze"* (hold your position without moving). When your teacher calls "puncture," let the air escape as would a balloon punctured with a pin.

(2) Repeat, but this time lose air as a balloon slashed with a knife.

Balloon Toss

(1) Stand in a circle, facing in. The teacher will toss a real balloon to one person who will gently strike it towards another in the circle. Repeat until all have participated. Remove the balloon and redo with an invisible balloon, recreating the real situation.
(2) See an imaginary balloon floating immediately above your head. You jump and stretch to catch it, but it always bobs away. Move around the room in your attempts to get it.

Numbers

To soft slow music, print giant numbers from one to ten in the air. Using your whole body, stretch way up, kneel down, and travel a great distance in the room to make these huge numbers. Put your whole body into it. Don't worry if others finish before you. Just continue the consecutive printing until you are done.

Stamp and Tramp

Place one person at the end of the room. At the opposite end, you, with a group of nine or ten people, will advance towards that person while you and the group loudly say "Stamp" as you walk on the right foot and "Tramp" as you walk on the left foot. Repeat until your group is close to the single person. Stop, remain quiet, look at the person, and then intuitively retreat as a group in slow motion, repeating the word "Shuffle."

We're Coming

Divide into two groups, each at opposite ends of the room. If possible, have the stationary group standing on steps or levels. Starting in a bent-over position, the other group members advance, repeating, "We're coming," in a crescendo pattern as they slowly straighten up during their advance. When they are very close to the stationary group, that group raises its arms and loudly commands, "No." The advancing group now retreats slowly and quietly, while looking into the faces of those who said "No."

Music and Movement

(1) If possible, dim the lights or draw the shades. With eyes closed, sit quietly and listen to the recording of classical music your teacher will play. Concentrate on what the music says to you. Move your body to the music only when you completely feel it. Then get up, open your eyes, and move any way the music tells you. Do not dance. Just respond physically to the sound.

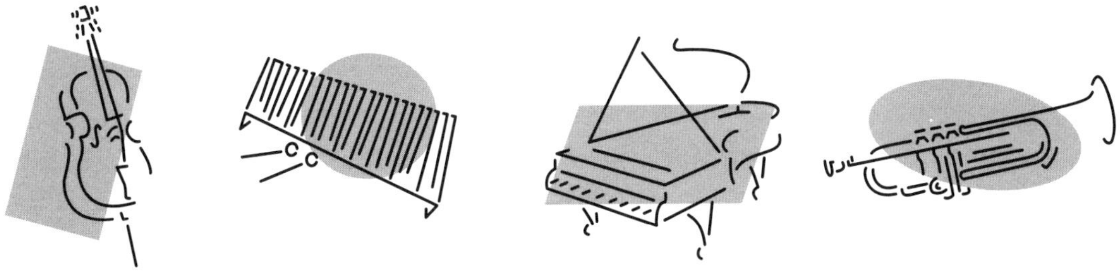

(2) Repeat, using sound effect recordings.

Exploring

One class member sits cross-legged in the center of the floor with head bowed. The teacher will use a sound maker—a guitar, tambourine, rattle, drum. You and your classmates should walk to the wall and stare at it. As the sound begins, it attracts you and the others. You move about the room, look at each other, exploring with the eyes, but never touching. As you explore, walk around the student sitting in the center on the floor. Pass by, but never look at that person. When the sound reaches a loud climax and stops, everyone "freezes." The center student slowly gets up and stretches arms toward the sky. Those close, touch the student's arms and the arms of other actors, until everyone is touching another person's arm.

Chapter 2

Trapped

WORD BANK

concentration **imagination** **flexible** **"curtain"** **inner resources**

Watch for these valuable words wherever you see the word bank icon. 

BRAIN TEASERS

(1) How can an actor's training help you, even if you don't intend to become an actor?
(2) What is involved in training an actor?
(3) Why must an actor believe what he or she is doing?
(4) What is the value of warmups?

CUE SHEET

Acting is fun, and so is the training that goes along with it. An actor's training aims at stimulating the powers of imagination, observation, sensory recall, and concentration. These are the *inner resources* from which actors draw material for evolving a role. Actors must have a vivid imagination in order to put together every day qualities in a unique way. They must be able to observe life situations and store them up for later use on stage. They must be able to recall at will how things taste, smell, feel, etc. And they must be able to concentrate deeply on the scene situation in order to create a believable character.

Besides working on these inner resources, an actor conditions his or her body and voice to be flexible, coordinated, and expressive in countless situations. Only with such training can actors meet the strenuous demands of long intensive hours of rehearsal and performance.

What an actor learns, any individual can use and be the richer for it. The more sensitive our inner resources and the more expressive our bodies and voices, the better we can meet life.

So hop upon the actor's trunk. Learn how to extract meanings from the world around you, how to transform these impressions into something that is uniquely yours, and finally how to communicate these special feelings and ideas inside you to your fellow humans for a shared experience.

The first thing to learn about acting is *you must believe whatever you do*. Only when your actions are believable to *you* can they be believable to anyone else—a fellow actor or an audience member. So you must see within your imagination everything about the scene—where you are, what things look like, who you are, what you want, and who the others are. In the following exercises, strive to believe whatever you are called upon to do.

WARMUPS

The class procedure should be as follows. Upon entering class, immediately and quietly do the basic body warmup routine detailed in Appendix A. Class members may participate simultaneously. Don't skip this step, as it is most important to condition yourself for the other activities.

After warming up, as a class do each of the following group warmup improvisations that prime you for the main project.

Tug of War
Count off into teams of equal number. Team members should stand in front of each other in a line, facing a similarly placed team. Using an imaginary rope that you can believably see and feel in your mind, pull together as hard as you can to take the rope from the other team. Be careful that the rope does not stretch. Following your teacher's side coaching, when one side gets the advantage, the other must give. Make the tug so believable to you, that at the end of the game, you'll feel tired from the strong physical exertion. Think only of what you are doing. Don't talk. Put all your energy on the tugging.

Focal Point: See and feel the imaginary rope until it becomes real.

Ladder Climb

Simultaneously with your classmates, climb a tall, imaginary ladder. Stretch your arms and hands to the rung above, pulling yourself up and balancing with your feet on the rungs below. Concentrate completely on what your body is doing. Feel your shoulders lift and your arms move up. Feel your fingers stretch to grasp the ladder. Feel your feet heavy on the rungs. Climb to the top and look down, surveying the situation below. Then climb slowly down, concentrating on every move, believing what you are doing.

Focal Point: Feel every muscle you have as you climb and descend the imaginary ladder.

Grandstand

Count off into two or three teams. Each group decides a sport they want to watch. When the first group is ready, it goes to the playing area, calls *"curtain"* and begins. Each team member *individually* watches the sport that is taking place some distance away.

Focal Point: Actually see the sport. See it with your arms, your feet, your face, your whole body. Make it believable to you.

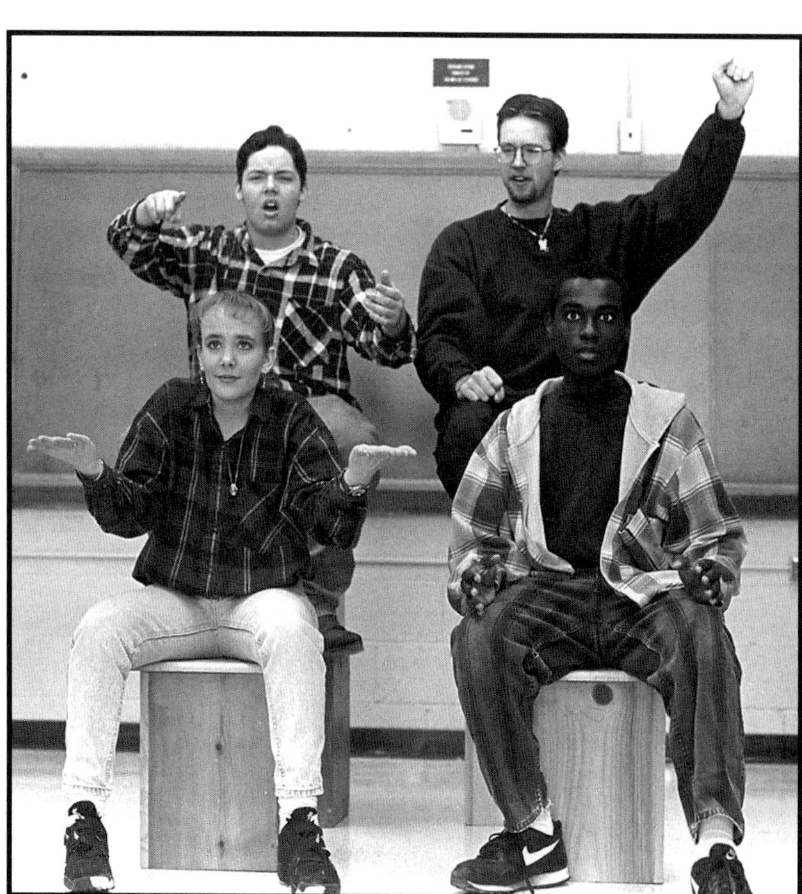

ACTIVITY AND ITS PURPOSE

Trapped
In this one minute improvisation you are to make believable your efforts to escape from a place where you are trapped.

Focal Point: Use your whole body in trying to escape.

HOW TO PREPARE

Decide where you are trapped and in your mind see everything about that place. Is it a box, well, a pit, a telephone booth, a cave? Of what is it made? Is it concrete, earth, steel? What does it look like and feel like? What is its size? Are the sides straight? Do they slant? Is there light? How did you get there? How long have you been trapped?

Fill in the activity sheet distributed by your teacher and hand it in.

HOW TO PRESENT

After the whole class warms up, your teacher will call on you for the "Trapped" project. Hand in your activity sheet and quietly go to the playing area. With your back to the class, close your eyes and see the place that entraps you. When you can believe it, open your eyes, call "curtain," turn towards the class, and begin your attempts to escape. Concentrate intensely on escaping from the enclosure. Do not worry about how you look. This is an acting exercise and not a performance Make everything you do believable to yourself. Strain, grunt, scream, claw, climb, dig—whatever is necessary to escape. Use your whole body. Escape with your elbows, your ears, your back, your legs, your face—the whole you straining to get away.

An actor is as great as their imagination.

Chapter 3

The Machine

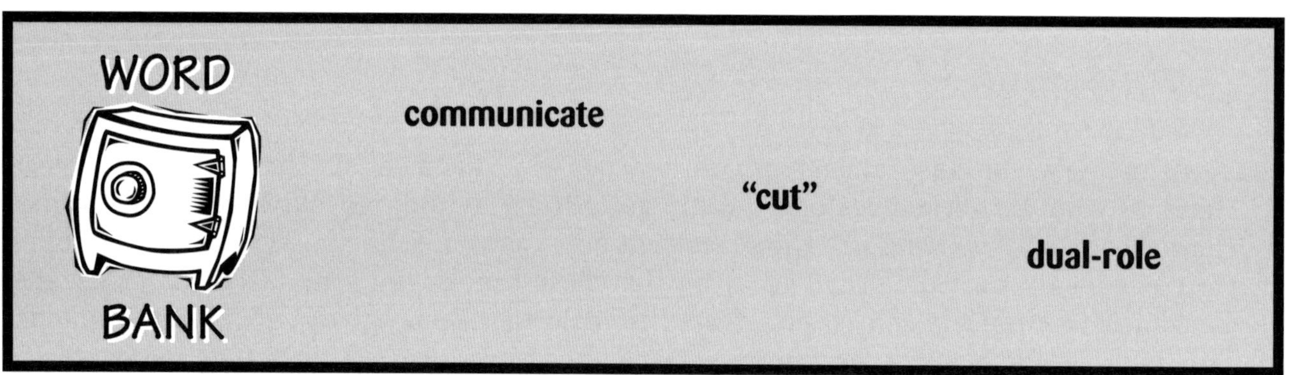

Watch for these valuable words wherever you see the word bank icon. 

BRAIN TEASERS

(1) What does communication mean?
(2) How does an actor generally communicate?
(3) What is an actor's dual-role?

CUE SHEET

Not only must actors believe what they are doing, they must communicate that belief to the others around. By communicating we mean you share or transfer your thoughts and feelings so that your fellow actors and audience members can think and feel as you do. To transfer thoughts and feelings, an actor relies mainly on *physical action*. This differs from a public speaker who relies more on the telling than on the showing. Both actors and speakers communicate—they must stress different methods.

When actors show a message through the use of the body, they must be aware not only of what they are doing in the scene, but also on how they are interrelating. Acting is seldom a solo performance. It is a group endeavor where every player is needed to show the story.

To achieve group playing, you must perform a *dual-role* of concentrating on your own contribution, while at the same time being aware and responding to others in the scene. A spirit of teamwork must prevail.

WARMUPS

Upon entering class, immediately and quietly complete the basic body warmup routine in Appendix A. Then as a class, do the following warmups to condition yourself for the main project.

No Hands
Count off in groups of three or four. As a group decide on an inanimate object that you can move without the use of your hands. Example: a large trunk, a big boulder, a car, a piece of furniture.

Focal Point: Move the object without using hands.

Ball Toss
Count off in groups of three or five. As a group decide the size and weight of an imaginary ball. Toss the ball among yourselves, being sure you see and feel the ball. Use your whole body in tossing it. When the game is in progress your teacher will side coach, suggesting different weights and sizes for the ball. Respond accordingly.

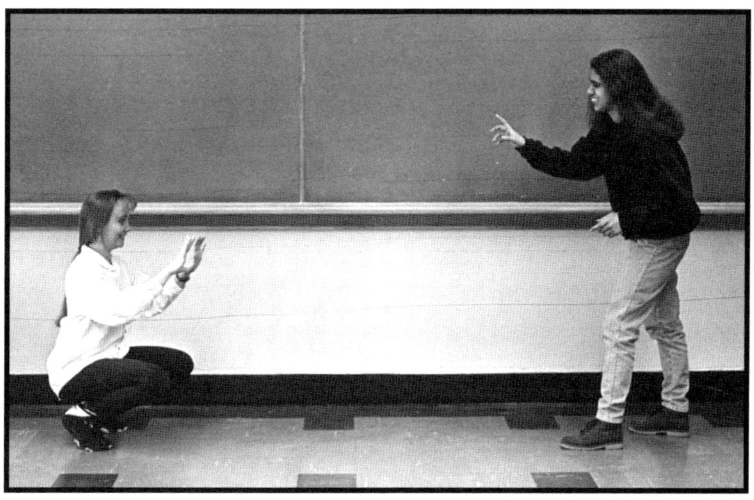

Focal Point: Concentrate on the size and weight of the ball.

ACTIVITY AND ITS PURPOSE

The Machine
You are to move as if you are a working part of a machine. Make your actions so believable that your classmates will know what you are doing. As you continue your action, others will approach one at a time and add another part of the machine.

Focal Point: Concentrate on your body's movement as it mechanically duplicates a working machine part, coordinating with the other players.

HOW TO PREPARE

Outside of class, watch at least two machines work—perhaps a car, a cement mixer, a lawn mower, a clock. Notice the various moving parts (piston, gears, wheels, etc.), their placement, rhythm, sound. Choose one machine and fill out the activity sheet to this chapter.

HOW TO PRESENT

Hand your activity sheet to your teacher. After warmups, your teacher will select someone to start the game. If you are selected, quietly go to the playing area and begin moving as one part of the machine you have chosen. Continue your movement as other players add to your machine until your teacher calls "cut." Repeat with a different player starting and moving as a different machine.

If you are not chosen to begin, carefully watch the actor at work. As soon as you think you know what he or she is doing, quietly go to the playing area and become another working part, coordinating with the action that is already going on. Concentrate on your movement. Do not waste energy in talking or giggling.

Chapter 4

Double Image

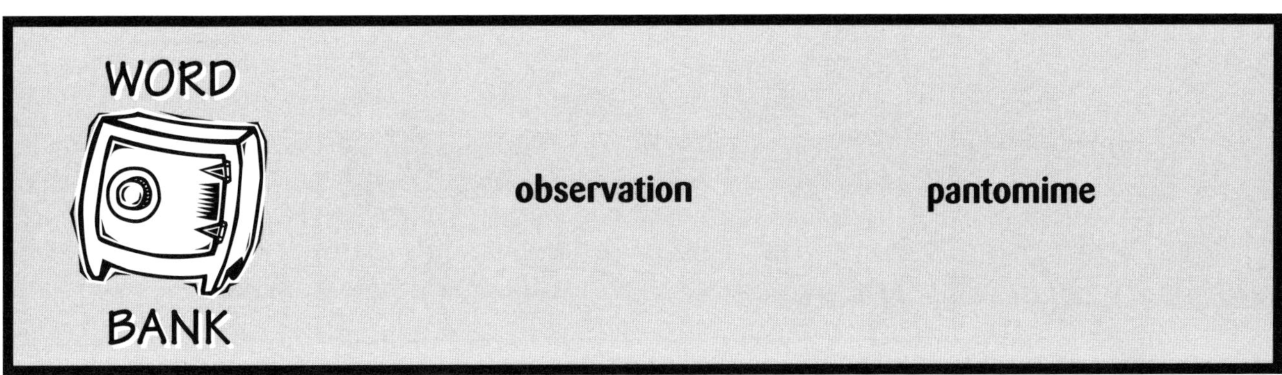

Watch for these valuable words wherever you see the word bank icon. 

BRAIN TEASERS

(1) What is the difference between "seeing" and "observing"?
(2) What are the advantages to developing your powers of observation?

CUE SHEET

People who can see are sometimes still "blind," for they have not learned how to *observe*. Observation means more than just seeing. It means to study closely whatever you are looking at, with the intent of remembering the details. Developing your powers of observation will not only make you a more sensitive, well informed person, but will give you a storehouse of ideas to use in acting. If you portray a machine, having closely observed one will give you ideas of what to do. If you must create on stage an old person, you will have a better idea of how to do so if you have scrutinized old people as they walk, sit, laugh, read, eat, and talk.

How accurate an observer are you? Close your eyes and right now see if you know what is on the bulletin board of your classroom. What was your mother wearing at breakfast this morning? What one beautiful thing did you notice on your way to or from school today?

Most people have neglected developing their powers of observing accurately. Conflicting reports of witnesses to an accident prove this. Test your powers of observation by studying the pencil drawing below for just one minute. At the end of that time, list the "wrong" things you find in the drawing. There are 9 of them. The answers are printed at the end of this chapter.

The following improvisations will help you to become a better observer.

WARMUPS

Upon entering class, immediately and quietly begin to go through the basic body warmup routine. Then as a class, do each of the following to condition yourself for the main project.

Quick Switch
Divide the class into two groups that sit and face each other in a row. Without talking, carefully observe the person opposite you as to dress, hair, jewelry, etc. On a signal from your teacher, turn your back to your partner. Each player is to make three changes in his or her appearance, such as untying a shoelace, switching a ring to another finger, buttoning a sweater, changing the hair style. Face your partner again and take turns identifying the alterations. Change partners and repeat, making four changes this time. Continue to change until you reach four or five changes.

Focal Point: Carefully observe your partner's appearance to detect changes.

Table Objects
Divide the class into two or three groups that can encircle a table on which the teacher has placed 15 to 20 everyday objects such as a pen, vase, toothbrush, hammer, stick of gum. You have just one minute to study the objects before your teacher covers them and you return to your desk, listing as many as you can on paper. Check to see who has the most accurate list.

Focal Point: Observe and remember all of the objects on the table.

Magic Object
Count off into groups of eight to ten, with each group standing in a large circle. If space does not permit several groups working simultaneously, use one group at a time with the other class members sitting inside the large circle and quietly observing. The first player selects an imaginary object and uses it. When the player on the right knows what the first player is doing, he or she picks up the action and repeats it. When that person obviously has the action, player one stops. Now the second player continues the original action until it gradually works into a similar but different movement. When the third player knows what the second action is, he or she begins it, uses it, and then alters it slightly. Continue around the circle. Example: casting a fly fishing rod may develop into directing with a musical baton, that may be altered to painting with a brush.

Focal Point: Concentrate on the movement you copy and gradually let it change of its own accord into something different.

Eye Spy
Count off into partners. Sit close together, facing each other. Look directly and closely into your partner's eyes, describing what objects you see reflected in them. Reverse roles.

Focal Point: Put all your powers of observation on reporting what reflections you see in your partner's eyes.

Mirror
Stand and face a partner, establishing direct eye contact. Begin slow under-water-like movements of arms, hands, and body—bending, twisting, walking, using the space around you. Your partner is the mirror and must reflect exactly all of your movements. Do this quietly without talking or laughing. Try to communicate with your eyes the new action you will initiate. Strive to work together as a unit, being careful not to trick your partner with quick movements. At a command from your teacher, reverse roles. In later sessions, mirror facial expressions, sounds, or have five or six players serve as mirrors that stand diagonally to the initiator.

Focal Point: Observe your partner to create exact mirror reflections of the whole body.

ACTIVITY AND ITS PURPOSE

Double Image
You are to present a one-minute prepared pantomime (a scene without words) in which you do a short simple everyday activity. Your classmates will observe your actions, and when you are through, one of them will be called upon to repeat exactly what you have just done. This exercise checks your powers of observation.

Focal Point: As the actor, concentrate on your action, making everything you do believable to you and the audience. As the spectator, carefully observe the scene so you can recreate it.

HOW TO PREPARE

(1) Choose a simple and short everyday activity that demands clear-cut actions. Examples include:

(a) Brushing your teeth
(b) Sewing on a button
(c) Dialing a phone number
(d) Putting on a coat
(e) Making a peanut butter sandwich

(2) Using the real article, actually do what you have chosen. Really brush your teeth or really put on your coat. As you do the action, carefully observe what you do. With which hand do you pick up your coat? How heavy is it? What does it feel like? Do you sling it over your shoulder? Which arm goes in first? Do you button it up or down? How many buttons? Is there a zipper or a hook? Repeat the activity until you know exactly every movement you do.

(3) Outline the step-by-step actions on the activity sheet to this chapter.

(4) Now without the real object, rehearse the pantomime. Make the imaginary situation real to you. Reconstruct it vividly in your mind. Pay attention to details. Don't walk through doors. Don't leave items in midair. Carefully communicate with your body, so the spectators will recognize your actions. They must know what you are doing, not just make a guess at it.

HOW TO PRESENT

Hand your activity sheet to your teacher. When you are called on, quietly go to the playing area. Set up necessary chairs or tables, making sure their position will place you facing the audience. Now turn your back to the class and take a moment to prepare yourself. Call "curtain." Turn around and do your pantomime.

When you are finished and return to your seat, your teacher will call on a classmate to reproduce exactly what you have done. Afterwards, the class may wish to discuss briefly the degree of accuracy.

Carefully observe the other class pantomimes, as you will be called on to recreate one of them.

Answers To Observation Puzzle On Page 16.

1. The birthday banner says 12th birthday, and the cake says 11th.
2. The exclamation point on the banner is upside down.
3. The second P in Happy on the banner is backwards.
4. There is a balloon missing from one of the strings the girl in the middle is holding.
5. The boy on the left is holding his gift upside down.
6. The boy on the left has one pants leg shorter than the other.
7. The table is missing one leg.
8. The girl on the right is wearing her party hat on her face.
9. The girl in the center has on one low top shoe, and one high top shoe.

Chapter 5

I Sense It!

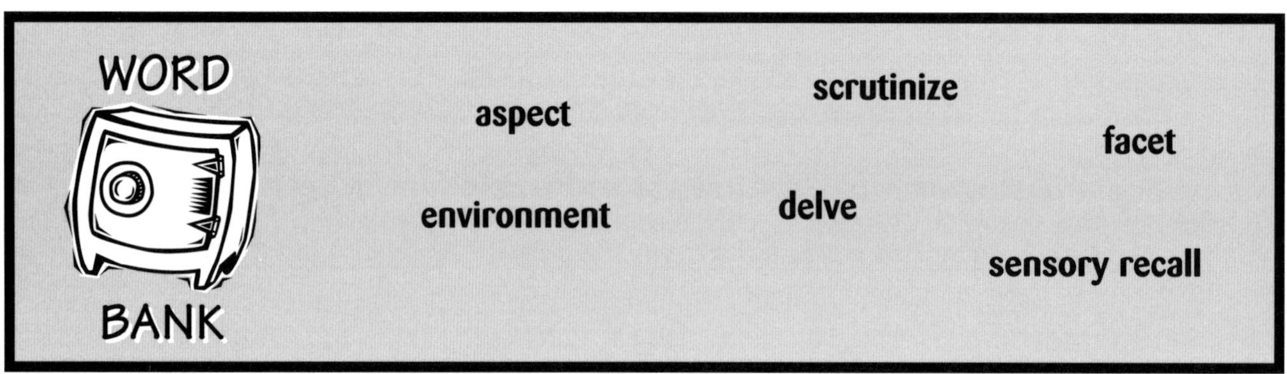

WORD
BANK
aspect
scrutinize
facet
environment
delve
sensory recall

Watch for these valuable words wherever you see the word bank icon. 

BRAIN TEASERS

(1) What are the five basic senses?
(2) What benefits will you get from sharpening your senses?
(3) How does an actor use sensory recall?

CUE SHEET

How do you perceive the world? You look. You hear. You taste. You smell. You touch. These are the basic five senses that channel the environment into you. The more aware you are of what your senses tell you, the more informed you are to communicate.

Besides receiving the material, the ability to *recall* sensory experiences is important to an actor. The theatre features artificial scenery and properties, but the actor must respond as though they were real. The forest on stage may be painted canvas, but the trained actor recalls the smells and sounds of a real forest, in order to communicate in a believable way.

The improvisations in this chapter will help you to sharpen your senses, as well as to stimulate your powers of imagination, observation, and concentration.

WARMUPS

Upon entering class, immediately and quietly complete the basic body warmup routine. Then as a class, do the following:

Listening

(1) Close your eyes and quietly sit for one minute, listening to the sounds around you. After the minute is over, compare the sounds you heard.

Focal Point: Really hear the sounds around you.

(2) One person will start humming a tune, then another will hum a different tune until each class member is simultaneously and quietly humming a tune. At first listen only to yourself. Then try to concentrate on the tunes being hummed around you, while continuing to hum your own.

Focal Point: Repeatedly hum a tune while listening to those hummed by your neighbors.

Tasting

(1) Count off into groups of four or five, with each group deciding on something simple to eat. The groups will take turns going to the playing area, calling "curtain" and proceeding to eat, taste, and smell the food they decided on. No talking. Just action. Feel the food in your mouth, feel it as you swallow. Chew it. Taste it.

(2) Your teacher will call out different tastes. Truthfully recall them to yourself. Examples include:

(a) Chocolate
(b) Dill pickles
(c) Popcorn
(d) Honey
(e) Onions
(f) Mint candy
(g) Root beer
(h) Barbecue sauce

(3) Recall your favorite food and savor its taste in your mouth.

Focal point: Taste and smell the imaginary food.

Smelling

Your teacher will name many items and places that have varied smells. Try to recall their aroma. Examples include:

(a) A pizza baking
(b) A doctor's office
(c) Fish frying
(d) Hot baked cookies
(e) A gymnasium

Focal Point: Truthfully distinguish each odor.

Touching
Close your eyes and concentrate on feeling various objects, liquids, and fabrics that either your teacher or you and your classmates bring. Notice the shape, size, texture, and weight. Examples include:

(a) Cold ice cube tray
(b) Velvet
(c) Sandpaper
(d) Water
(e) Syrup
(f) Burlap

Focal Point: Touch and feel objects.

Candy
Your teacher will distribute one piece of candy such as a lemon drop, or an orange slice to each student, with half of the class receiving one kind and the other half a different kind. For three minutes quietly study the candy, being aware of every facet—shape, weight, color, texture, smell, taste, and the associations it calls forth. (Does the orange slice remind you of a seashell, a Halloween adventure, an eraser?) After three minutes, quickly write down your impressions in phrases. Read aloud your description and compare it with those of others. What impressions are similar? Which differ? Notice that some descriptions are more complete than others, suggesting greater sensory awareness.

Focal Point: Become aware of the total sensory impression of the piece of candy.

ACTIVITY AND ITS PURPOSE

I Sense It!
To continue training your sensory awareness and recall, you are to select a small object outside of class, scrutinize it carefully, and then write its description *from memory* on the activity sheet given to you by your teacher. Bring your object to class where it will be assigned to a classmate who will study and describe it. Compare the two descriptions.

Focal Point: Use all of your senses to achieve a complete awareness of the object and then to recall it accurately and vividly.

HOW TO PREPARE

(1) Select a small object that you can bring to class. It may be something as common as a cup or as unusual as an electric back scratcher. Suggestions include a:

(a) Key chain
(b) Candy bowl
(c) Spear of broccoli
(d) Hammer
(e) Flower
(f) Perfume bottle
(g) Half a walnut in its shell
(h) Driftwood

(2) Using your ears, nose, tongue, hands, and eyes, inspect the object carefully. Even if you choose a familiar piece, scrutinize it as though you were seeing

it for the first time. For four minutes delve in deeply, remembering each aspect.

(3) After four minutes, cover the object. Write three or four paragraphs recalling your sensory impressions. *Don't peek!* This exercise is valuable to you only if you recall the description from memory.

(4) Bring your article and description to class. Your teacher will arrange a trade of objects, giving yours to someone else and giving you an article from a fellow classmate.

(5) For four minutes the class will study simultaneously their assigned individual objects, noticing shape, weight, color, texture, smell, taste, sound, and associations called forth. Work quietly without talking.

(6) After four minutes, your teacher will place the articles in a large box. You will be given four minutes to write a description of the object. Try to recall everything you noticed. For speed, write in phrases rather than sentences.

HOW TO PRESENT

When your teacher displays the object you brought, hand in the bottom part of the activity sheet (be sure your name is on it), take the top part—your description—to the front of the room. The student who studied your article in class will accompany you with his or her description.

Your partner will hold the article in full view while you read your recall written at home. Then you will hold the article and your classmate will read aloud his or her description of it.

When you are both through, your teacher will ask for a brief discussion on the differences and similarities between the two analyses. Taking into account the discrepancy between the home and class work, which description shows the more sensitive awareness? How do personality and background influence the descriptions?

In like manner, you will later read the description of the article you studied in class and compare it to that written at home by a classmate.

Chapter 6

Distinguish the Difference

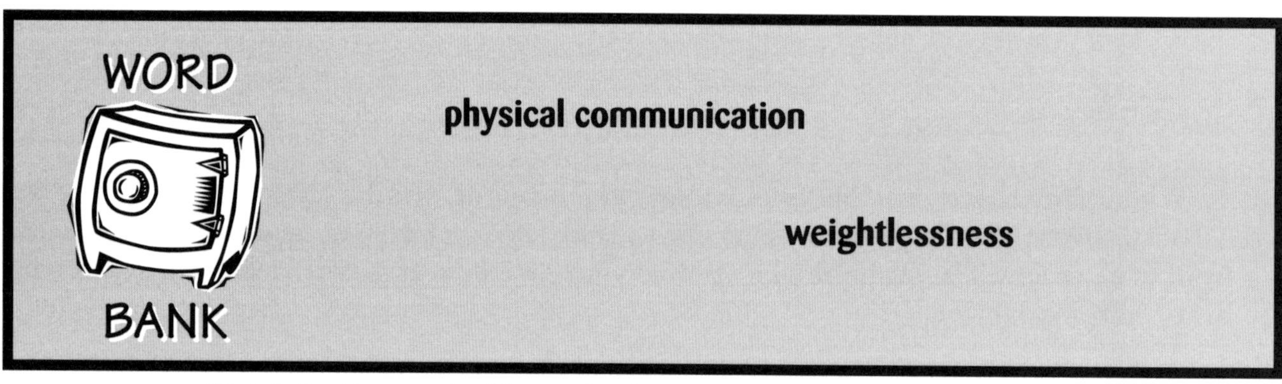

Watch for these valuable words wherever you see the word bank icon. 

BRAIN TEASERS

(1) What mental preparation must an actor have to communicate believability without words?

CUE SHEET

Now that you have awakened your powers of sensory recall, you need practice in physically communicating your impressions. With body movement alone, you can show the same activity under varying circumstances.

In the following exercises, activate your sensory recall and command your body to respond accordingly. Work quietly in your own special way. Do not copy the other players. Concentrate on believability within yourself.

WARMUPS

Upon entering class, immediately and quietly complete the basic body warmup routine. Then as a class, do the following:

Take a Walk
If space permits, the whole class will participate at once. If not, divide into two or three groups that will take turns. Stand in a huge circle, all facing one direction. As you walk around the circle, respond to your teacher's side coaching that covers the following:

(1) Walk leisurely, enjoying a warm summer day.
(2) Walk briskly to be on time for an appointment.
(3) Walk barefoot (feel your feet bare even though your shoes are on) in sticky, squishy mud that oozes between your toes.
(4) Walk barefoot on hot burning pavement.
(5) Walk barefoot on fine hot sand.
(6) Walk on slippery, smooth ice.
(7) Walk through piles of dry, crackling autumn leaves.
(8) Walk in a shallow stream that is pebbly, icy, and clear.
(9) Walk in shoes that are too small for you.
(10) Walk on the moon with weightlessness.
(11) Walk with your right foot stuck in a bucket.
(12) Walk with a thumb tack stuck in your shoe heel.
(13) Walk on thick foam rubber.

Focal Point: Respond with vivid recall to each suggestion.

Suitcases
Count off into groups of ten or twelve that will take turns participating. Respond to your teacher's side coaching by moving from one side of the room to the other, or from one corner to the other. Two or three of you should begin the move and when you are about halfway across, two or three more should follow in like fashion until the whole group has taken part.

(1) Carry an empty suitcase out of a store and down the street to your car. Show its size, shape, and weight.
(2) Carry to your car that same suitcase now filled with vacation clothing.
(3) Carry that same suitcase filled with heavy books.
(4) You are in the lobby of an air terminal. Carry that same suitcase along with a large heavy box.
(5) That suitcase is now a wire cage that contains a poisonous snake being shipped to a zoo. Carry it to the delivery truck.

Focal Point: Really see and feel the case in each situation.

Eraser Creator
Divide into circles of eight to ten people, standing. You are to handle and give a chalkboard eraser to the person on your right as though it were the object your teacher suggests. Continue around the circle. Examples include:

(1) A hot potato
(2) A butterfly
(3) A full cup of hot chocolate
(4) A tiny puppy
(5) A raw piece of liver

Focal Point: Really see, feel, and hear the article you hold and give. Make it believable to you. Adjust to the weight, shape, size, and other features.

ACTIVITY AND ITS PURPOSE

Distinguish The Difference
You are to decide on a basic everyday physical activity and at least six corresponding variations that can be created in class.

Focal Point: Communicate as many different messages as you can within the same basic structure.

HOW TO PREPARE

(1) Select a simple physical activity around which you can create numerous variations. Suggestions include:

(a) Reading a book
(b) Threading a needle
(c) Reading a letter
(d) Sitting on a chair
(e) Eating a cookie

(2) On the activity sheet to this chapter list at least six variations to the activity. Use your imagination to create vivid and different situations. For example, read a book as if:

(a) It were a cookbook and you are going over a tasty recipe.
(b) It were a telephone directory and you are searching for a number.
(c) It were a 200-year-old manuscript in the rare book section of the library.
(d) It were a difficult textbook you have to study.

HOW TO PRESENT

When your teacher calls on you, take your activity sheet to the front of the room and stand to one side. Your teacher will choose a fellow classmate to accompany you and to communicate with physical action only each situation you read aloud from your paper.

Announce the first situation, and the player will act it. Your teacher may ask for a brief discussion before continuing to the next variation. Depending on available time, your scenes may be limited to just a few on your list.

When you are called on to be the player, hand the teacher your activity sheet. Quietly approach the front and concentrate on vivid recall to communicate the situation. Give yourself a few seconds to create in your mind the scene before you begin to play it.

2 LEGS ... OR 3?

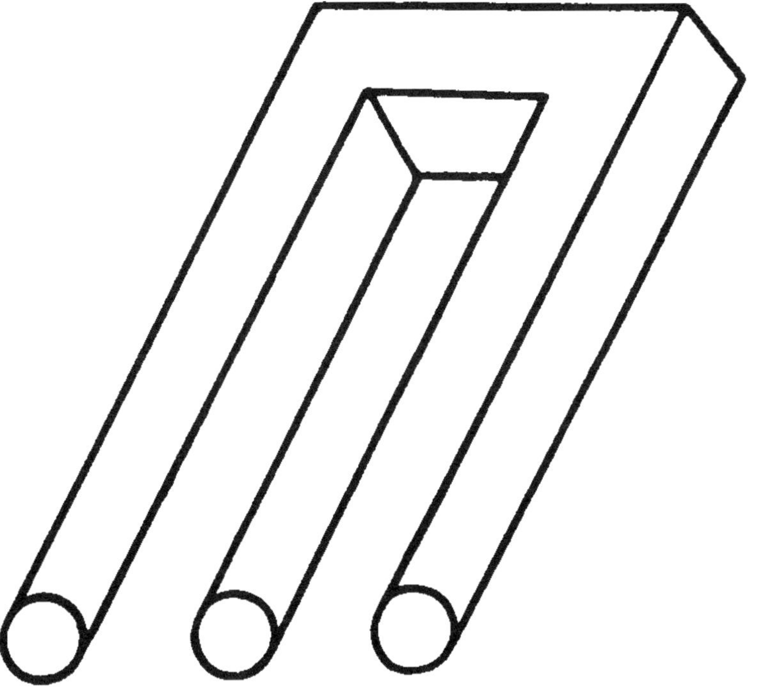

COVER THE TOP HALF OF THE FIGURE, AND IT APPEARS TO HAVE 3 LEGS.
COVER THE BOTTOM HALF, AND IT APPEARS TO HAVE 2.

Chapter 7

Conflict

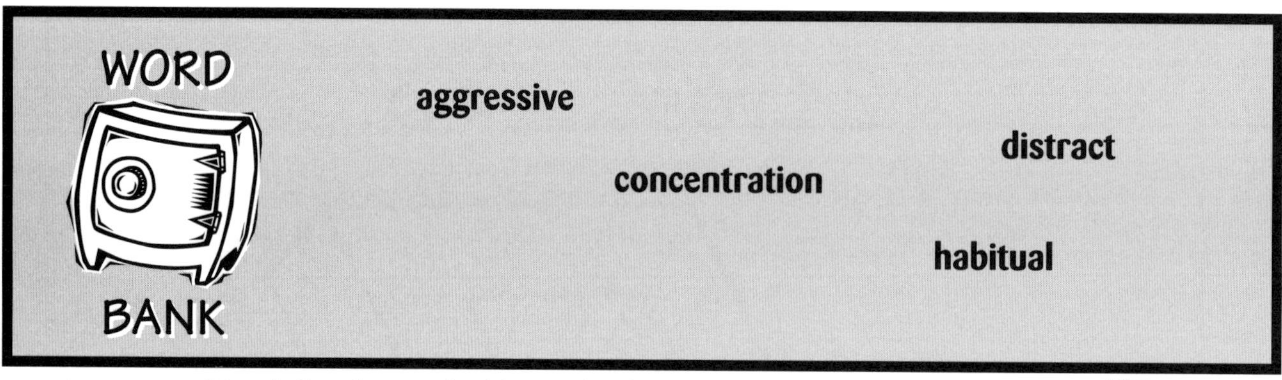

Watch for these valuable words wherever you see the word bank icon. 

BRAIN TEASERS

(1) How can increased powers of concentration help you in everyday life?
(2) How can concentration help an actor?
(3) What are some of the rules in improvising a scene?

CUE SHEET

When no one is looking, try this: Pat the top of your head with one hand and at the same time rub your stomach in a large circular motion with the other hand. If you have trouble doing this bit of nonsense, it means you need to strengthen your powers of concentration.

Concentration (another one of your inner resources) means absorption— giving your complete attention to the matter at hand. You already know how important concentration is in studying. It is equally vital in communicating. We have previously said that actors must believe what they are doing in order to make the audience believe in it also. They achieve this belief primarily through concentration, by focusing their minds on the problem. Remember, to whatever aspect actors give their attention, so will the audience. To prove this, stand on a busy street corner and look intently and obviously up at the sky. Notice what happens to those who walk by.

In the earlier chapters you have already had some practice in concentration if you achieved your focal point in each exercise. You may also have noticed that when you were working on observation, you had to concentrate in order to retain what you saw. In this chapter, you are to continue improving concentration skills that will reward you not only in acting but in everyday life.

WARMUPS

As soon as you enter class, immediately and quietly complete the basic body warmup routine that should now be habitual with you. Then as a class, do the following:

Double Interview
Count off into pairs with each having an "A" and a "B." Using two pairs at a time, place them about two feet apart. Two interviews are to be conducted simultaneously. "A" in each pair is to question the partner on school, hobbies, etc. "B" must reply to each question asked, while at the same time concentrating on the answers given by "B" of the other pair. After one minute, your teacher will call "cut" and each "B" will relate what the other "B" answered. Now reverse roles.

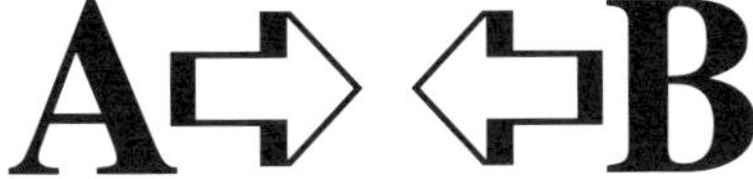

Focal Point: Completely concentrate on two simultaneous interviews.

Quick Quarrel
Divide into partners. Pairs may play one at a time or several may participate simultaneously, depending on class size and time available. Your teacher will give one partner a sentence to be used to start a quarrel. Each couple must carry on the argument, determined not to give in to the partner. Begin your quarrel in control and finally lose your temper. At the end of 1 to 2 minutes, your teacher will call "cut." Be sure you are constantly arguing during this time. Beginning sentence suggestions include:

(1) Where have you been? I've been waiting for you.
(2) You never like any of my friends.
(3) Turn off that TV.
(4) Why do you always wear brown?
(5) Your room is always messy.
(6) You are always eating — munch, munch, munch.

Focal Point: Maintain your side of the argument through concentration.

Argument Express
Working with a partner, decide on one situation where you can argue on opposite sides. The two of you are to carry on an argument simultaneously without any pauses. No matter what happens or is said, carry on your own side of the question without stopping and without giving in to your partner. Situation examples include:

(1) Teenager and parent argue about curfew
(2) Drivers argue about an accident
(3) Husband and wife argue about an invitation list
(4) Coach and player argue about training rules
(5) College roommates argue about cleaning

Focal Point: Avoid letting your partner interrupt your argument. Concentrate only on your side.

Thief
Working with a partner, improvise a "polite" quarrel scene where the two of you are arguing but are trying to be nice about it. One of you is to wear a hat that your partner will attempt to grab and wear.

Focal Point: Throughout the scene maintain a sensible argument while trying to distract your partner so you can snatch and wear the hat.

ACTIVITY AND ITS PURPOSE

Conflict
With a partner you are to decide on a situation where each of you wants to buy the same article. The store has only one of the articles, but neither of you is willing to give it up to the other.

Focal Point: Concentrate on getting your own way. Do not give in to your partner.

HOW TO PREPARE

(1) Your teacher will assign you a partner and allow you a few minutes in class to decide on a situation. Do not plan together what you will say or do. Only determine where the scene takes place and what article it is that you both want. For example, you both want to buy the same:

(a) CD player at a music store
(b) sweat shirts in a clothing store
(c) old uniform at a rummage sale
(d) pair of shoes at a shoe store

(e) crystal vase at an antique store
(f) puppy at a pet store

(2) Now, working alone without your partner, fill in the activity sheet to this chapter. On it, list four physical *actions* you can do to get the article, and four *reasons* you can use to persuade your partner to let you buy it.

(3) Have your plan of attack well in mind so you can go into battle armed for action.

(4) Decide which one of you will introduce the scene.

HOW TO PRESENT

Hand your activity sheet to your teacher before doing your scene. Walk quietly to the playing area and arrange necessary chairs or tables, placing them so both of you will face the audience. Introduce the scene by announcing clearly and loudly where it is set. Take a few seconds to prepare yourself mentally for the first action you will take. Then call "curtain" and begin. Get into the scene *immediately* by coming on stage and *doing* something specific. Concentrate on achieving your goal physically. Perhaps you will try on the shoes, jump up on the stool, snatch the coat, or storm towards the clerk.

Use one of the actions you planned and don't go on to the next until you have exhausted its every possibility. Then try another. If something better comes to mind during the scene, do it. Concentrate throughout on getting your own way. Quarrel, persuade, plead, suggest, offer alternatives, be aggressive, but do *not* give in to your partner.

After two or three minutes, your teacher will end the scene by calling "cut." Remember, only your teacher can end an improvisation, so keep playing until you hear the end signal.

Conflict.

Chapter 8

It's All Greek To Me

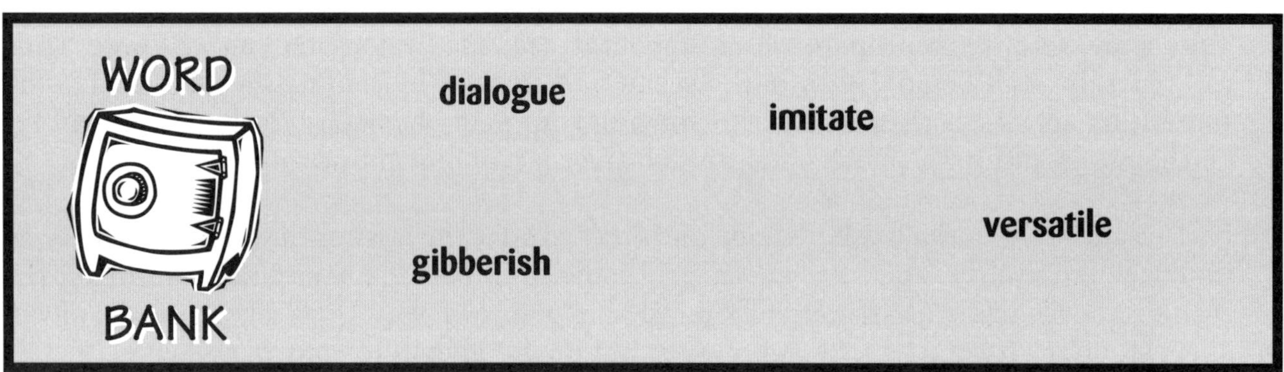

Watch for these valuable words wherever you see the word bank icon. 

BRAIN TEASERS

(1) What does the term "acting" mean?
(2) Besides using movement and words, how else does an actor communicate?

CUE SHEET

The word "acting" is taken from a Latin term meaning "to do." Thus, an actor's primary job is to *do* something, to *show*, to use the body with its versatile actions to convey a message. Frequently, of course, an actor must also speak or use dialogue. But sometimes the words used are not the important factor in communicating. Instead, the message is carried by the *sound of the voice*: the tone used, the emphasis put on words, and the rate of talking. *(See the dog experiment in Chapter 31.)*

It is a challenging and valuable game to communicate with body and voice without incorporating real words. It can be done, as you will discover in the following exercises.

WARMUPS

Do the basic body warmup routine as soon as you enter class. Then, with your classmates do the following:

Mocking Bird

In groups of 12 to 15 sit on the floor in a small circle, facing out. Link your little fingers with those of your neighbors on both sides. Now close your eyes and concentrate on what you hear. A designated student will begin by making any type of vocal sound, which the neighbor to the right will imitate. Then that student's neighbor will mimic what he or she heard from the second student—not as it sounded from the first one. Continue around the circle, each student imitating the sound heard immediately to the left. What is the sound like when it reaches the originator? Is there change? If so, why?

Focal Point: Exactly reproduce the sound you hear from the person on your left.

Gibberish

Gibberish means you communicate by using nonsense syllables instead of real words. When you use gibberish, you are creating your own language. For example, "goo-ga-gee," "da-la-pah," "eshapifenuk" are all gibberish. Just be sure not to use any words—English or foreign—that you know. You should be thinking in English but speaking with the sounds you make up. Concentrate on communicating with your vocal tone and expression. Use spontaneous physical action, but do not plan gestures as a sign language.

(1) While seated at your desk, carry on a conversation in gibberish with a neighbor. Although you are using an unknown language, make yourself understood. Use a variety of different sounds. Let your voice and body bridge the communication barrier.

Focal Point: Make yourself understood with gibberish.

(2) Repeat the conflict scenes that were used in the main project of the previous chapter, but this time play the scenes with gibberish instead of real words. What difference does this make? Is there more physical action than before? If so, why?

Focal Point: Communicate with gibberish.

(3) Divide into groups of three. Using either actual news items or your own ideas, improvise a scene where an English speaking television announcer interviews a foreigner about:

(a) a product he or she has invented,

or

(b) a discovery he or she has made,

or

(c) an adventure he or she has had.

Since the foreigner speaks only gibberish and the announcer speaks only English, an interpreter translates the English questions to the foreigner and those gibberish replies to the announcer. If time allows, rotate the roles.

Focal Point: Communicate with gibberish.

ACTIVITY AND ITS PURPOSE

It's All Greek To Me
Using gibberish, you are to sell and demonstrate a product that you bring to class. During your 1 to 2 minute speech, class members will ask you questions in English in an attempt to understand what you are saying. You will reply in gibberish.

Focal Point: Use your body and voice in such a way that you communicate with gibberish.

HOW TO PREPARE

(1) Select an article to sell and demonstrate. Examples:

(a) potato peeler
(b) shoe polish kit
(c) athletic shoe
(d) back pack
(e) canine choke collar
(f) calculator
(g) egg separator
(h) catcher's mitt

(2) On the activity sheet to this chapter, outline a 1 to 2 minute speech by:

(a) announcing your product
(b) explaining why the audience needs it
(c) demonstrating its features
(d) giving information on how to buy it: cost, place, etc.

(3) Memorize the sequence of your material, so you will know in what order to present it.

(4) Practice giving your speech in gibberish while thinking in English.

HOW TO PRESENT

When you are called upon, hand your activity sheet to your teacher and go to the front of the room with your product. Begin your speech in gibberish. As you talk, think in English but make up the sounds. Be sure to use only nonsense words. If necessary you may repeatedly use the same gibberish, but try to be creative and explore many sound combinations.

Employ all powers of your voice and body to get your meaning across. Gesture and move, make your vocal tone coordinate with your ideas.

During your talk, class members will interrupt you and ask questions in English to understand your product better. Don't let the questions upset you. Just reply in gibberish, earnestly trying to communicate. Then pick up your speech where you were interrupted and continue.

Your teacher may allow you to finish your speech or may call "cut" at the end of two minutes.

τί σοι μαθήσομαι;
Greek Translation:
What would you have me learn?

Chapter 9

Say It In Song

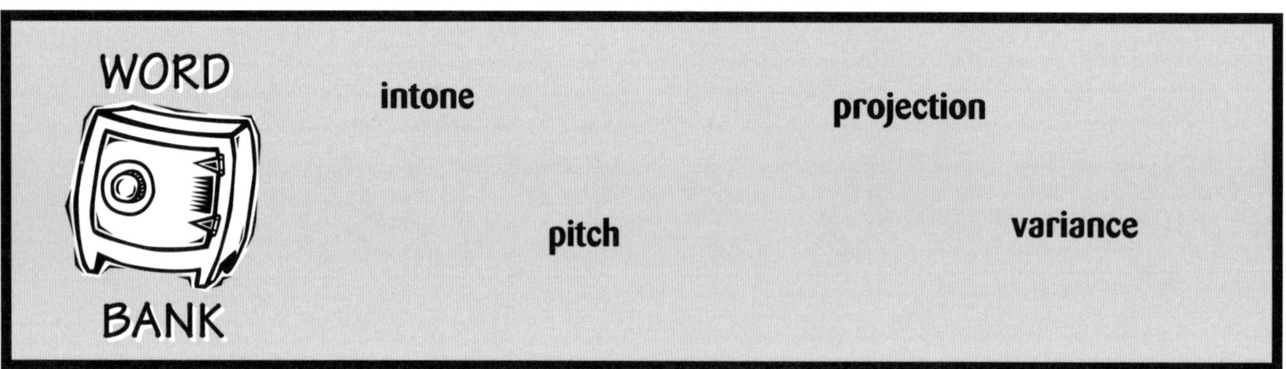

Watch for these valuable words wherever you see the word bank icon. 

BRAIN TEASERS

(1) How do you achieve vocal versatility?
(2) How do you achieve projection?

CUE SHEET

By now you should be aware that the voice and body work together in most communication situations. Just as your physical actions must be flexible and clearly understood by your audience, so must your voice be versatile, easily heard, and understood.

Vocal versatility is achieved when you become aware of variances and when you practice disciplined exercises. You may wish to refer to Chapter 31 that discusses the four major aspects of a flexible voice.

The quality of making yourself heard by everyone in the room is achieved through *projection*. Projection does not mean that you shout. Instead, it means that you heighten or exaggerate your voice and words to enable the "little old deaf person on the very last row" to hear you—whether you whisper or yell. Success in projection greatly depends on your state of mind. You must have a strong desire to be heard and understood. You can learn skills in projection and in versatility—both of which the following exercises will help you acquire.

WARMUPS

As a class, do the basic body warmups to activate your muscles. Then do the basic voice warmups. When you have completed them, go to the following:

Intone
Together as a class sustain "ahhhhhhhhh" on a pitch that is comfortable for you. Your teacher will side coach to direct you to intone louder, softer, higher, and lower in a variety of combinations.

Hi-Count
As your teacher counts, shout "hi" in class unison on the odd numbers. Repeat and shout on the even numbers.

Adverb Versatility
Your teacher will give the class a sentence such as "The box has come," "Everything is the same," "Today is Monday," or "Now is the time." As a class say the sentence aloud according to each of the following adverbs your teacher calls out. Be sure you distinguish a difference between every emotion and allow your voice to communicate each variance:

happily	joyously	exuberantly	sadly	shyly	cautiously
expectantly	sternly	irritably	threateningly	sarcastically	eagerly
airily	sleepily	wistfully	haughtily		

Focal Point: Change your voice and attitude to communicate each emotion.

Quick Change
As a class say aloud, "Where are you going?" or another similar sentence according to the following situations as your teacher calls them:

(1) As a cross parent talking to a teenager
(2) As an excited coach talking to a ball player
(3) As an employer dictating a letter
(4) As a frightened child questioning his or her mother
(5) As a burly policeman questioning a driver
(6) As a grandparent talking to a cute puppy
(7) As a foreigner just learning to read English
(8) As a flirt questioning a football star

Focal Point: Adjust your voice and attitude to communicate each circumstance believably.

Counting

Take turns counting aloud from one to ten, following your teacher's side coaching. Suggestions include:

(1) Counting off in an exercise routine
(2) Counting pennies as you drop them into a piggy bank
(3) Counting the girls at a crowded party
(4) Counting out a man in the boxing ring
(5) Reciting as though giving a telephone number over a bad connection

Focal Point: Count believably for each situation.

Calling a Distance

Divide into small groups. Each group decides a situation to improvise in which the players are forced to call back and forth to each other over a wide distance. Determine *where* the scene takes place, *who* you are, and *what* is happening. Examples include:

(1) Where: Coal mine
Who: Miners and supervisor
What: Miners in the mine report to supervisor above ground on the cave-in conditions.

(2) Where: Long tunnel
Who: Tourists and a guide
What: Guide is separated from the tourists

Focal Point: Call to the other players as though over a wide distance.

Stage Whisper

Divide into small groups and decide on a situation where you must whisper to each other and yet be heard by a large audience. Examples include:

(1) Where: A house late at night
Who: Robbers
What Robbers have broken into the house and are trying to find where the occupants have hidden their valuables.

(2) Where: Airport
Who: Undercover agents
What: Agents are plotting to arrest a spy

Focal Point: Whisper to be heard by all of the audience.

ACTIVITY AND ITS PURPOSE

Say It In Song
For an additional experience in vocal projection and variety, you are to improvise a 2-3 minute scene involving two or three players having an argument. Rather than speak the dialogue, you are to sing your sentences as is done in opera. You needn't carry a tune. Just explore the highs and lows (pitch) of the scale, according to what you think fits your ideas and words.

Focal Point: Sing—do not speak—the dialogue.

HOW TO PREPARE

(1) Meet with your small group and determine the where, who, and what for a scene to improvise. Be sure the "what" incorporates a conflict. Do not plan what you will say or do. Only plan the basic three *W's*. Examples include:

(a) Where: Living room of a small house
Who: Landlord and tenant
What: Landlord demands the rent, which the tenant cannot pay

(b) Where: Sidewalk
Who: Two pedestrians
What: Two pedestrians, walking toward each other, simultaneously claim a twenty dollar bill on the sidewalk.

(c) Where: Bargain counter in a department store
Who: Two customers and a clerk
What: Two customers want to buy the same sale sweater from the clerk

(d) Where: Pet store
Who: Customer and clerk
What: Because the clerk wants to give to his girlfriend the store's only poodle, he is trying to talk the customer out of buying the poodle.

(2) Fill out the activity sheet for this chapter.

HOW TO PRESENT

When it is your turn to participate, hand your activity sheet to your teacher. With your group, quietly go to the playing area and set up any furniture you need, placing it so you can face the audience as you play the scene. When you are ready, call "curtain" and immediately get into the scene by singing a beginning line. Don't hesitate because you feel silly. Opera stars get paid huge salaries to "sing their sentences." Keep your mind on the focal point and get on with the scene.

No one cares whether or not you carry a tune. What you must do is to explore all the sounds you can and sing them out. The more you exaggerate your singing, your gestures, and your movement, the better. In this exercise, you are permitted to "ham" it up as long as you maintain your focal point.

At approximately two minutes, or when the action has played out, your teacher will call "cut," and you will stop the scene.

Chapter 10

Voice Dubbing

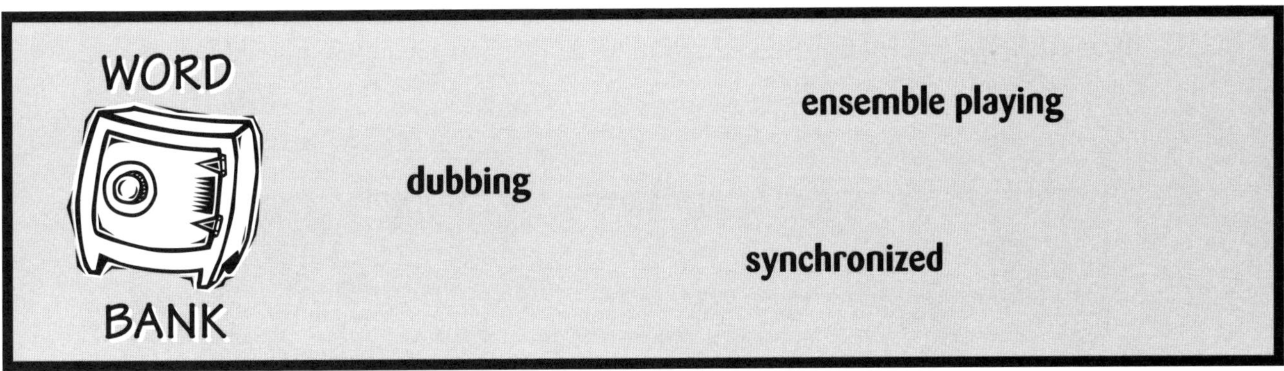

Watch for these valuable words wherever you see the word bank icon. 

BRAIN TEASERS

(1) How do you achieve ensemble playing?
(2) Why is ensemble playing necessary?

CUE SHEET

"Keep on the alert" is a good motto for you to follow whenever you communicate. Whether you are acting, speaking, or discussing, you must constantly use your powers of observation and concentration to be aware of what is going on inside both participants and spectators. Only then can you properly adjust what you say or do to meet the needs of the situation.

In acting, this ability to relate and adjust to fellow performers is called *ensemble playing*. Everyone in the scene cooperates toward achieving the goal. Again, you bring into use the dual-role discussed in Chapter 3: You concentrate on your part while at the same time you are aware and respond to what is going on around you.

The following games require ensemble playing with attention to dialogue.

WARMUPS

As you enter class, do the body warmups located in Appendix A. Then simultaneously as a class, run through the voice warmups, also in Appendix A, before doing the following:

Spin a Yarn
Divide into groups of eight or ten and sit facing each other in a circle. Your teacher will give one person in each group a ball that consists of varying but short lengths of string or yarn. The starting person begins a story while unwinding the ball. He or she continues the story until coming to the end of the yarn. Then the player on the right takes the ball and begins to unwind it while at the same time continuing and advancing the story line. Repeat around the circle, keeping contributions short so all can participate more than once. Make your story as fantastic and imaginative as you can, having wild adventures described with vivid adjectives.

Note: This may be played without the yarn ball. A leader should call "cut" to each contributor after 45 to 50 seconds.

Tug of War
Repeat this ensemble warmup as described in Chapter 2.

Mirror
Repeat this ensemble warmup as described in Chapter 4.

ACTIVITY AND ITS PURPOSE

Voice Dubbing
With one or two other players you are to improvise a short, (1-3 minute) well known folk tale. One team will act the story and the other team sitting on the sidelines will provide the voices, as though dubbing in for a synchronized sound track. To achieve this ensemble playing requires strong concentration and quick observation.

Focal Points: *Actors:* Physically create the story.
Voices: Anticipate the actors' movements and synchronize your dialogue with their actions.

HOW TO PREPARE

(1) Your teacher will assign you a group. Each "acting" group must have a twin "speaking" group.

(2) Together, the twin groups decide on a 1 to 3 minute folk or fairy tale to play and a role for each participant. Choose a story that has only two to four characters. It may be necessary to play just one scene—perhaps the climax—rather than the complete story. (Or the class as a whole could choose one longer story and each twin team act out one scene only, with the whole story being given in sequence by successive teams.) Be sure that for every actor there is a speaker. To save time, your teacher may appoint stories and roles. Some story suggestions might be:

Three Billy Goats Gruff
Three Little Pigs
Little Red Riding Hood
Goldilocks and the Three Bears
Jack and the Beanstalk
Hansel and Gretel

(3) As a group, review the story to familiarize everyone with the plot and the part that each character plays. Do not plan, however, what you will say or do.

(4) Outside of class complete the activity sheet to this chapter.

HOW TO PRESENT

When the teacher announces your story, hand in your activity sheet and go quietly to the playing area. The actors should set up necessary furniture. (Keep it to a minimum.) The voices should sit on the floor, placing themselves in front and slightly to the side of the actors.

The actors begin the scene immediately, getting right into the action. At first they may have to proceed at a slow tempo until the voices become adjusted to the action. The actors should concentrate on sharing the scene with each other and should not turn around to look at the voices.

Each voice should concentrate on the scene, synchronizing loud, clear dialogue each time the actor "talks." Make your voice sound like the character. For example, a troll may have a deep, gruff voice; a baby bear may have a light high voice.

Depending on the time available, your teacher may call "cut" before the scene has ended. If time allows, reverse the roles with the actors becoming the speakers and vice versa.

Chapter 11

Connections

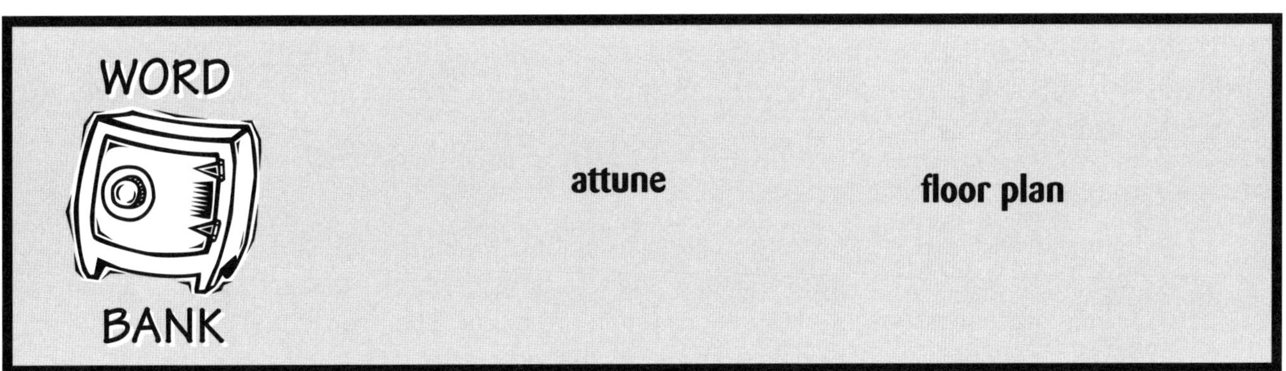

Watch for these valuable words wherever you see the word bank icon. 

BRAIN TEASERS

(1) How can you tell where you are?
(2) Why should you be aware of the stage setting?
(3) How do you relate to stage furnishings?

CUE SHEET

If someone were to blindfold you, lead you into a room in an unfamiliar house, and then remove the blindfold, how could you tell what room you were in? If you saw a stove, a sink, and a refrigerator, you'd realize you were in a kitchen. If you saw a ping-pong table, a television set, and lounge chairs, you'd conclude you were in a recreation or family room. The physical objects placed in an area tell you where you are, or at least they indicate the general nature of the room.

In real life you relate to the objects in your environment. You put your feet on the coffee table (if Mother isn't looking), you sit backwards on the chair, you lean your shoulder against the wall, press your nose to the window, finger the knickknacks on the mantle.

In acting, you must relate not only to your fellow players but also to where the scene occurs. Your identification with the furnishings will help make the action believable. Otherwise you will look like an uncomfortable, wooden actor placed in a newly constructed and unfamiliar area, rather than as a settled individual who is supposed to have lived in the room for ten years. Or if your character is to be in a new place, he or she still must react to the objects, communicating their unfamiliarity.

To adjust to the play's "where," (where the action occurs) you should be aware of the objects on stage and then imaginatively use them. The "where" projects in this chapter will attune you to these demands.

WARMUPS

Warmup with both the basic body and voice routines in Appendix A. Then as a class do the two following exercises for stimulation and concentration and do the other activities for relating to the "where."

Skip Rope
Using an imaginary rope, skip and jump around the room. Be sure you are aware of the weight, texture, and length of the rope, and also of your muscles that are working. Jump in one place until you can believe what you are doing. Then concentrate on a steady, smooth pattern as you quietly move around the room.

Focal Point: Concentrate on the rope and your muscles used in jumping it.

Jump Rope
Divide into groups of three. As above, use an imaginary rope, but this time two people turn the rope and one player jumps it. Rotate roles.

Focal Point: The two rope turners must coordinate their actions and see the rope in order to work as a unit. The jumper must see the rope and time his or her movements to jump over and not step on it.

Guess Where

A volunteer player decides on a "where" and then goes on stage, using an object that is associated with the place. When other class members think they know where the first actor is, they each become a character, entering the scene, and using another relating object. Additional class members join the scene in like manner. Repeat with a different player initiating the "where." *Example:* One student begins to check out groceries. A second student enters and begins filling the sacks. A third student enters and starts pushing a cart, etc.

Focal Point: Concentrate on where the scene is taking place.

Change Location

With a partner, improvise a scene in a specific "where." Then change the "where" and redo the same scene. Notice that there will be definite changes in the playing because of a different location. Examples include:

(1) Where: Living room
Who: Husband and wife
What: They argue loudly and move freely in a dispute over monthly bills.

(2) Redo the scene with the same who and what but changing the where to a busy restaurant.

Focal Point: Concentrate on where you are.

ACTIVITY AND ITS PURPOSE

Connections

With a partner you are to improvise a 2-3 minute scene within a simple floor plan, and during the scene each of you must touch every article on stage so that the audience knows why you are doing so.

Focal Point: Show where you are by using all of the objects within the floor plan.

HOW TO PREPARE

(1) Outside of class determine and arrange on paper a simple floor plan. By floor plan we mean the arrangement of furniture and objects within an area or room. Keep the number of articles between four and six. Use squares, rectangles, and circles to denote objects and then label each one by printing on it. You may choose any room you wish. Make the furniture arrangement interesting and usable.

The following are sample floor plans of a living room and a meeting room.

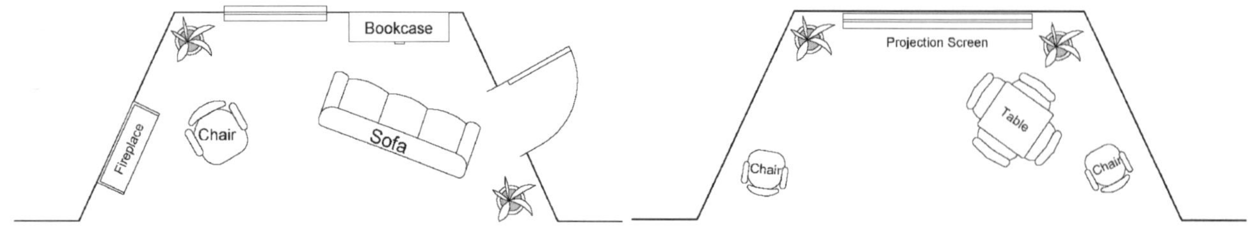

(2) Decide on two characters (who) and a situation (what) that can be played in the floor plan. Examples include:

(a) Where: Living room
Who: Shy man and dance teacher
What: Teacher is giving the man a private dance lesson in his home.

(b) Where: Meeting room
Who: Sales manager and salesperson
What: Sales manager is introducing a new ad campaign to salesperson.

(3) Transfer this information to the activity sheet for this chapter.

HOW TO PRESENT

When the teacher calls on you, hand in your activity sheet, go to the front of the room and announce the where, who, and what. Then on the chalkboard, quickly draw your floor plan, making it extremely large. Label each article. Using class chairs, place them in the playing area to represent all of the furniture on your plan. Now return to your seat and observe two players whom your teacher will select to enact the scene as you prescribed.

When it is your turn to play another student's scene, study the floor plan on the chalkboard. Then assume the role given you and after calling "curtain" immediately plunge into the action with your partner. Concentrate on *where* you are. Imaginatively determine how you can handle every object in the room without succumbing to a built-in activity such as dusting every article or moving the furniture around. If you use such devices, you are not meeting the assignment. Instead, as your scene develops, use the objects within the floor plan. If you forget what some of the objects are, quietly refer to the chalkboard drawing again.

Use the objects, don't talk about them. Relate to them in varied ways. Remember, there is more than one way to sit on a chair—or maybe you won't even want to sit on it. Perhaps you'll plop on the floor and lean your back against the chair. Instead of turning on the lamp, you may toss your jacket over it as you enter.

Your teacher will end the improvisation by calling "cut" when you both have touched all of the objects or when the time seems appropriate. The class may wish to discuss how well you achieved your focal point and if you communicated to them what you were doing with each article.

Dance Lessons.

Chapter 12

Before And After

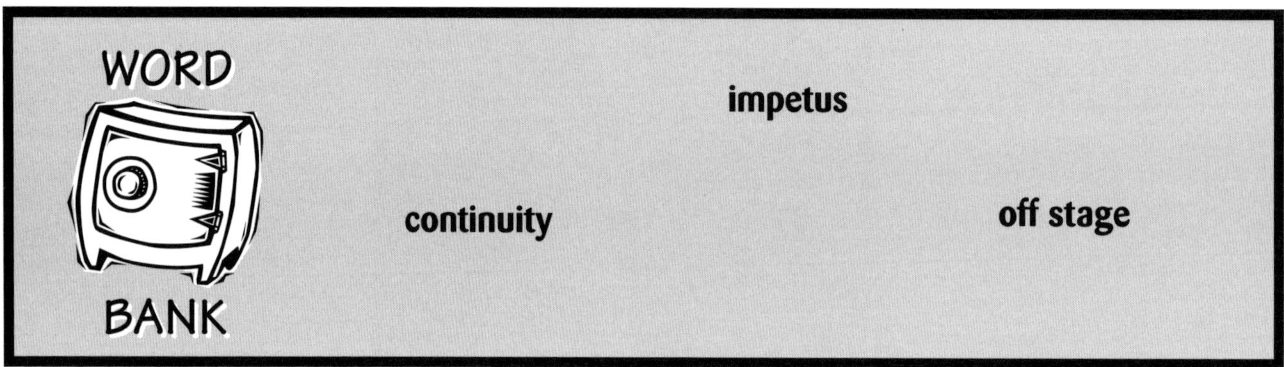

Watch for these valuable words wherever you see the word bank icon. 

BRAIN TEASERS

(1) Why must the actor be concerned with where the character has been and what the character has been doing before entering the scene?
(2) What must an actor communicate as the character exits?

CUE SHEET

We live in a world of chain reactions. If your first period teacher scolds you, you enter second period in a disgruntled mood. If you receive an "A" on your term exam, you are probably exuberant for the rest of the day. If you have a dreaded dental appointment after school, you leave the building reluctantly.

So it is in life, and so it must be in the theatre. What a character does on stage is dependent upon where he or she has been and what has happened *before* he or she enters. So while actors are waiting off stage to begin the scene, they must mentally and physically create within themselves *where* the character is and *what* happens before entering. For example, if the character, upon entering the stage, announces that he or she has been running from the post office to proclaim the news, the actor may make this believable by running before entering, so that breathing and actions suggest prior activity.

In like manner, as the actor leaves the scene, he or she must indicate to the audience where the character is going.

The following projects will help you develop this skill that gives continuity and life to the role.

WARMUPS

Do the body warmup routine as you enter class. Then participate in the following:

Statues

(1) In groups of three or four, move freely and spontaneously to a spirited musical recording played by your teacher. Run, leap, wiggle, dodge, writhe and stretch, using your whole body in active and total movement. When your teacher side coaches "freeze," stop instantly, holding your position. You may be in a very unique or silly position, but "freeze" anyway. When the teacher calls on you, describe a logical reason for that pose. For example, if you freeze on tiptoe with one arm high above your head, you may justify your position by believing you are picking apricots.

(2) Using groups of three or four, a designated class member will swing each of you around with great impetus. When he or she releases you, you must "freeze" in the random position in which you light. Then quickly determine what you are doing. Begin improvising a scene around that position. All members of the group must imaginatively relate their position to whatever situation the first student suggests.

ACTIVITY AND ITS PURPOSE

Before And After
You are to do approximately a one-minute solo scene in which you enter and leave the stage showing only from what room you have come and to what room you are going.

Focal Point: Concentrate on where you have been and where you are going.

HOW TO PREPARE

(1) Outside of class determine how you can show the room from where you are coming and the room to where you are going. The stage itself is to be merely an empty hallway between the two rooms. *Example:* You quietly and cautiously enter the hallway, dig into your pocket, produce what appears to be a cookie, and proceed to eat it. You then feel stickiness on your face and see your chocolate covered hands. Hurriedly you walk into the next room to wash off the evidence.

(2) Fill in the activity sheet to this chapter.

(3) Rehearse your brief scene.

HOW TO PRESENT

Hand your activity sheet to your teacher when called upon and go quietly to the playing area.

Give yourself a few seconds to adjust your mind and body to the situation you will play. Then call "curtain" and enter the scene, showing us only what room you have come from and what room you are going to. Don't tell us. Show us.

After you have finished, your teacher may ask for a discussion as to what you communicated.

Chapter 13

Guess Who

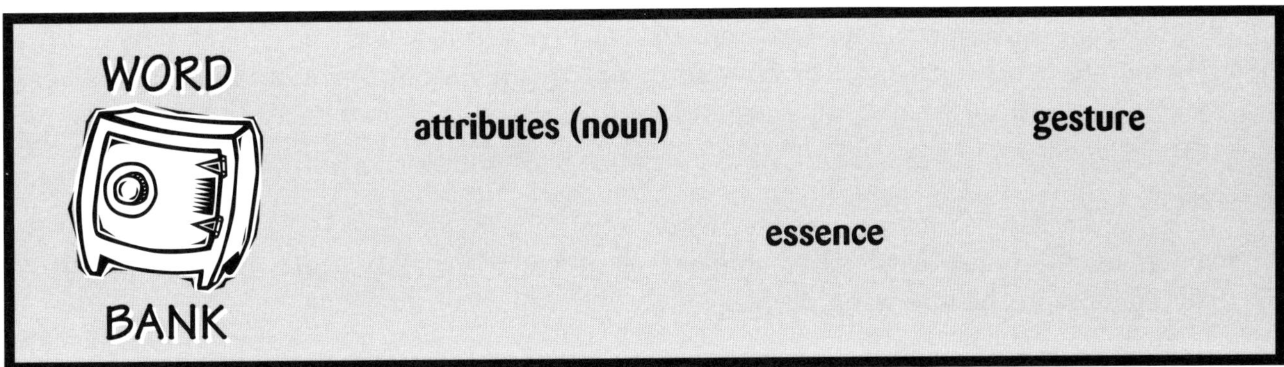

Watch for these valuable words wherever you see the word bank icon. 

BRAIN TEASERS

(1) How does age influence character?
(2) How do people show us who they are?
(3) Why is it necessary to individualize a character?

CUE SHEET

In most of the previous projects, you have been acting as yourself in developing your inner resources. Only in a few of the assignments have you assumed a character to play—someone different from yourself. An actor's job, of course, is to communicate character. Plays are about people doing things. When an actor has initial control of the body and voice, he or she can then concentrate on creating a specific role.

Age is an important aspect of character. Basically our age influences how we move. The older we become, generally the slower our body reacts. Gestures become smaller and closer to the body. Muscles become slack. Age also influences what we do and what we think is important. A small child may be fascinated by a butterfly, while an adult may not even notice.

Observe various people to discover how their age influences them. Be aware that age qualities are not all physical. Mental attitude towards life can make a young person seem old or an old person appear young.

Notice, too, that while you can detect general attributes within each age, every person is unique and complex. All old people do not walk with a cane in bent-over fashion. All young people do not skip and jump on their way to play. As an actor your goal is to show the essence of an age, while yet contributing individualized features. Maybe your old person will walk straight, though slowly, and the individualized quality will be fumbling hands that are swollen and disfigured with arthritis.

Behavior is also an important aspect of character. *The way people behave or relate to others shows us who they are.* Have you ever sat in a busy restaurant and observed people? If you see a teenage boy and girl, how can you tell if they are boyfriend and girlfriend or brother and sister? How can you tell if a man and woman meeting in a cafe are husband and wife or if they are business associates? You can almost always guess correctly because of the way people respond to each other.

An actor, therefore, can communicate to the audience who the character is by the way he or she behaves to other characters in the scene. Let's put these principles to practice now in the following projects.

WARMUPS

Do the basic body warmup routine before continuing.

Guess My Age
Individually or in groups of two or three you are to show the specific age of a person who is standing and waiting for a city bus. Write on a piece of paper the age you are depicting and hand it to your teacher as you approach the playing area. Show us, don't tell us your age. Your teacher will side coach, announcing if the bus is approaching, if it is held up in traffic, or if it turns a corner before it gets to you. Respond accordingly.

Focal Point: Concentrate on your character's age.

ACTIVITY AND ITS PURPOSE

Guess Who
With a partner you are to improvise a one-minute scene involving a character's behavior. You will know who you are and what your relationship is to your partner, but your partner will not know these things. By the way you relate, your partner must discover who he or she is.

Focal Point: Show your relationship to your partner. Your unknowing partner's focal point is to discover his or her character.

HOW TO PREPARE

(1) Determine a situation involving two characters. Decide which role you will play, the state of your unknowing partner, where the scene takes place, and what occurs. Suggestions include:

(a) Where: Gift shop.
Who: You are a clerk. Your unknowing partner is the manager.
What: You have broken an expensive candy bowl.

(b) Where: Campus Center.
Who: You are a college student. Your unknowing partner is an attractive college student of the opposite sex.
What: You are trying to get acquainted with your partner in hopes of getting a date.

(c) Where: Bank
Who: You are new in town and unemployed. Your unknowing partner is a bank manager.
What: You want to make a good impression so you will be offered a job.

(d) Where: Living room
Who: You are a teenager. Your unknowing partner is your parent.
What: You have come in an hour later than your deadline.

(2) Since *how* you behave, not what you say, is the aim of this project, decide several things you can *do* to clue your partner into knowing who he or she is.

(3) Fill out the activity sheet to this chapter.

HOW TO PRESENT

When you are called upon, hand the teacher your activity sheet and announce whether you need a boy or a girl to be your partner. Your teacher will appoint someone to join you. Set up necessary furniture in the playing area. Then enter and immediately begin an action to carry out the scene. Show, do not tell, your relationship. Your partner will know who he or she is only by how you behave. As soon as the discovery is made, play out the scene until the teacher calls "cut." Later in class you will serve as a classmate's unknowing partner and must discover your role through behavioral clues.

Scene example follows:
Your unknowing partner is standing on stage. You enter, look at him, and begin to sob a bit. Wiping your eyes you say "I'm sorry, I didn't mean to cry." Then you open your purse, take out a small package, and walk over to the bench. You gently ask your partner

to "come here." He does so. You ask him to sit down and he sits. You take his hand and place the package in it. "We fought over this as children. Take it with you now as a memory of home. And please be careful." You adjust his tie, flick off a piece of lint on his lapel, and kiss his cheek. When your partner knows that he is your brother going off on a dangerous government assignment, he continues the scene.

Note: If there is too much telling and not enough showing, your teacher will have you play the scenes in gibberish as an added challenge.

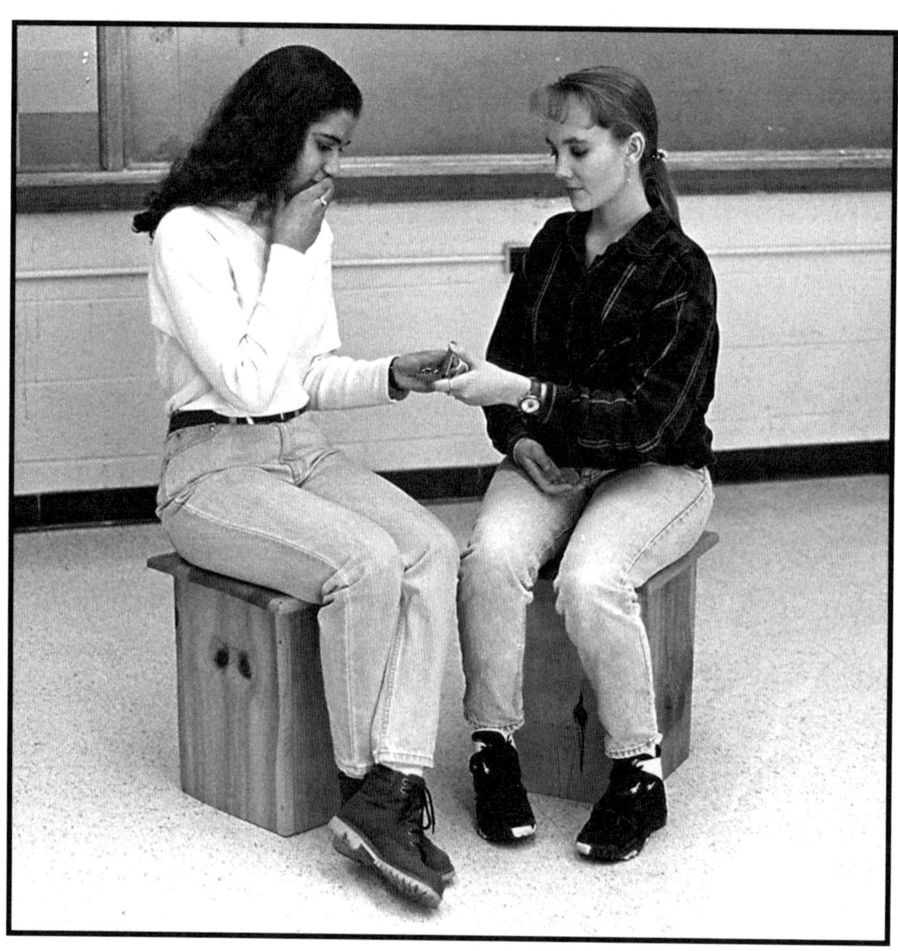

Chapter 14

Knock Knock

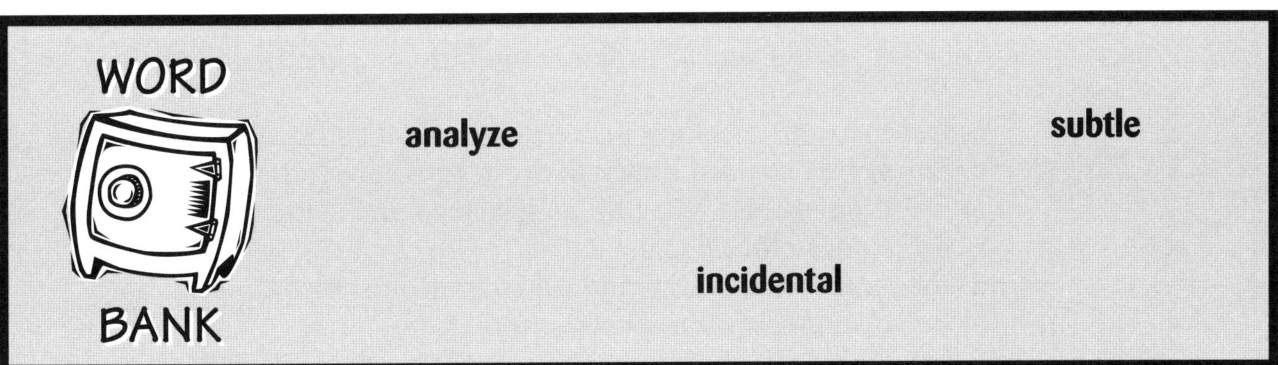

Watch for these valuable words wherever you see the word bank icon. 

BRAIN TEASERS

(1) In creating a character, why should you work on incidental items?
(2) How can your inner resources help you develop character details?

CUE SHEET

Even seemingly incidental items can help you to create a stage character. You have applied age and behavior in establishing a role. Now your challenge is to create a "who" in a "what" by using *sound* only. This may seem difficult, but if you have developed sensitivity to your environment and have stored up sensory impressions, you should have ample material for communicating subtly with sound.

WARMUPS

Do the basic body and voice warmups. Then select favorite warmup activities from previous chapters and redo them.

ACTIVITY AND ITS PURPOSE

Knock Knock
While standing behind a drape or a screen out of sight from the audience, you are to communicate a character (who) in a situation (what) solely by knocking on a door.

Focal Point: Communicate who and what by door knocking.

HOW TO PREPARE

(1) Determine who, where, and what. Analyze the situation to decide the quality and type of door knocking your character would do. Suggestions include:

(a) Irate parent knocking at a child's locked bedroom door.
(b) Spy giving a coded knock in order to receive admittance.
(c) Frightened child who has been sent to and is knocking on the principal's office door.
(d) King's messenger demanding entrance to the duke's castle.
(e) Rejected lover at his sweetheart's door.
(f) Florist boy delivering a bouquet of flowers.
(g) Gossipy woman at her neighbor's door.
(h) Prim lady paying a social visit.
(i) Prizefighter wanting to get in his agent's office.
(j) Nurse on night duty knocking at patient's door in hospital.

(2) Fill in the activity sheet to this chapter.

(3) Rehearse your knocking until you are sure it communicates what you intend. If possible, record it on tape and listen carefully to the playback. Or ask a member of the family to hear you knock in character. Do not tell friends in class what character you are doing. It should be a surprise for all.

HOW TO PRESENT

Hand your activity sheet to your teacher when you are called on to participate. Quietly, without talking or giggling, walk to the designated area near a door or wall but behind a curtain or a screen. Place yourself so you are entirely hidden from the audience. Take a few seconds to get into character and then knock on the wall or door as you rehearsed. Pause five seconds and repeat. Pause again for five seconds and repeat a third time. Then walk to your desk. Your teacher will lead a brief class discussion on who and what you communicated.

Chapter 15

Foot Feature

Watch for these valuable words wherever you see the word bank icon. 

BRAIN TEASERS

(1) Why must an actor exercise specific parts of the body when working on characterization?

CUE SHEET

All parts of your body must contribute to a unified picture of your character. For instance, if you are to depict a prim individual, it must show not only in the way you hold your torso, but in your lip line, your hands, where you position your elbows, how you place your knees, and what you do with your feet. All elements must contribute to the intended effect.

In working toward total physical communication of a character, it is often helpful to exercise isolated parts of the body—to make them flexible and responsive. Like a typist who drills the weak fourth finger in order to make it strike with proper force, so can actors condition their problem features to obey character demands. The improvisations that follow help you practice communicating with your feet and legs.

WARMUPS

Do the rhythm hop to stimulate your body. Then to throw focus on your feet, do the *Skip Rope* and *Jump Rope* exercises described in Chapter 11.

ACTIVITY AND ITS PURPOSE

Foot Feature
You are to improvise a brief scene in which you use your feet and legs alone to show who you are, where you are, and what is happening.

Focal Point: Show who, what, and where, with feet and legs alone.

HOW TO PREPARE

(1) Choose a partner. Together decide a character for each of you and a place and situation that you can show with your feet and legs.

Scene example:
A boy's feet clad in tennis shoes are seen bouncing up and down, forward and backward in quick succession. Then they stop and retreat a bit in hesitation. A man's feet appear in highly polished business shoes, walking with authority. He stomps as he makes a demand. The tennis clad feet show nervousness. The man's feet turn and forcefully leave. The boy's feet kick up dirt as he reluctantly follows.

Scene suggestions:

(a) Girl and boy dancing, with the boy being awkward and the girl getting stepped on.
(b) Two students playing one-on-one basketball.
(c) A couple finding a seat in a movie and then watching that movie.
(d) A couple on the doorsteps saying good-night after a date.
(e) A mother walking her small child in the park.
(f) A young man calling on a girl to take her for a walk.
(g) A nurse assisting a blind person to cross a street.
(h) A thief in a warehouse being caught by a night security guard.

(2) Basically plan your scene. Also determine what shoes you will wear that fit the character's personality and the situation.

(3) Fill out the activity sheet to this chapter.

(4) Rehearse the scene with your partner, but avoid setting specific movement. You are to play the scene as spontaneously as possible.

HOW TO PRESENT

For these scenes a special setting is needed to cover the body from the knees up. If possible, play on a platform behind a raised curtain. Or hang a large cloth knee high and attach it to two poles. It is important that the audience see only the player's feet up to the knees.

When you are called upon, hand your activity sheet to your teacher, change into your character's shoes, and with your partner walk quietly to the playing area. Go behind the covering and when you are ready, call "curtain" and begin your scene. *Do not* use dialogue. Use only movement to communicate. You may do things you rehearsed and any other spontaneous and imaginative activity that comes to mind.

When your scene is finished, your teacher will ask for class discussion on who and what you communicated. The class should not guess their answers. They should definitely know because you showed the message so clearly.

Note: This assignment can be done by one person instead of in couples, and it can be done barefoot.

Chapter 16

Hand It To You

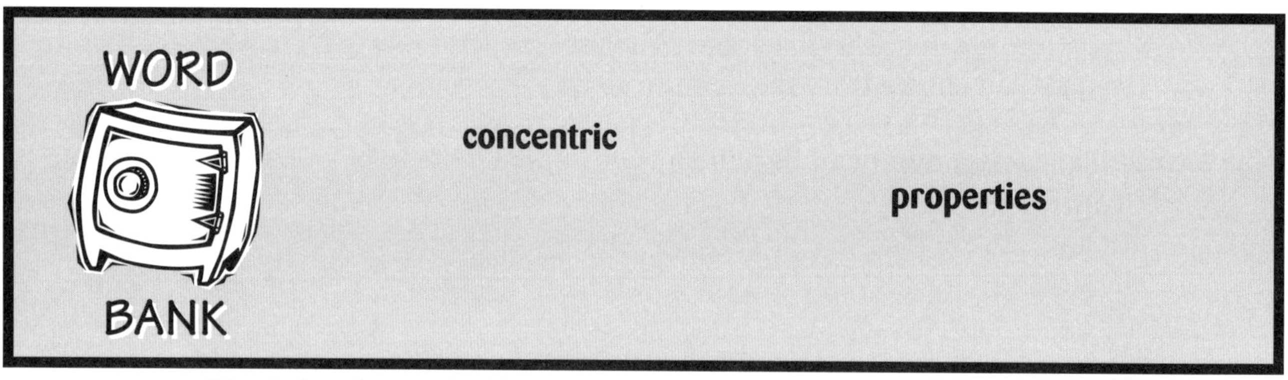

Watch for these valuable words wherever you see the word bank icon. 

BRAIN TEASERS

(1) What do a person's hands communicate?
(2) Why should an actor study a person's hands?

CUE SHEET

"But what do I do with my hands?" is often the cry of the actor. Hands, like feet and legs, must be in harmony with your role. If you are truly portraying a calm character, you must not have nervous hands. If your role is that of a muscular, athletic individual, you must exhibit strength in all parts of your body, including the hands.

Hands are a looking glass into people. They show your state of mind by being calm, agitated, clenched. Hands show what work you do. Rough calloused ones announce hard manual labor. Smooth soft hands indicate "white collar" work—or perhaps no work at all. Hands show age as Hollywood and television stars know. When you are old, you can have your face surgically lifted, but your wrinkled and spotted hands can still give your age away.

Be aware of people's hands. Study them. Remember them. Give yourself a storehouse from which you can draw to create special characters.

WARMUPS

Go through the basic body warmups before doing the following as a class.

Handling Hands
Divide the class into two evenly numbered groups. Form two concentric circles, facing each other. Take hold of the hands of the person in front of you. Examine them, feel them, clasp them. With side coaching, your teacher will suggest aspects to look for. Determine to yourself what the appearance of the hands communicates. Your partner will examine your hands in like fashion. When your teacher commands, the inner circle should move one step to the right to give everyone a new partner. Repeat the scrutiny. Continue until you have observed several classmates' hands.

Locked Hands
Clasp your hands together and close your eyes. Now opening your eyes as though you had just awakened, discover that your hands are locked tightly together. No matter how you struggle, they remain solidly clasped. Only after strenuous effort do you succeed in freeing them.

ACTIVITY AND ITS PURPOSE

Hand It To You
With a partner, improvise a short scene showing who, where, and what with hands only. If you wish, you may use hand properties (small items you handle in the scene).

Focal Point: Communicate who, where, and what with hands only.

HOW TO PREPARE

(1) Your teacher will assign you a partner. Together, decide whom each of you will play, where the scene occurs, and what happens.

Scene example:
We see the efficient hands of someone counting packets of paper money on a table, noting the sum on a calculator at the side. The hands hesitate, interrupted with a sound—apparently a knocking at the door, for a second pair of hands enters. These are nervous hands. They hesitate, then delve into a pocket and produce some more paper bills, which the efficient hands readily accept. As the first pair of hands turns to leave the table to use the calculator, we see the nervous hands quickly grab a few bills and return them to his or her pocket.

Suggestions:

(a) Piano lesson with teacher and pupil
(b) Manicure session with gossiping ladies
(c) Video game
(d) Grandparent and baby playing
(e) Criminal signing a confession in the police station
(f) Husband comforting his distressed wife as they await word about their kidnapped child

(2) Fill out the activity sheet to this chapter.

(3) Rehearse with your partner a few times to get the feel of the scene. Do not set definite action, however, as you are to play the scene with spontaneity.

HOW TO PRESENT

These scenes require that you stand behind a curtain or screen where only your hands and arms will show. If you have a puppet stage, use it.

When the teacher calls on you, hand in your activity sheet and go to the playing area with your partner. Position yourself to show only your hands and arms to the audience. Give yourself a few seconds to get into the mood and then call "curtain" and begin the scene. Do not use dialogue. You must communicate solely with your hands.

At the end of the scene, your teacher will ask the class to discuss your success at communicating who, where, and what.

Chapter 17

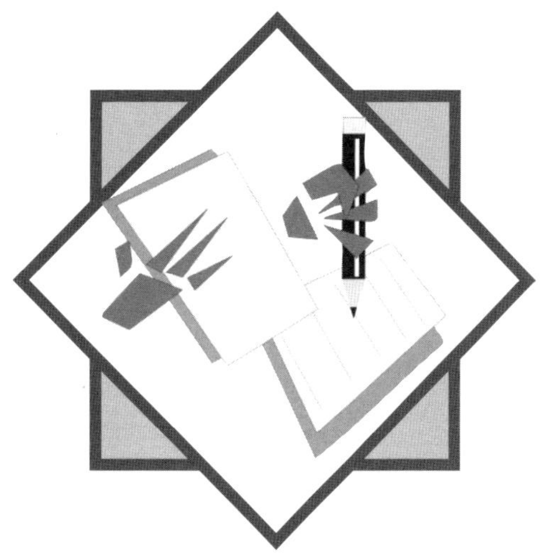

Character Sketch

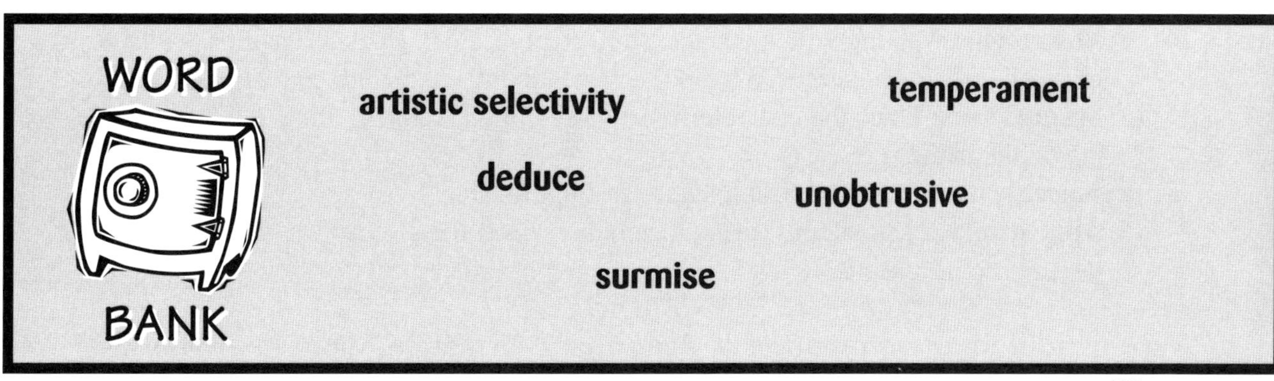

WORD
BANK
artistic selectivity
temperament
deduce
unobtrusive
surmise

Watch for these valuable words wherever you see the word bank icon. 

BRAIN TEASERS

(1) What are the internal qualities of a character?
(2) What are the external qualities of a character?
(3) How does an actor use artistic selectivity?

CUE SHEET

Nothing is harder and yet more exhilarating in the theatre than when you create a breathing true-to-life character. Using the only tools of your trade—your voice and body—you can learn to fashion an individual that becomes a person distinct from you and yet one that does not live without you.

Character creation demands intensive study. Primarily you need a knowledge of people. Past experiences with family and friends and close observation of individuals either in life or in books will provide inspiration. Stored sensory recall and a vivid imagination will add further material.

As you create a specific role either for an improvisation or for a scripted play, you should analyze that character's internal and external qualities.

Internal qualities will give you a basic idea of personality. They include:

(1) **Background:** What can you discover about the character's family, education, job, hobbies?
(2) **Mentality:** Is the character intelligent, average, dull, clever?
(3) **Attitude and Values:** What does the character believe in? What are the character's ideals, attitude toward people, outlook on life, goals in life?
(4) **Temperament:** Is the character shy, confident, bitter, happy, sullen? What are the likes and dislikes?

External qualities include those outward aspects an audience can readily see. Externals are important in that they usually communicate inward traits. They include:

(1) **Posture:** Tall, slumped, stiff, relaxed?
(2) **Movement:** Walking with a bounce, shuffle, plod, float, stride? Gestures: awkward, graceful, exact, hesitating? What do they tell about age, health, and attitude?
(3) **Mannerisms:** Does the character repeatedly cough, scratch, chew gum, bite nails, tap on the table?
(4) **Voice:** Is it high, low, pleasant, harsh, grating, musical?
(5) **Appearance:** Neat, sloppy, prim, clean, dirty? Are the clothes fashionable, in good taste, extreme, casual?

Such careful analysis produces a wealth of information, more than you need. You must learn, therefore, what to use and what to discard. We call this *artistic selectivity*. In creating a role, decide how little you can use and still *communicate the necessary ideas and emotions*. Your aim is a clear cut, yet believable, person.

WARMUPS

Run through both the body and voice warmup routines before doing the following:

Blind Move
Use as large a group as space will allow. With your eyes kept constantly closed (no peeking) or with a blindfold on them, move freely around the room by crawling, running, hopping, jumping, and rolling, in as many variations as you can. As you move, be careful that you do not touch anyone. If you do, you must remain solidly stuck to the other person at the point where you contacted and from then on move together as a unit. Game winner is the last person who is not glued to someone.

Focal Point: Move blindfolded but without touching anyone. If you touch, remain glued to that person and move as a unit.

ACTIVITY AND ITS PURPOSE

Character Sketch
Without being obvious, you are to observe at length and analyze a real person, before creating that person in a 3 to 4 minute group improvisation.

Focal Point: Move, speak, listen, and react as the person you observed.

HOW TO PREPARE

(1) From the following suggestions or from a list your teacher provides, choose a public place where you can observe an individual at length. No more than two or three should choose the same place.

(a) restaurant
(b) bus stop
(c) airport
(d) museum
(e) doctor's waiting room
(f) public library
(g) church
(h) subway
(i) auction sale
(j) grocery store
(k) video arcade
(l) shopping mall

(2) Commit to memory the internal and external factors, so you will know what to observe.

(3) Go to the place you have chosen. If you attend with another classmate, separate from each other to prevent its being obvious what you are doing. Carefully look around until your interest focuses on one person. Then using your developed powers of observation and concentration quietly study everything you can about that individual. If possible, spend 10 to 15 minutes observing. Observe all of the external qualities. Try to deduce internal qualities from the behavior. Be unobtrusive. The person you scrutinize should not know you are studying them. If it is possible, take notes. Otherwise, store the information in your mind.

(4) At home, fill out the activity sheet. Do not do this at the time of observation. Do it later. You can be specific about the externals, but you will have to surmise the internal qualities, basing them on intuition from observation.

(5) Determine what qualities you will use to communicate the essence of the person.

(6) Rehearse your creation by doing the following in character:

(a) sit in a chair
(b) eat a hamburger
(c) put on a jacket
(d) open a letter

HOW TO PRESENT

Your teacher will divide the class into groups of five or six. When your group participates, hand in your activity sheet.

As a warmup, your teacher will call on each member of your group to do in character one or two of the situations you rehearsed at home: sit in a chair, eat a hamburger, put on a jacket, or open a letter.

When each group member has presented, your teacher will quickly describe a situation in which you assume your observed character. Suggestions include:

(1) Characters waiting in a doctor's office. One person is the secretary.
(2) Characters waiting to board an airplane that is late. One person will be the airline agent.
(3) Characters in the waiting room of a hospital.
(4) Characters gathering for a school board meeting.
(5) Characters gathered for a garage sale.
(6) Characters gathered at a class reunion.

Get immediately involved in the situation, creating necessary action. Keep your mind on your focal point: move, speak, listen, and react as the person you observed.

At the end of 3 to 4 minutes, or when the scene is played out, your teacher will call "cut." Your group and the audience should discuss what was communicated and what needs to be improved.

Art is a lie that makes us realize the truth.
—Pablo Picasso

Chapter 18

The Trouble Is

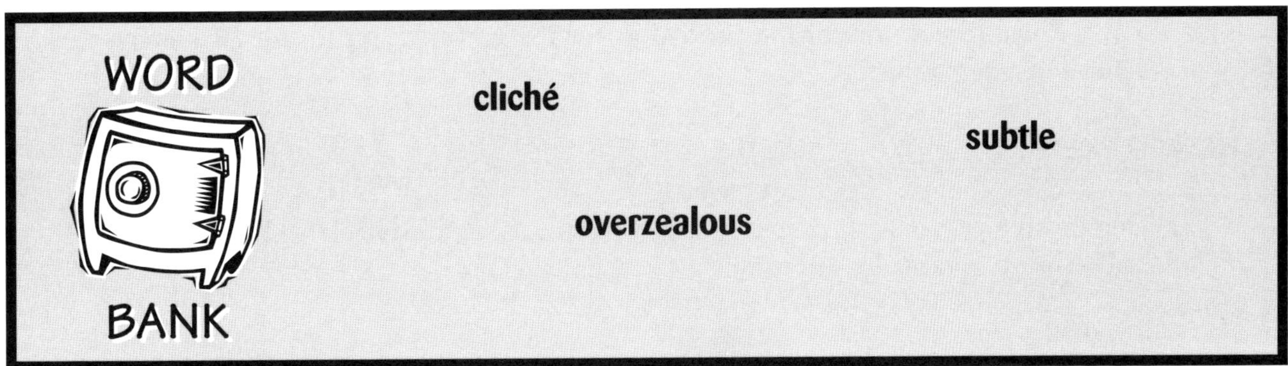

Watch for these valuable words wherever you see the word bank icon. 

BRAIN TEASERS

(1) In their eagerness to communicate, what two "no no's" should actors avoid?
(2) In addition to those cited in the chapter, what cliché movements can you list?

CUE SHEET

Sometimes actors are so intent on making their ideas clear that they overdo an action— "ham" it up—or exaggerate beyond what is necessary for audience understanding. Or, the overzealous actor uses unimaginative cliché movements, which are actions that have been so frequently repeated as to become commonplace and ineffectual. Rubbing your hands together to denote coldness, putting your hand to your ear to suggest deafness, pointing to the sky with a happy smile on your face to indicate that a brilliant idea has occurred to you, are examples of clichés. Avoid them!

Instead, search for imaginative action that shows your character's individuality in an artistically subtle message (one that the audience gets without feeling beaten over the head with it). Try your hand at this artistic theatrical touch in the following projects.

WARMUPS

Do the basic body and voice warmups. Then repeat *Magic Object* described in Chapter 4.

ACTIVITY AND ITS PURPOSE

The Trouble Is....
You are to give a 1 to 2 minute personal experience speech during which you are bothered with a physical irritation that you cannot openly remedy because of the people watching you.

Focal Point: Concentrate on the discomfort you feel and on trying to hide all attempts to relieve that discomfort.

HOW TO PREPARE

(1) Decide on a personal experience that you can easily and briefly (1 to 2 minutes) talk about. Examples include:

(a) A fishing trip
(b) A day at the zoo
(c) The time my dog ran away
(d) A shopping spree
(e) My first lesson in bowling
(f) How I broke my leg
(g) My slumber party
(h) A trip to Yellowstone National Park
(i) A day at the dentist
(j) The time I was a hero

(2) Determine a physical irritation that is supposed to be bothering you during your speech. Suggestions include:

(a) An itchy nose
(b) A too tight collar
(c) A sneeze that won't quite come
(d) An itching between the toes of your left foot
(e) A shoulder strap that has fallen and hampers gestures
(f) A contact lens that has slipped into the corner of your eye
(g) A piece of chicken caught between your teeth

(3) Fill out the activity sheet to this chapter.

(4) Rehearse your speech and physical irritation in front of a full length mirror.

HOW TO PRESENT

Hand your activity sheet to your teacher when you are called on. Then go to the playing area and begin your speech. While talking, focus on the discomfort you feel because of the physical irritation. Let the irritation move you rather than the other way around. Try to remedy or relieve the discomfort as you speak, but as you do so, attempt to conceal your efforts from the audience. Your teacher will call "cut" after 1 to 2 minutes or when the scene seems over.

Chapter 19

Many Meanings

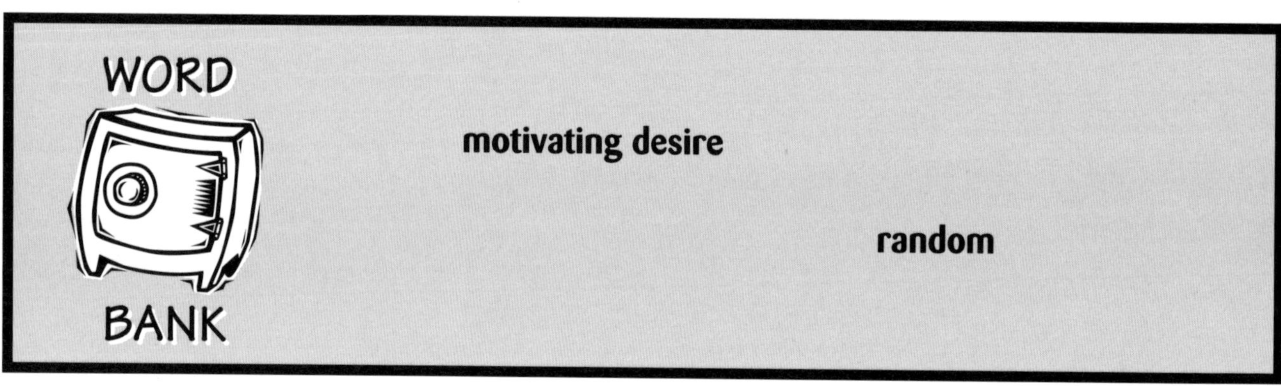

Watch for these valuable words wherever you see the word bank icon. 

BRAIN TEASERS

(1) Of what importance is it for you to know your character's desire or wants?

CUE SHEET

You are asked to play a scene. You know *who* you are to be, you know *where* the scene takes place, you know *what* the basic action is, but you are still puzzled. You ask, "*How* do I do it?" The answer is a valuable principle you may already have realized from past projects: Actors know *how* to do something if they know *why* the character is doing it.

For example, suppose your teacher tells you to go to the front of the room and move around, looking at the floor. If you do this for a few minutes, you are probably going to feel rather silly because your movements are random and meaningless. You lack a specific purpose. You don't know what to do because you don't know why you are there. But if you are told that you have lost a diamond out of your ring and you heard it drop, your looking at the floor takes on meaning. If you are told that there is a secret trap door in the floor and you want to hide some money in it, you will scrutinize it in yet another way. If you are hired to refinish the floor and must estimate size, cost, and material, you will move and observe quite differently from the other two situations.

Remember, knowing *why* will assist you in knowing how to do something. So it is important for you to concentrate always on your character's why — which is his or her *motivating desire* or want.

You do this in everyday life. You are usually more concerned with the *reason* for an action rather than with the action itself. You clean the living room because you want to impress your date. You wash the car because you won't get your allowance until you do. You mow the lawn because you want permission to go fishing. So transfer this everyday truth to the stage and concentrate on what your character wants.

WARMUPS

Practice the routine body and voice warmups before doing the activity.

ACTIVITY AND ITS PURPOSE

Many Meanings
You and a partner are to improvise three different short scenes with the same memorized dialogue. How you do each scene will be determined by your character's *why* or motivating desire.

Focal Point: Concentrate on your character's desire.

HOW TO PREPARE

(1) Your teacher will appoint you a partner and assign both of you one of the two following dialogues:

Dialogue I:
(a) You're late.
(b) I know. I couldn't help it.
(a) I understand.
(b) I thought you would.
(a) I have something to give you.
(b) Really?
(a) Yes, this.

Dialogue II:
(a) Now is the time.
(b) Yes.
(a) I hadn't planned it this way.
(b) Neither had I.
(a) Well, that's the way it goes.
(b) Yes.

(2) You and your partner will now prepare separately outside of class. Determine where each of your scenes takes place and who each of you is. Then using the same place and characters, list three variations the scene could take and list the character's motivating desire (why) for each. Examples include:

	WHAT	*WHERE*	*WHO*	*MOTIVATING DESIRE (WHY)*
(a)	PARTING SCENE	PARK	MAN	WANTS TO LEAVE IMMEDIATELY
			WOMAN	WANTS TO DELAY HIM
(b)	CRIME SCENE	PARK	MAN	WANTS TO GET CLOSE ENOUGH TO GRAB HER PURSE
			WOMAN	WANTS TO AVOID HIM AND LEAVE
(c)	LOVE SCENE	PARK	MAN	WANTS TO KISS HER BUT IS EMBARRASSED
			WOMAN	WANTS TO KISS HIM BUT IS EMBARRASSED
(d)	QUARREL SCENE	PARK	WOMAN	WANTS TO HURT HIM WITH SARCASM
			MAN	WANTS TO CALM HER BUT IS BEWILDERED

(3) Fill out the activity sheet to this chapter.

(4) Memorize the assigned dialogue, learning *both* parts so you can take either role. Do not plan or rehearse actions. You and your partner are to improvise the movement and meaning behind the lines as you say the memorized dialogue.

HOW TO PRESENT

Hand your activity sheet to your teacher when called upon. Proceed with your partner to the playing area.

From your list or that of your partner's, your teacher will select and announce the scene (with its where, who, what, why) that you are to play. He or she will also indicate which lines each of you is to speak.

Using your memorized dialogue, play the scene as suggested, concentrating on your character's why: the desire. Knowing the why will help you to determine how you move and how you say the lines.

When the dialogue is finished, your teacher will ask for class discussion on what you communicated. You will then be assigned another scene variation listed on one of your activity sheets. Use the same dialogue to play this scene.

Your teacher will have you do other variations if time allows. You may even be asked to play the same situation but to switch dialogue, with you saying the lines your partner previously used. Notice throughout that the *why* determines the *how*.

Chapter 20

Evolving Emotions

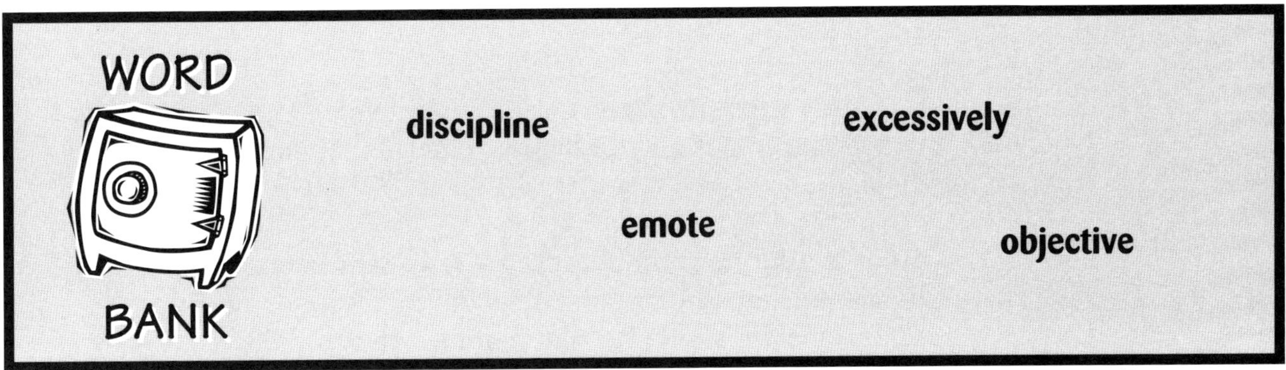

Watch for these valuable words wherever you see the word bank icon. 

BRAIN TEASERS

(1) What is meant by "theatrical reality?"
(2) Why must an actor use controlled emotions on stage?
(3) What are the two basic principles of stage emotions?

CUE SHEET

Do not confuse theatre and life. Good theatre is *not* life; it is an art that presents a highly concentrated interpretation of life. Like artificial fruit it is not real—it only *appears* to be real.

Everything on the stage evolves around this "theatrical reality." Actions are carefully selected; time is compressed; character traits are focused; and emotion is controlled. All of this makes it possible for the audience to see a person's lifetime in the span of two hours, or to clearly witness cause and effect because of the careful distillation of events that focuses attention on a specific aspect.

In real life it may take an hour for dinner, on stage perhaps five minutes. In real life people's actions are generally cluttered and busy. On stage the artistic selectivity we discussed in Chapter 17 predominates to present a heightened effect that "zooms in" on the core. In real life we often emote excessively during our high and low times. We exhaust ourselves with a tantrum, or we uncontrollably giggle our joy. This is not so on the stage. There, emotion is objective, handled by a disciplined actor who adjusts feelings to the demands of the role.

False is the idea that a good actor uses the theatre for his or her own emotional release. Personal "hang ups" have no place on stage. Truly fine actors must handle emotions with discipline to maintain theatrical reality. They must always be in control, ready to turn on or shut off the emotion, ready to give just the right touch to enable the audience to experience the feelings too.

Your participation in past projects has included some emotional response. In this chapter, you are to continue learning how to control emotions so that *you* rather than they will be the master. In order to do this, you must learn the following basic principles of emotion:

(1) Emotions start first with an inner action or response that comes before all outward movement and dialogue. Something dynamic must happen inside of you.

(2) Having this inner feeling, an actor must then physically communicate it to the audience. Perhaps he or she raises an eyebrow, or perhaps throws a vase, but a controlled and noticeable activity must occur.

WARMUPS

Do the basic body and voice warmup routines before participating in the following:

Emotion Talk
As a class discuss and experiment with the following emotions:

(1) *Laughter* and the various emotions it can show, such as joy, sarcasm, embarrassment, nervousness, hysteria, hate. If you have trouble manufacturing a laugh, try expelling your breath with explosive spurts from your diaphragm.

(2) *Crying* and the various situations it can express such as sorrow, hysteria, happiness. Produce crying by inhaling with little gasping sobs. When talking, sob between words rather than on them. Be sure to put some tears in your voice too.

(3) *Anger* and the various ways your body communicates this emotion.

(4) *Other emotions* such as love, hate, fear, exasperation, depression and how your body communicates them.

Inner Scream

While seated at your desk scream silently. As you do this, make sure you scream with your whole body—your back, arms, toes, stomach, wrists. If you accomplish this scream correctly, you will have experienced the basic principle of inner action we discussed above. Now repeat the inner scream, and at the ripe moment, when your whole body is primed, your teacher will side coach you to scream out loud.

Focal Point: Concentrate on your whole inner self screaming.

Danger Freeze

In groups of two or three improvise a scene in which all of you are unable to move because of an outside danger. Examples include:

(1) Fugitives hiding from the searching police
(2) Soldiers finding themselves in the midst of a mine field
(3) Passengers in a train accident

Fugitives

Focal Point: Concentrate on your inability to move.

Continuous Chant

Divide into groups of 5 to 10. One group stands quietly in the playing area. Another group congregates to the side and begins chanting one word such as a :

(1) Torture word ("shame," "hate," "jealous").
(2) Worry word ("fear," "doubt," "ridicule").
(3) Soothing word ("gentle," "caress," "contentment").

Whether the chant crescendos to a loud climax or diminishes to a soft whisper, it must be constantly spoken. The listening group should respond to the word in any way they feel.

Focal Points: *Chanters:* create a mood that the word suggests.
Listeners: respond to the word any way you wish.

ACTIVITY AND ITS PURPOSE

Evolving Emotions
By yourself you are to improvise a scene in which you handle certain objects while feeling a specific emotion. Then something happens to change your emotion and you rehandle those objects in reverse, showing that changed emotion.

Focal Point: Communicate your inner feeling by the way you handle objects.

HOW TO PREPARE

(1) Decide on a simple 1 to 2 minute scene that requires activity and an emotion. Then, determine what occurs within your scene to change the emotion and make you reverse the activity. Examples:

Where: Gymnasium
Who: High school student
What: Hanging a large "Welcome Winner" banner

Beginning inner action:
Happiness at the thought of welcoming a winning basketball team

Second inner action:
Disappointment at learning that the team lost their final game

Scene:
Happily you unfold a large banner and pick up the rope at one end. You climb a ladder and tie the rope to the ceiling beam. Then you climb down, carry the ladder to the other end, pick up the rope, climb the ladder again, and secure the sign. After climbing down, you are proudly looking at the banner when a friend enters to tell you that the team has lost, not won, its final game. Your emotion (inner action) changes to disappointment as you look at the sign. You show this changed inner feeling, as you reverse the steps in the activity: climb the ladder again, untie the ends, and fold up the banner.

Activity suggestions:

(a) Pack a suitcase; then discover you can't go.
(b) Wrap a package to give to a special friend, and then for some reason you must unwrap it.
(c) Arrange in a vase some flowers that were sent to you. Then something occurs that makes you replace them in the box.
(d) Prepare for a special party and then learn that your date has cancelled.

(2) Fill out the activity sheet to this chapter.

(3) Rehearse your scene. Work on showing how you feel by the way you handle the objects in the scene.

HOW TO PRESENT

Give your activity sheet to your teacher before going to the playing area. Set up necessary furniture. Announce the "where" but do not tell anything else about the improvisation. Then allow yourself a few seconds to create your beginning inner action before calling "curtain" and starting the scene. Communicate your emotions to the audience by total body response, facial expression, and the way you handle the objects.

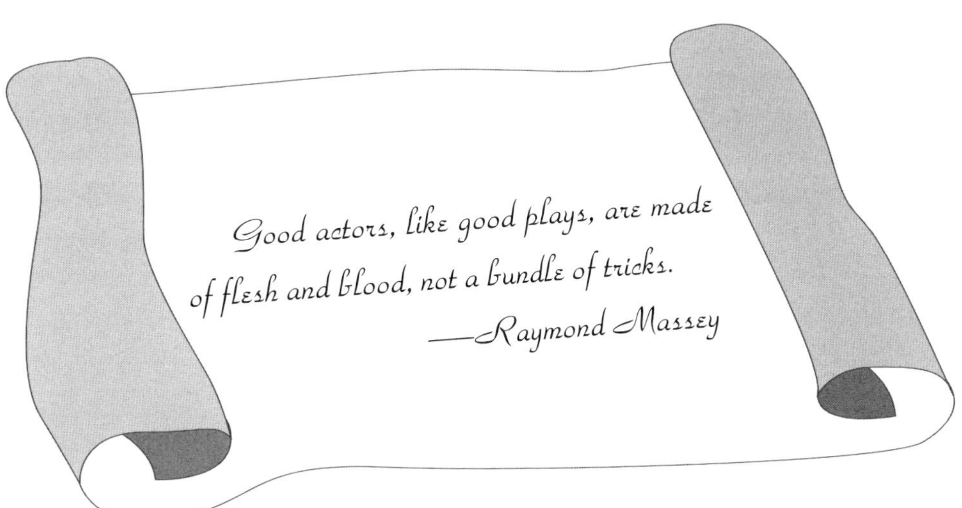

Good actors, like good plays, are made
of flesh and blood, not a bundle of tricks.
—Raymond Massey

Chapter 21

Disaster Strikes

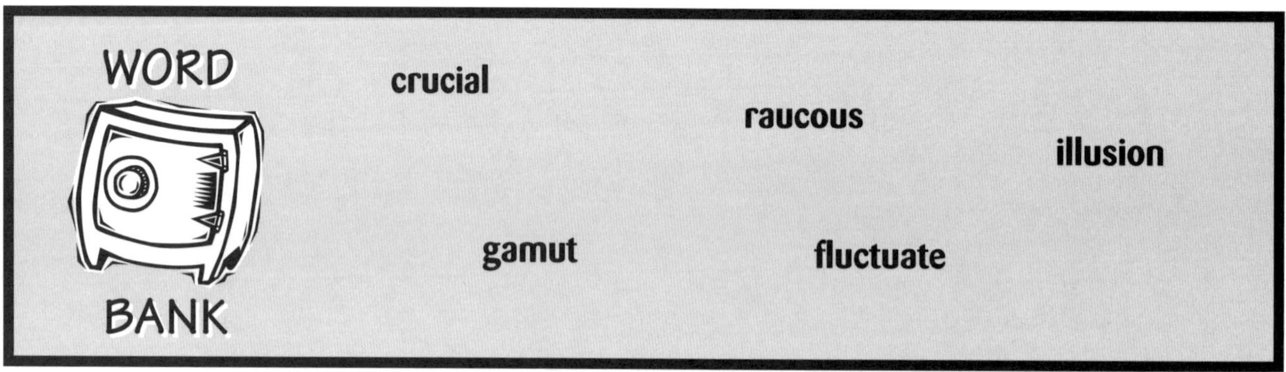

Watch for these valuable words wherever you see the word bank icon. 

BRAIN TEASERS

(1) How does an actor achieve emotional control on stage?
(2) What is the difference between acting as *if* you were a character, and trying to become a character?

CUE SHEET

Controlled emotion on stage does not imply an absence of hysteria, screams, raucous laughter, foot stomping or glass smashing. On the contrary, intense outbursts are frequent in theatrical reality, for drama usually depicts crucial moments in life that require impassioned outbursts.

Control means that actors have been trained to always be in command of their functions. They can start, maintain, and fluctuate an emotion. Perhaps even more important, they can stop it. They are skilled artists who communicate only the degree of feeling necessary for that particular scene. And when the role is finished, they can easily be themselves again. Stage control allows actors to be objective, working as *if* they were the character. They do not try to become the person. They know, and so does the audience, that they are not really the character. They are not actually dying on stage. Tomorrow night, and as long as the play runs, they will "die" each performance. But through imagination the audience accepts this illusion. Through control the actors achieve it. They should be able, therefore, to run the gamut of emotionality without feeling a personal drain.

WARMUPS

Practice the body and voice warmup routines and then do the following exercises:

Emotion Gamut Game
Divide into groups of five or six. One person begins a scene with a definite where, an activity, and an emotion. A second character enters and immediately presents a different mood, place, and activity. The first person then changes to that emotion, activity, and locale and continues the scene with the newcomer. Character three enters and again alters the mood, setting, and action to which the others respond. Continue until the whole group has participated.

Focal Point: Physically communicate each emotional change.

Silence
Choose a partner and improvise a scene in which there is such a great emotional stress neither of you can talk. Determine the where, who, and what. Then play the scene without dialogue but with great meaning. Scene suggestions include:

(1) Where: Living room
Who: Husband and wife
What: Have just received word of their son's death.

(2) Where: Family room
Who: Spouses of two astronauts
What: Waiting to see on TV if the spacecraft landing is successful.

(3) Where: Cafe
Who: Long time business partners
What: Each has learned that he or she has been betrayed by the other.

Focal Point: Communicate your character's feelings through the silence.

ACTIVITY AND ITS PURPOSE

Disaster Strikes
You are to improvise a short scene that evolves around a disaster, an accident, or a grieving situation. One student will begin the scene and when others know what is going on, they will enter as characters and participate.

Focal Point: Concentrate on physically communicating your inner action (emotion) of grief, hysteria, remorse, anger, etc.

HOW TO PREPARE

(1) Outside of class, decide on two disaster scenes and their where, who, what. Determine what activity you can do to initiate each scene. Suggestions include:

(a) Where: Swimming pool
Who: Small child
What: Child has been pulled unconscious from the water.

Other players: Lifeguard, eyewitness, policeman, doctor, other swimmers, pool manager

(b) Where: Forest
Who: Lumberjack
What: A large tree has pinned him or her to the ground.

Other players: Co-workers, supervisor, ambulance driver

(c) Where: Outside a burning apartment house
Who: Mother
What: Her baby is in the burning building.

Other players: Neighbor, fire chief, apartment manager, paper boy

(2) Fill out the activity sheet to this chapter.

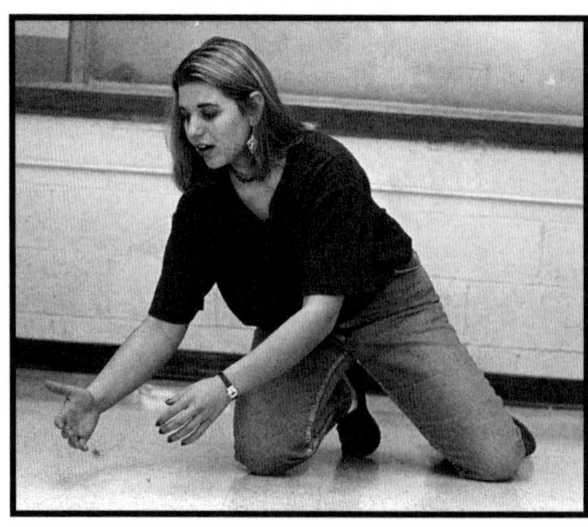

Swimming pool.

HOW TO PRESENT

When the teacher calls on you, hand in your activity sheet. Decide which of the scenes you will do (depending on what has been previously played) and then go to the playing area. Begin by doing something specific that starts the scene. Other class members will take definite roles and enter the action, advancing the emotion and the story.

When a classmate initiates a scene, you should observe carefully and then when you know what is occurring, assume a character and enter the scene. Let your inner action create outward movement that contributes to the improvisation. Do whatever is necessary—cry, scream, sob, quarrel. Just keep in control.

At the end of 2 to 3 minutes or when the action is played out, your teacher will call "cut." Then the class should discuss the scene and the communication that occurred. Did all characters relate to the scene? Did they each show their feelings by the way they handled objects and by their facial expressions? Did they maintain the scene emotion by keeping in character? Did they show their inner action rather than talk about it?

Burning apartment house.

Chapter 22

Instant Scenes

CUE SHEET

By now your imagination should be stimulated to create numerous scenes for class improvisation. The following are suggestions upon which you can build for any number of sessions. As a group, determine the focal point before each improvisation.

ACTIVITIES

Position Playing
Four to five players are required for this activity. Your teacher will assign each group member certain body positions such as pointing, kneeling, hands on hips, bowing, or hand covering eyes. While improvising you must at least once work your assigned position into a meaningful character action that advances the scene.

Unrelated Words
Three to five players are required for this activity. Your teacher will assign your group three unrelated object words that you must incorporate into an improvised scene. You must not just say the words during the scene. Instead, the objects should become key factors in the story around which the action evolves. Word suggestions include:

(1) Hammer, Zebra, radishes
(2) Ink, bracelet, bucket
(3) Turnip, clock, ball
(4) Seashell, zipper, elevator
(5) Tractor, monkey, trumpet
(6) Diamond, rosebud, dice

Character Object

Three to five players are required for this activity. Bring to class an object and place it on a table along with those objects supplemented by your teacher. Decide on a where, who, and what. Improvise a scene with each player spontaneously choosing and using an object at the instant in the scene when he or she needs it to show a relationship or an emotion. For example, a young happy couple might toss a balloon between them during their light frolicsome scene. An angry father might select and use a horn to show his loud disapproval.

Tag Line

Two players are required for this activity. Your teacher will assign you a sentence that you or your partner must use as the tag line (final sentence) to your scene. Determine a where, who, and what, and work up to using that final sentence logically. Final sentence examples include:

(1) "But it was Harry all of the time."
(2) "So it's hello again."
(3) "Silly. That was the surprise."
(4) "If you come closer, I'll scream."
(5) "There goes the last one."

Animal Antics

Three to eight players are required for this activity. Scrutinize an animal or bird in the woods, on a farm, at a zoo, or in your neighborhood. Observe its body rhythm and action. Study individual movements of its head, wings, tail, and paws. In class portray that animal with action and sound in an improvised scene. Finally, transfer your animal's characteristics into human sounds, movements, and mannerisms. For example, a woodpecker may suggest a gossipy person; a frog may develop into a fat, solid business person.

Proverb Play

Three to seven players are required for this activity. Select a proverb that will suggest a scene. With as much imagination as possible, improvise it. Proverb suggestions:

(1) A bird in the hand is worth two in the bush.
(2) A rolling stone gathers no moss.
(3) Birds of a feather flock together.
(4) Too many cooks spoil the broth.
(5) A stitch in time saves nine.
(6) Nothing ventured, nothing gained.
(7) Look before you leap.
(8) He who laughs last laughs best.
(9) Experience is the best teacher.
(10) Out of sight out of mind.
(11) When in Rome, do as the Romans do.
(12) Haste makes waste.
(13) A fool and his money are soon parted.
(14) Don't count your chickens before they are hatched.
(15) The early bird catches the worm.
(16) A watched pot never boils.
(17) Charity begins at home.

Attitude Action

Four to seven players are required for this activity. State a sentence that embodies an attitude. From that sentence, create a character and improvise a scene where all of your reactions are governed by that initial attitude.

Examples of attitude sentences include:

(1) "Nobody likes me."
(2) "The world is beautiful."
(3) "She thinks she is so smart."
(4) "Leave me alone—just leave me alone."
(5) "I'm so undecided."
(6) "Don't tell me what to do."

Wax Works
Five to eight players are required for this activity. Two players are wax sculptors. The others are globs of wax. The sculptors fashion each piece of wax into an entity which, when molded, remains in that position. When all are complete and the sculptors think they are through, each wax player begins to get warm, soften, and melt. The sculptors frantically try to keep their figures molded.

Happening
Five to ten players are required for this activity. Your teacher will give you a short poem that you are to take to the playing area and read aloud with meaning. Other readers will join you when the teacher indicates. Reading and rereading the poem, relate to the others. Communicate with them. Use no dialogue other than the poetry lines. Move all around, using what is in the room: proclaim from the steps, kneel on the floor, climb the ladder. Your teacher will hand various players a prop such as a banner, bell, drum, broom, whistle. Use these with your selection and pass them among yourselves. Your teacher may add background music and stage lighting to help create this happening.

Retirement Center
Five to ten players are required for this activity. Improvise a scene during a "recreation" period in a retirement center. Use only numbers and letters of the alphabet to communicate in gibberish. Start the scene with three players. Others join as they feel the need for additional characters and occurrences.

History Tale
Two to eight players are required for this activity. Improvise stories in history, or events leading up to the actual happenings. Do research to base your improvisation on facts.

Literature Tale
Two to ten players are required for this activity. Divide favorite literature stories into scenes and then improvise the story, adding scene on scene until the whole tale is created.

Chapter 23

The Play's The Thing

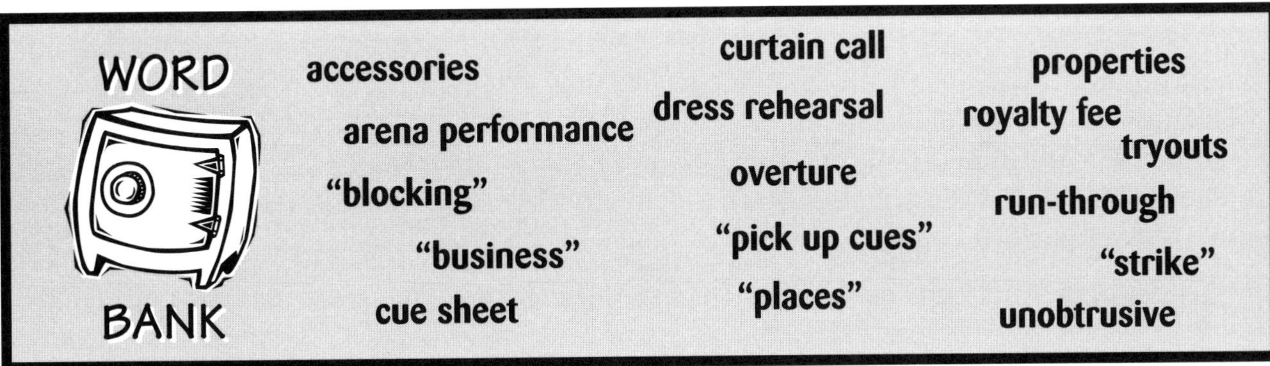

WORD
BANK
accessories
arena performance
"blocking"
"business"
cue sheet
curtain call
dress rehearsal
overture
"pick up cues"
"places"
properties
royalty fee
tryouts
run-through
"strike"
unobtrusive

Watch for these valuable words wherever you see the word bank icon. 

BRAIN TEASERS

(1) What relationship is there between improvisation and formal theatre?
(2) What should you consider in selecting a play for production?
(3) What procedure is used for casting a show?
(4) What backstage crews are needed for a show and what are their duties?
(5) What is the order and purpose of the six types of rehearsals?
(6) What theatre courtesies should you observe when working on a play?

CUE SHEET

"Places," the stage manager yells. That is your cue to be ready for the curtain and for your entrance. As the house lights are dimmed, you can hear a hush fall over the audience who eagerly await out front. You await in the wings, checking last minute details. You have theatrical makeup on your face, a costume on your back, and butterflies in your stomach. But you have studied long on the play, memorizing your role, developing your character, and rehearsing each scene. Butterflies or not, you are prepared and can do your part. Such is formal theatre.

The improvisation projects you have been previously doing in class have served two purposes: (1) they have been a learning situation in themselves—training your inner resources, teaching you how to communicate with body and voice, and giving you opportunity to cooperate with others in a creative effort—and (2) they have prepared you to step into formal theatre with a flexible body, voice, and imagination that can respond to the demands of the play, director, and role.

Like improvisations, formal theatre is fun. And like improvisations, it has its own special set of rules and regulations that you need to know in order to work effectively within the boundaries. Let's look into the procedures of formal theatre.

PLAY SELECTION

First, your director (who is usually your teacher) or you and your classmates should choose a play. It should be one that both cast and director like and one that is worth the many hours to be spent on it. This means that it should be well written with vivid characterization, expressive dialogue, and a clear chain of events that leads to a strong climax. The play should also be suitable to the available talent, equipment, and budget. The better and newer scripts demand a royalty fee for the author that must be paid in advance of performance.

TRYOUTS

In order to select actors for each part, your director will hold tryouts, preferably in the place where the play is to be presented. He or she will give you a casting sheet to fill out.

At the beginning of tryouts the director will briefly discuss the play's plot, characters, and setting. He or she will then announce the first tryout scene and choose those who wish to read. The scenes will be short and characteristic of each role. When you tryout, take the script, go to the stage, read aloud the best you can, and try not to be nervous. Your director is eager to listen to you and give you serious consideration for the part. You may also be asked to do a brief improvisation or to participate in movement exercises. When you are not trying out, listen to and carefully watch the others. You may learn from them and do better a second time.

In choosing a cast, directors will consider your physical appearance, movement, and rhythm as they relate to the part. They will listen to your voice and its ability to be flexible and to be heard. They will also judge your vitality and imagination as suited to the role, and will observe emotional intensity that can be developed. In addition, they want dependable actors who will attend rehearsals, study their parts, and cooperate with cast and crews.

BACKSTAGE CREWS

Since a play cannot be produced without reliable stage crews, your director will select crews and chairmen during the tryouts. Backstage crews are as important as the actors, and your director will choose them with care. He or she will be looking for competent people who can develop a flair for scene construction, costumes, and lights. Each crew member will be responsible to the crew chairperson who in turn is responsible to the stage manager and director. The following is a list of backstage crews and their duties. The type and number of crews, of course, will depend upon the play you are presenting and the number of people available.

(1) *Assistant director* helps the director in conducting rehearsals, typing out notices, or doing research, and sees that the practice room is ready and set up for each rehearsal.

(2) *Stage manager* has charge of all stage crews and sees that they keep to schedule. During dress rehearsal and performance he or she has supervision of the stage, giving warning calls for lights, effects, and curtain. Before opening the curtain for each scene or act, reports of "O.K." from each crew chairperson will be given to the stage manager, who also assists in setting up the scenery before the show and in taking it down afterwards.

(3) *Prompter* attends all rehearsals, taking charge of the prompt script and becoming familiar with the play. During rehearsals he or she writes in the script each character's movement that the director sets. The prompter also marks all intentional pauses in the dialogue to avoid prompting during them, marks all crew and entrance warnings, and at rehearsal cues those actors who forget their lines, using a medium voice, not a whisper. At dress rehearsal he or she times the show and scene shifts with a stopwatch. During the play if anything goes wrong on stage, the prompter should be able to assist the actors with lines when they need help. If the cast has done its job well, though, it should not need a prompter during performances and many schools prefer not to use one during the run of the show.

(4) *Stage crew* builds, paints, and puts up the scenery. If there is a scene change, the crew shifts the scenery during the show. After the last performance members "strike" the set, which means that they take down the scenery and put it in storage.

(5) *Light crew* prepares a cue sheet for light changes. Crew members also hang, focus, and connect the lights. During the technical rehearsals and the performances the crew runs the light board and dimmer.

(6) *Sound effects crew* prepares a cue sheet and provides the necessary sound effects by actually making the sound or by playing a tape of it. The crew also selects and has the director approve of mood music to be played for the overture and transitions.

(7) *Costume crew* plans each character's costumes, listing them on a chart. Crew members borrow, rent, or make the costumes. During dress rehearsals and performances, they hang each actor's costume in scene or act sequence with accessories (hats, gloves, ties) gathered in a marked box. The crew keeps all costumes mended and pressed and assists

actors in dressing and making quick changes. In addition the crew helps actors keep their dressing rooms clean, and after the show they assist in returning costumes to the proper places.

(8) *Makeup crew* plans makeup for each actor and obtains necessary supplies. During dress rehearsal and performances the crew arrives at the makeup rooms early, spreading newspapers on tables and setting out makeup and mirrors. They assist the actors in applying makeup. This crew keeps the makeup rooms clean and puts the supplies away after each show.

(9) *Property crew* prepares an accurate list of properties (set furnishings including furniture, ornaments, drapes, and pictures) for each scene and obtains them for use. The chairman will assign each member specific props to set up and strike. The crew organizes the props in a separate basket for each scene. After the final performance the crew returns all borrowed props and stores all of those belonging to the school.

(10)*Publicity crew* advertises the play by giving news stories to the school and local newspapers. Stories should have the director's approval and should contain title and author of play, dates, place, time of performance, and director, cast, and crew names. If possible, the crew makes arrangements for newspaper pictures. With the director's permission the crew may use other publicity sources such as making and placing posters in store windows, mailing post cards to interested people, or hanging over a main street in town a banner that advertises the play.

(11)*Ticket crew* designs the tickets and orders them early (specifying a different color for each performance, if possible). When the printed or duplicated tickets are ready, the crew should number each in the upper right-hand corner in order to keep a record of those sold and by whom. The ticket crew should sell tickets in advance, being assisted by the whole company. Remaining tickets may be sold at the door. The following is a ticket sample:

Name of School
presents
PLAY TITLE
Author
Place
Date
Time
Price

(12)*Program crew* designs and organizes the printed program. Attractive programs on colored paper can easily be made using a computer and printer. Programs usually include a title page or cover that names the play, author, producing group, date, time and place.

The cover should also have some design or sketch that fits the play and its mood. Inside, the left page should list cast in order of appearance and tell the time and place of each scene or act. The opposite page should list all backstage members by crew and acknowledge the play's publishing house and any local business firms or individuals who have loaned items for stage use. The back of the program should list any necessary information about the play and any other coming events in your school. Be sure your programs look neat, smart, and professional with all names spelled correctly.

(13)*Ushers* greet the audience with a friendly smile and a "good evening," or "good afternoon." Ushers stationed at the door will hand out programs and take tickets. Other ushers will escort the audience to their seats. Since plays are festive occasions, ushers should dress up in good clothes or in appropriate costumes planned and approved by the director. As soon as the theatre empties after each performance, ushers should check all rows for lost articles and turn these items in to the teacher. They should deposit used programs and rubbish in waste or recycling containers.

REHEARSALS

During the weeks that the backstage crews are planning and carrying out their duties, the director rehearses the cast. Prior to the first rehearsal, the whole production has been carefully planned. Not only does the director know the exact goal for each backstage crew, he or she knows the play thoroughly—its theme, its mood, its climaxes, and each character's motivating desire. The director has divided the play into workable rehearsal scenes and has scheduled rehearsals to utilize the actor's time efficiently. When called to a practice, the actor knows it is for working rather than waiting. At the first session, the director will mount a rehearsal schedule on the stage bulletin board and will hand out duplicates to cast and crews. Seldom will this schedule be changed, so plan to meet it!

How you behave at rehearsal greatly determines your success in the play. You must expect to maintain standard theatre policies by attending all rehearsals when you are called. You should also be prompt and be on your best behavior. Practicing a show is serious work, but if everyone cooperates as a team, rehearsal provides adventuresome fun.

Rehearsal time varies according to the length and difficulty of the play and the experience of the actors. Three-act plays will need five or six weeks for rehearsing three hours a day, five or six days a week. For one-act plays, schools need at least three to four weeks of rehearsal, three or four times a week. Thus, if time is short or acting experience limited, one-act plays are a good choice. You will learn more, have more fun, and achieve greater success if you present a one-act or a series of them rather than if you try to sustain a long play. Besides, one-act plays are becoming increasingly popular. Many current playwrights are creating one-acts that are played by professionals on and off Broadway.

Your director will plan specific goals for each rehearsal period. A standard rehearsal sequence that your director may use is listed below:

(1) *Reading* rehearsals immediately follow casting. All cast and crews attend and sit around a large table. The purpose of this rehearsal is to help the group gain an understanding of

the play. The director discusses his or her interpretation of the play and the concept of the characters, the theme, and climaxes. A drawing of the floor plan is shown and possibly a watercolor sketch of the scenery. Each actor reads his or her part, with the director correcting any mispronunciation or misinterpretation. The director may ask questions like "Why does your character say that? What does he want? What does this reveal about her?" You should also ask questions that will help you understand the characters and the play better.

(2) *Blocking* rehearsals follow reading rehearsals. Here the director blocks the scene, which means you are given specific basic movement—crosses, groupings, entrances, and exits—that will coordinate with your lines. As the director indicates your moves, write them in your script with a pencil. Do not use ink, as you may need to erase if the blocking is later changed. Always take a pencil to rehearsal when you have books in hand and notate all directions. Your director will block one scene at a time and repeat it to help you set it in your mind. After each scene is set, you should begin memorizing your lines for that scene.

(3) *Developing* rehearsals are conducted after blocking is set for the whole play. During the first rehearsal without scripts, your director will help you with stage business (detailed bits of action such as dialing a phone, sewing, or writing a letter, as distinguished from stage grouping and crosses). Other developing rehearsals will be devoted to characterization, motivation, concentration, relationship of characters, and projection of emotion and voice. During these rehearsals you can begin using dummy props—anything that will work until the actual properties are available closer to production date. At these sessions your director may be on stage with you part of the time, going out front when an overall view is needed. At times concentration will be on certain scenes. At other times the director will have a complete run-through of the play.

(4) *Polishing* rehearsals perfect the play. They are what many groups never take time to have, and yet these are the rehearsals that make the difference between mediocre and high quality performances. While polishing, the director works out front in the auditorium where it is easier to test stage grouping and check for those details that make a believable play. He or she insures that you say your lines loudly and clearly, emphasizing the important ones. The director deletes any unnecessary movement, coordinates group scenes with the rest of the show, encourages ensemble playing, and refines the tempo to create vigorous climaxes that alternate with less intense scenes. The director sees that you "pick up your cues" which means that no time elapses between when you begin your line and when your partner's speech ends. And he or she checks to be sure your acting is believable at all times.

(5) *Technical* rehearsals coordinate backstage and acting aspects. The first technical rehearsal is held on stage without the actors. Crews set up scenery, mount lights, place furniture, and hang curtains. They also practice any scene and prop shifts or lighting changes. The second technical rehearsal is with the cast. Those places in the script having changes are repeatedly run-through until the crews can manage quietly and quickly. The stage crew now marks furniture positions on the floor with masking tape so furniture will be placed in the same spot each time. The stage manager practices opening and closing the act curtain.

(6) *Dress* rehearsals coordinate all aspects of the play. There are usually three dress rehearsals. A list of their times, procedures, and regulations should be handed to each cast and crew member before the first dress. Each dress rehearsal—like other rehearsals—should begin and end promptly.

Undoubtedly there will be some confusion at the first dress rehearsal when every element is brought into harmony with the whole. But the last dress rehearsal should go smoothly if previous work has been efficient and if cast and crews cooperate. Contrary to belief, a bad final dress generally means a bad performance. So never leave details to the last minute. Everyone involved deserves a perfected final dress rehearsal that will provide the confidence to produce a strong performance.

The first dress rehearsal uses sound, lights, scenery shifts, and properties. The cast wears full costume but no makeup. The director sits out front, and in order to watch the show constantly and to avoid any interruptions, he or she may dictate notes which the assistant will write down. The prompter will time the show and scene shifts. After the play, the director will gather cast and crews out front to discuss the notes for improvement.

The second dress rehearsal adds makeup to the other technical aspects. Also, the cast rehearses a planned curtain call. When the curtain opens for the first call, all supporting roles should be on stage in specified places. Then the major roles enter in pairs. Actors should smile and bow in character, maintaining poise and suppressing giggles. The stage manager shuts and opens the curtain again as the whole company bows. The curtain is closed each time after applause reaches a climax, refraining from additional curtain calls when applause diminishes or when house lights come on.

Third or final dress rehearsal should be run exactly like performance. There should be absolutely no interruptions and every detail should be complete. Some directors invite a few guests to this rehearsal so that the cast can become used to an audience.

PERFORMANCE

This is the specific goal towards which you've been working. Before and during performance only those who have specific jobs should be allowed backstage. Crews should arrive early enough to have the stage completely set up about an hour before curtain. The cast should come about an hour before performance in order to warmup, dress, makeup, and check their hand props. About 15 minutes before curtain, your director will talk to the assembled cast and crews, reminding you to do the show as rehearsed and to give your best each time.

As in dress rehearsal, the stage manager has charge of performance. This enables the director to sit out front, observing the audience reaction and taking necessary notes. The stage manager should always start the show on time. If necessary, late comers may be seated after the first scene or act.

After each performance, actors remove makeup and costumes and tidy the dressing rooms. They should never leave a mess for the crews. After the final show, while enthusiasm is still keen, crews should immediately strike the set, properties, and costumes. They should return borrowed items the next work day. It is fun to have a party for cast, crews, and faculty directors. This is often held on stage after strike, or if the hour is late, at another time.

THEATRE ETIQUETTE

When you participate in shows you should observe the following specific theatre courtesies:

(1) Always be prompt for rehearsals.
(2) Come to rehearsals prepared to work.
(3) Study your part when you are not on stage; also study it at home.
(4) When not studying your part, actively watch the others on stage. You will learn from their errors and achievements.
(5) Don't leave rehearsals until you are dismissed by the director.
(6) Cooperate with all cast and crew members. There are no "stars" in a show; each person is needed to create a good production.
(7) Accept criticism cheerfully.
(8) Allow the director to direct. When he or she gives you direction, listen.
(9) Avoid a display of temperament. Be patient and pleasant. Don't criticize others.
(10) Be quiet backstage and in the rehearsal room when a practice is in progress.
(11) Be ready for entrances without having to be called. Never be late for an entrance.
(12) Remain in character whenever on stage. *Never* break and laugh.
(13) Don't look at the prompter if you forget a line. Remain in character and wait for the prompt. Listen to it carefully.
(14) Do not "mouth" other actors' lines.
(15) When the director interrupts rehearsal for another actor, stand quietly in character, ready to start again when the interruption is finished.
(16) If anything accidently falls on the stage floor, pick it up unobtrusively.
(17) Never appear in makeup or costume except backstage and on stage.
(18) Don't touch items such as lights or props that are under the management of another crew.
(19) When entering the theatre, leave personal problems behind.
(20) Give your best performance for every audience.
(21) Don't confuse acting with living.
(22) *Never* peek through the main curtain at the audience!
(23) Keep up your grades. If you can't participate in theatre and simultaneously maintain good grades, don't accept a role.

ACTIVITY AND ITS PURPOSE

"The Play's The Thing"
With your teacher serving as director, you and your classmates are to work together producing a one-act play for an assembly or evening performance. If the class is small, do one play, and each member will have either a role or a backstage job, or both. If the class is large, do two one-acts with every student having at least one job. If you have a stage, use it. If not, do the show in a large room for an "intimate" theatre presentation in arena style with the actors playing in the center and the audience sitting around the playing area on either three or four sides. This assignment will take about four weeks of class time: one week for casting and other preparations, and three or four weeks for rehearsals. Extra out of class rehearsals will probably be necessary.

HOW TO PREPARE

(1) Your teacher will provide two or three acceptable scripts from which you and the class will choose the one you wish to do. (For play suggestions see Appendix C.)

(2) After tryouts your teacher will cast the play and appoint crews and crew heads. You and each of your classmates will have a responsible job to do, either on stage or backstage.

(3) If you are cast in a part, you will rehearse during class and at other times when called by your teacher. Apply yourself to the part—write down the blocking and learn it, develop your characterization, and memorize your lines by the deadline. Your teacher will follow a rehearsal schedule similar to the one discussed in this chapter.

(4) If you are a crew member, discuss your responsibilities with your teacher and organize your duties into a schedule. Some work can be completed in class. Other jobs you will need to do after school. Remember, crew work is every bit as important as acting, so do your job with pride.

(5) If you are not going to be occupied throughout the rehearsal weeks, your teacher will assign you extra work as listed below under additional activities.

(6) You will be rated according to the checklist on the activity sheet in the Teacher's Manual. Your teacher will hand the activity sheet out now so you can see what is expected of you.

HOW TO PRESENT

Follow the basic procedure as discussed in this chapter. Work towards giving a good show. If you present the play for a very small invitational audience of parents and friends, your class may wish to serve punch and cookies afterwards or during intermission between the one-act plays. If possible, have programs to distribute at the door. Ushers should dress up to make this a special occasion.

ADDITIONAL ACTIVITIES

(1) Write a report on a past famous actor or actress such as:

(a) Edmund Kean
(b) Coquelin
(c) Talma
(d) Richard Burbage
(e) David Garrick
(f) Edwin Booth
(g) Ellen Terry
(h) Sarah Siddens
(i) Sarah Bernhardt

(2) Conduct interviews and from them write a report on a community or summer theatre group in your area. Discuss its purpose; how it is organized; how actors, crews, and directors are selected; how plays are chosen; audience size; and the group's contribution to the theatre and the community.

(3) Collect and arrange material for an interesting bulletin board on theatre. For inexpensive and good prints on actresses and actors, theatres, costumes, and Shakespeare's world, write University Prints, 21 East Street, P.O. Box 485, Winchester, MA 01890.

(4) See a professional or amateur three-act play and write an evaluation on it as though you were a professional critic. In your paper discuss the play, the acting, the production, and audience response.

(5) See and study the following videos. (For addresses, see Appendix E.)

(a) *Shakespeare and the Globe* (Films for Humanities)
Shakespeare's life and workings of the Globe.

(b) *The Origin of the Drama and Theatr*e (Insight Media)
Discussion of Greek Drama

(c) *Blocking a Scene* (Insight Media)
Basic staging in step-by-step procedures.

(d) *Page to Stage* (Insight Media)
Producing a play from first rehearsal to production.

(e) *The Directing Process* (Insight Media)
How to select, organize, and direct a play.

(f) *Lighting* (Insight Media)
Details about lighting instruments, proper handling, and how lighting affects faces and costumes.

(g) *Setting the Stag*e (Insight Media)
Three videos on preparing, painting, and texturing scenery.

(h) *Sets, Props, and Costumes* (Insight Media)
Explains basic stage equipment.

(i) *Auditioning for the Actor* (Insight Media)
How to choose material, how to create favorable impressions and how to handle readings.

(j) *Unarmed Stage Combat* (Insight Media)
Three videos on basic techniques of punches and falls, and how to perfect them.

(k) *Building a Character* (Insight Media)
Demonstrates process of creating a character and the choices available.

(l) *Creating Drama Improvisation* (Insight Media)
Shows how to unleash the imagination and the creative process.

PEANUTS® by Charles M. Schulz PEANUTS® Reprinted by permission of UFS, Inc.

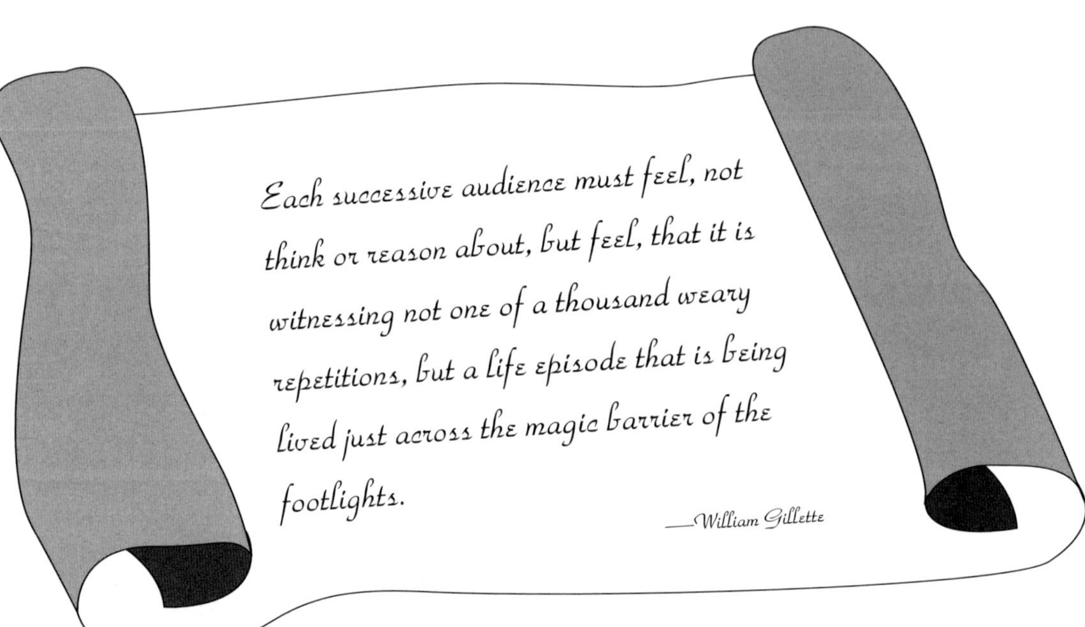
Each successive audience must feel, not think or reason about, but feel, that it is witnessing not one of a thousand weary repetitions, but a life episode that is being lived just across the magic barrier of the footlights.
—William Gillette

UNIT II

Speech

Chapter 24

Presenting

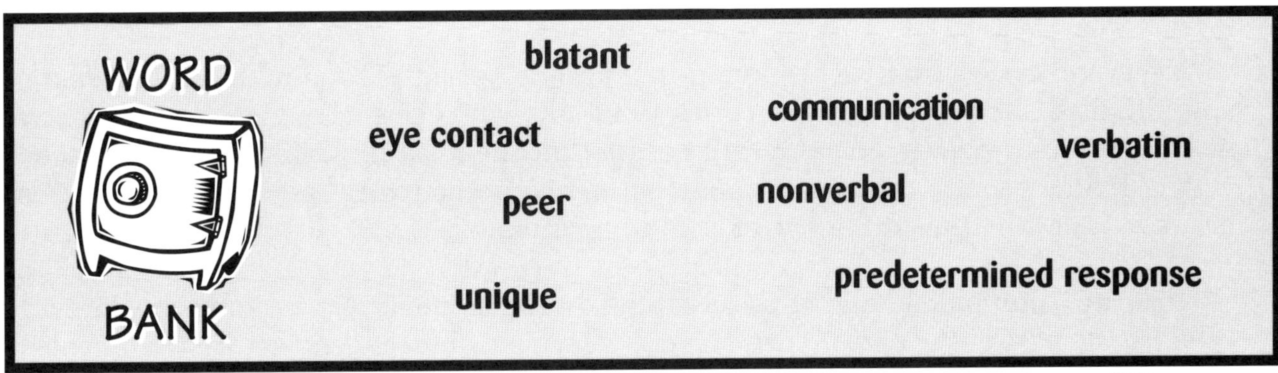

Watch for these valuable words wherever you see the word bank icon. 

BRAIN TEASERS

(1) Why is speech important?
(2) Why do we talk?
(3) How can we improve?
(4) What is the social function of speech?
(5) What does one's speech reveal?
(6) What is communication?
(7) What are the many ways we communicate?
(See "Student Introduction" on page xii.)

PLATFORM NOTES

"Buzzzzzzzzzzzzzzzz." The sound comes at you as through depths of time. You move. Perhaps you cover your ears. But the buzzing continues—nearer. And now you identify the noise. You grumble. Then with a swift, definite gesture, you reach for the blatant intruder and switch off the alarm clock. Soon you hear mother calling you. "I'm coming.

Be down in a minute," you assure her. Your day has just begun and already you have used the one major tool that connects you to every person you encounter throughout each day. That tool is speech.

Can you imagine your life without speech—the difficulty of constantly getting across your ideas with your mouth taped shut? True, you are used to some nonverbal communication: the raised eyebrow, the kick under the table, the toothpaste smile, the elbow in the ribs, the hand on the shoulder. But you would have to be a skilled mimist to achieve in silence continued subtle, detailed interaction with your associates. Even then, you would probably find such a quiet run a tremendous handicap and a frustrating barrier. For humans, speech is an integral part of life. Let us discuss this tool by focusing on its three P's: (1) *P*revalence, (2) *P*urpose, and (3) *P*romise.

Everyday you talk—all day—at breakfast, en route to school, between classes, at work. If a friend were to follow you for one day and tabulate on a manual-counter each word you spoke, you would probably both be amazed at the daily total—at the *Prevalence* of words.

Everyone knows that we are living in a unique period of time with nuclear energy, space flights, and computers. Centuries from now, when historians look in perspective at our present day, they probably will decree that the most important influence on our way of living was the total communication network encircling the earth. Our present era may indeed be called the Age of Communication.

Pick up your phone, and it is possible to talk immediately to someone in every inhabitable part of the earth. Turn on your television, and you can see instantaneously anything from a soccer match in Australia to an earthquake in Italy, watching it right now as it is happening right now, halfway across the globe—thanks to the numerous communication satellites. Walk into the nearest bookstore and you find a multitude of printed communications, mainly paperbacks, in greater quantity than humans have ever known. Scrutinize the software for your home computer and you encounter a wealth of sophisticated, current information, and networking. Even our rapid air travel brings previously unheard of communication opportunities as we breakfast in San Francisco, lunch in Honolulu, and dine in Tokyo. Very accurately, we live in an Age of Communication, with talk usually taking prime time.

Why do we talk? What is our *Purpose*? We talk to communicate, to fulfill a social need. The most important function of speech is its *social function*. Have you ever noticed that when you talk there are almost always other people present? For without people, who needs speech? The social function of speech is exhibited in at least three ways. One, *we learn to talk under social influence*. When you were born and the doctor spatted you to induce that first breath of air, you didn't look around, smile, and say "What a nice birthday party." No, you couldn't talk. All you could do was cry, loudly. Speech had to be learned. During your random babblings as a baby, certain sounds you accidently made were similar to English words. You babbled "bah," and the adults around you repeated that sound with smiles. "Ball," they said and placed a soft round object in your hands. "Bah," you mimicked. Through repetition you began to see a relationship between that funny sound "bah" and the soft round thing you wanted. All you had to do to get it was to say "bah." In this way you (and all other humans) learned speech. But if you had no social influence, no speaking humans around, you would not have learned to talk.

Two, *society develops and maintains its institutions through speech*. Whether that institution is business, education, religion, or the court system, speech is the life blood. For example, it would be difficult, indeed, to buy and sell without speech or to teach and inspire only through a book or a computer.

Three, *we gain cooperation and control of others largely through speech*. True, we can stick a gun in someone's ribs, point to his wallet, and obtain complete control without speech. But that method is not the socially acceptable way! Far better to use words that persuade him to freely offer us the money.

Yes, the social purpose of speech is to gain our listener's cooperation, or, more definitely, we talk in order to obtain a predetermined response from our listener. We want our listener, either (1) *to understand* certain information: a dance on Friday night, or how to get up on water skis; or (2) *to feel* a special way: laugh at our jokes, feel pride in the team; or (3) *to believe* in certain ideas: the high school should sponsor a car wash; our school should have exchange assemblies. In other words, before we talk we know what reaction we want from the group. If we succeed in getting that desired response, we have truly communicated. For the word communication, with its prefix "c-o-m" meaning "together," implies an interaction between speaker and listener. In simple terms, communication is an interchange of ideas, a "togetherness," a sharing process that allows the listener to understand and respond. On a more complex level we notice an interdependence among the various elements of communication. As we speak, we and our listeners simultaneously adapt to the number of people around us, to the environment (or place where we are), to the nonverbal cues we notice, and to the influences of our culture and society. Thus, we can extend the definition of communication to its being a transactional process, with all of the elements modifying the way a message is sent and received.

Now on to the third "P" in your speech study: *Promise*. Why study speech, you ask. You already know how to talk, having used words for many years. So why study speech? The reason is simple. You have the capacity to learn how to speak better. Earlier we showed that speech is a learned process. And anything learned can be changed, as you know if you have ever broken a bad habit.

Does your speech need to be changed? Just how do you sound to your peers? To your boss? To the date you are trying to impress? Every time you open your mouth and say one sentence, no matter what the words, you reveal much about yourself. Your speech tells the discerning ear as much about you as an X-ray tells your doctor about a broken bone. Say one sentence, and your speech—that X-ray—discloses the region where you were brought up, for every area has its own accents and uniqueness. Say one sentence, and you reveal your education by your ideas, vocabulary, grammar, and your sentence composition. If you are a "deese, dems, and dose" person, it shows! Say one sentence, and your personality is revealed. You show if you are timid or if you are confident, if you are a whiner, a bully, or if you are a pleasant, friendly soul. Say one sentence, and it can even indicate your state of health, for healthy or well rested individuals sound different from sick or tired people. Notice this difference the next time you visit a friend in the hospital.

So, if you don't like everything your speech and voice disclose each time you open your mouth, you can do something about it. If you have a sincere desire to improve, this speech section can offer you a promise: you can learn to be at your best, to achieve self confidence when you are talking in front of a group of people.

The practice and suggestions you will receive in this section will allow you to give talks more easily in other classes such as history, or in meetings at 4-H, a Y group, or a community club. It will help you when being interviewed by potential employers, or when presenting your nominee at a campaign rally.

In this section you can also learn specific skills such as how to build your speech with careful organization, how to cement your ideas with verbal support or evidence, and how to make the talk have style so that the audience will respond favorably with understanding and cooperation.

In addition, you will learn how to become a better listener, remembering what you hear and judging the words for their worth.

All of your days will be speech filled. You cannot alter that fact. But you *can* alter the way you speak. Let this section help you by giving freely of yourself to its varied assignments. Enthusiastically do each project given you. Then when next you hear "Buzzzzzzzzz" it will not be the sounding alarm, but the victorious buzzer signifying you as a Winner with Words.

ACTIVITY AND ITS PURPOSE

The sooner you become acquainted with everyone in this class, the quicker you will be able to profit from this section. Throughout these speech assignments you will be working closely with each member, sharing experiences, ideas, and suggestions. The class will be your audience when you speak, and their reactions to your talk will help you to determine what you must work on for improvement. Then when you are an audience member, it will be your turn to respond and be of help to the speaker. There must be a friendly give and take process in class, with members offering sincere and helpful suggestions when the teacher asks for them. When you give a speech, you will want your listeners to be attentive and quiet. When you hear your classmates, they will want your silent, undivided attention too. In this way, you will work as a team and your learning will be rapid.

During the first assignment in this section, you are to become better acquainted with the class. Although you may already know the students, there are undoubtedly things about each person to discover. In this assignment you are to give a speech to inform, telling the audience in detail about a fellow classmate. Your assignment emphasis, or the skill you are to work on especially, is eye contact. During your speech you are to look directly at your audience.

Your teacher will assign you a partner. You are to visit with this person and learn about his or her interests, background, and ideas. Then reverse roles, telling your partner about yourself. At home you will prepare a speech informing the class about the person.

HOW TO PREPARE

Your teacher will allow you and your partner 20 minutes to gather information about each other. Time yourselves so that each of you will have 10 minutes for questioning.

Refer to the activity sheet your teacher will give you. Quickly decide who will question first. When it is your turn, interview your partner according to the areas listed on the activity sheet, quickly filling in the sheet with the answers, using phrases rather than full sentences. Skip questions that do not apply, and add extra ones you feel are necessary. Do not waste time by getting sidetracked. Your purpose is to find out as much about your partner as possible in the time allowed you.

At home, take the activity sheet, and from it prepare a 1 to 3 minute speech. Your specific purpose is to tell the class what qualities make your partner special to everyone else in class. Every person *is* special, even when he or she doesn't think so. A person can be special for any number of reasons. Perhaps he or she has four sisters, or has traveled to distant places, or can teach dogs to "heel," or went fishing last summer and never caught a fish, or is allergic to bee stings, or can discuss football like a professional. Your job as speaker is to look through the information and *decide for yourself* why the person is unique or special.

Now plan your speech according to the following arrangement:

I. Introduce your partner by stating the name slowly and clearly.
II. Tell why your partner is unique, giving specific details and reasons.
III. State your partner's background:
   A. Birthplace
   B. Parent's occupation
   C. Others in family
IV. State discovered interests (add or delete items as needed):
   A. Hobbies
   B. Travel experience
   C. Awards or honors
   D. School activities participated in
   E. Pet peeve (something that really irritates him or her)
   F. Future plans
V. Conclude with a well planned statement that ties the speech together.

Now rehearse. You are to memorize only three things in your speech. You are never to memorize your speech word for word. That wastes time and limits you. Instead, memorize your first sentence in the introduction, so you can start. Memorize the concluding statement that you have carefully planned, so you can stop. Memorize the order or sequence of main points in your speech, so you know where you are going. For example, you might memorize that first you will say the name; next, why your partner is special, including background, hobbies, school activities. Your speech would include those main points in that order, and that would be all that you would talk about. As you rehearse your speech, you will know what information goes into each main point. Learning the sequence keeps your speech flowing. Remember, never learn your speech verbatim.

As you rehearse, stand in front of a full length mirror, if possible, and give your speech aloud. Say it over eight or ten times until you feel sure of yourself and the sequence of ideas. Ask a member of your family to listen to you give the speech, and as you do so, look right at that person with direct eye contact.

HOW TO PRESENT

Tear out the bottom portion of the activity sheet that your teacher will hand you, and when your teacher calls on you, hand it in. Now before you rise to speak, your partner is to walk to the front of the room and, writing large, sign his or her name on the chalkboard. Your partner will then sit down, and you will walk to the front. Turn, face your audience, pause, look right at the class, and give your speech loudly as rehearsed. When you finish, pause, and walk with poise back to your seat. Throughout the speech be businesslike and pleasant. Do not show your nervousness by giggling or making awkward noises.

ADDITIONAL ACTIVITIES

(1) Rent and show the following videos. (for addresses see Appendix E):

The Communication Process (Insight Media)
Elements of communication

The Communications Cycle (Insight Media)
Examine the basic communication process.

Communication Breakdown (Learning Seed)
Shows why conversation often ends in argument and how to unclog the channels.

Gender and Communication: She Talks, He Talks (Learning Seed)
How men and women use communication differently.

I know that you believe you understand what you think I said, but, I am not sure you realize that what you heard is not what I meant.

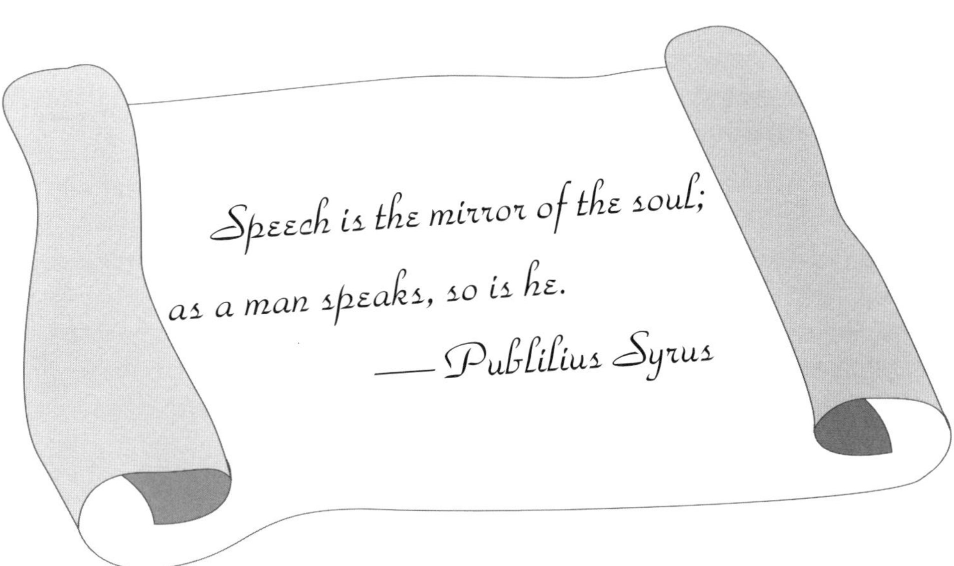

Speech is the mirror of the soul;
as a man speaks, so is he.
— Publilius Syrus

Chapter 25

Do It Yourself Kit

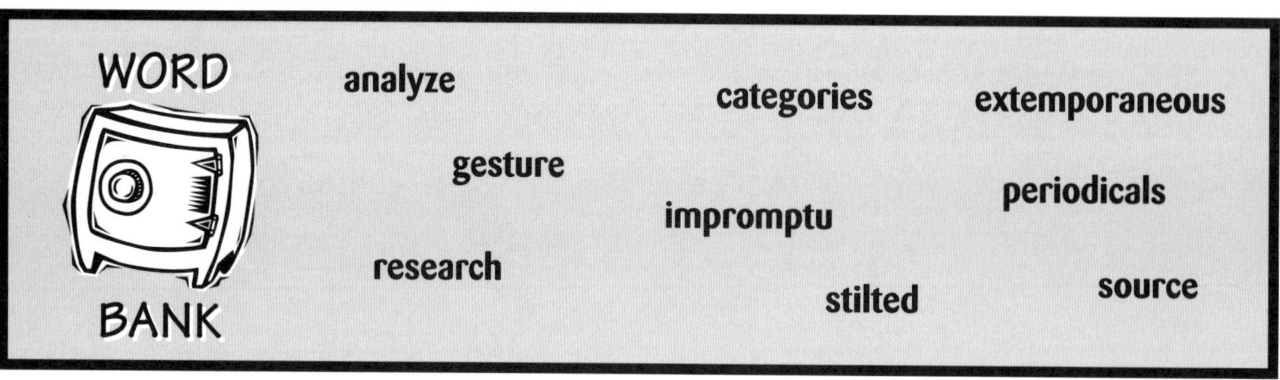

WORD
BANK
analyze
categories
extemporaneous
gesture
periodicals
impromptu
research
stilted
source

Watch for these valuable words wherever you see the word bank icon. 

BRAIN TEASERS

(1) What are the four methods of speaking?
(2) What is the preferred method and why?
(3) What are the three general purposes of speech?
(4) What is the order of the six steps in building a speech?
(5) What is the purpose of a speech to inform? To persuade? To entertain?

PROGRAM NOTES

Build your speech the easy way by using the right way. You know that it is easier to change a flat tire if you first jack up the car. In fact, most skills in life have a step-by-step procedure that, if followed, gets the job done correctly and rapidly.

So in building a speech, you should become accustomed to following six steps in their proper order. Six may seem like too many, but once you have made the process habitual, you'll find these steps are the shortest way to prepare extemporaneous talks.

Before we list the six preparation steps, let us discuss *extemporaneous* speaking, one of the four methods of speaking. This is the type you will be giving in class. It means that you carefully plan, outline, and rehearse your speech, but you never memorize the wording. As discussed in the previous chapter, you will memorize three things only—the first one or two sentences in your speech, the concluding statements, and the order of the main ideas. But do not memorize the words that you use to explain the ideas. The words may change with each presentation as you think of more exacting terms for communication. Of the four methods of speaking, extemporaneous is the most preferred because it allows the speaker this flexibility in adapting to each audience and occasion.

The other three methods of public address are impromptu, memorized, and manuscript reading. Impromptu means spur-of-the-moment. It should be reserved for emergencies only, such as when you attend an honors banquet and without forewarning the presiding officer presents you with an award and calls on you to speak.

Memorized speeches are those learned verbatim. This method is seldom recommended because the speaker is unable to adapt to his listeners, and his presentation tends to be stilted, with attention on remembering word sequence rather than on communicating ideas.

Manuscript reading is used on television, radio, and for extremely formal occasions when exact wording and timing are essential. To read a speech well from a manuscript requires special skill in establishing lengthy eye contact with the audience and in making the speech sound "talked" and not "read."

And now for that do-it-yourself speech-building kit with its six steps. When you are assigned a speech, progressively do each of the following:

(1) *Determine the general purpose* of your speech or the general reaction you want from your audience. There are three general purposes:

To inform: to make your audience understand an idea (How to swing a golf club. Lincoln's assassination. The enzyme).

To persuade: to influence audience beliefs (Straight "A" students should not have to take final exams. The lunch period is too short); to intensify feelings (Take pride in flying the flag. Lead a life of service to others); or to get immediate action at the end of the speech (Sign this petition right now. Buy these theatre tickets).

To entertain: to amuse the audience with humor and curious bits of information (Dogs and the people they own. Never say yes).

In this class, your teacher may assign you a general purpose, but if not, you must choose one to work toward.

(2) *Analyze your audience and occasion.* You can then custom-make your speech for that particular group. Consider the age, sex, interests, and attitudes of your audience. For example, if you give a speech on popular music to sixth graders, you would have to include more basic information than if you used that same subject for seniors in high school. The age makes the difference. Also consider gender. Male and female interests sometimes vary and should be accommodated. Audience attitude is important. If you are trying to get the PTSA to sponsor an after game dance, you'll have more chance to succeed if you know and adjust to their attitudes toward your subject. (Do they think previous dances have gone well? Do they believe such activities are important?) Furthermore, know the occasion. Is it serious, informal, dignified? Again, suit your speech to it.

(3) *Select and narrow your subject.* This is where you decide what specifically you will talk about—your *specific* purpose. Several factors should determine your choice. Select a subject that you know something about and that interests you. Remember, if you do not show interest in your subject, your audience won't listen. Choose a subject in which you *can* interest your audience. And most important, select a subject you can discuss adequately in the time allotted. Most students choose too broad a topic for the speech time limits. For example, if your speech is to be 3 to 4 minutes, you cannot adequately discuss "Animals." That topic is too broad for a 3 to 4 minute talk. So limit your subject. "Dogs?" Still too broad. What can you thoroughly discuss in four minutes about dogs? There are numerous topics:

How to bathe a dog properly.
Teaching a dog three basic commands.
My dog Rover.
Traits of the French poodle.
Training your dog to hunt.
Grooming of house dogs.
Dogs and their diets.

All of the above subjects are narrow enough to fit the needs of a short speech. Whatever subject you choose—limit, limit, limit!

(4) *Gather material*. While the library is the obvious storehouse for research, there are other avenues you need pursue. *Look at yourself*. What do you already know about the topic? Use that information. Where are the gaps in your knowledge? Plan to fill them in. *Observe*. If you are talking about split-level houses, do some firsthand observations on these homes. *Converse* with authorities. Discuss the split-level house with a person who lives in one, with a real estate agent who sells them, with an architect who plans them, with a contractor who builds them, with a designer who decorates them. Then *read* all types of literature about your subject. Newspapers, encyclopedias, magazines, pamphlets, and books may be source material. For magazine articles that pertain to your subject, consult the *Reader's Guide*, an index to all popular periodicals. In the *Reader's Guide*, articles will be listed by author, title, and subject matter. If you want to read magazine articles on split-level homes, look in the subject matter listing under "Houses, split-level," and following that entry will be all the pertaining titles, magazines, and dates within the period that the index covers.

When you find information that you want to use in your speech, such as an important quotation, or exact statistics, record it correctly. On 3 x 5 note cards write the information in the center, with source (name of book or magazine, date, and page) at the bottom. At the top of the card, label the material (history, advantages, or types). Before you begin writing your speech outline, stack identically labeled cards together and you will have all the same type of information neatly categorized:

Label:	Advantages
Information:	Herb Merrick, N.Y. architect says, "split level homes provide variety and conserve space."
Source:	Update. Jan. 3, 1996, p.34

(5) *Outline the Speech.* Use your previously determined categories as main points, arranging them in the order you feel is best to suit your specific speech purpose. Determine the information that supports the main ideas and list it under them. Shuffle points until the skeleton is in order. Then work out a detailed outline, using correct outline form. If you do not know how to outline, refer to Chapter 27 in this book or consult your English text.

(6) *Practice aloud.* With outline in hand, stand in front of a mirror, preferably full length, and give your speech. Practice until you have your outline well in mind, with the order of main points memorized. Now put your outline aside and present your speech without it. If you forget, look again at the outline, but continue to rely less frequently on it. In later rehearsals, when you feel more certain of your speech, concentrate on additional aspects. If you feel like gesturing (moving your hands, arms, face, shoulders) do so. Listen to yourself to be sure you are speaking loudly enough to be heard by every audience member. If you have a tape recorder, tape your speech, and then listen to be sure you are clearly enunciating the words and speaking slowly enough to be understood. Work with any visual aids you intend to use. If possible, video tape your speech and observe both your vocal delivery and your physical traits as you talk. Now say the speech to someone else and get his or her response. In your rehearsal period get the speech well in mind without becoming stale and mechanical. Most students are inclined, however, to practice too little instead of too much. Don't you fall into the unprepared trap.

Follow the above six steps in building a speech you will be enthused to give, and watch your audience sit up and take notice!

ACTIVITY AND ITS PURPOSE

The purpose of this written assignment is to give you practice in narrowing a speech subject. You are to select three general areas and for each one, write three properly limited subjects for a 3 to 4 minute speech. (An example of limiting a subject of "Dogs" appears above in the Platform Notes.)

HOW TO PREPARE

From the list below choose three subjects. Neatly fill out the activity sheet at the end of this chapter by writing the three subjects you have chosen. Underneath each one list three limited topics you could talk about that would pertain to the broad subject. Be sure you severely limit the subject to touch on just one small aspect of that area.

(1) computers
(2) basketball
(3) fashions
(4) safety
(5) recreation
(6) pollution
(7) video games
(8) vacations
(9) television
(10) government
(11) fish
(12) transportation
(13) books
(14) music
(15) disasters
(16) customs
(17) journalism
(18) airplanes
(19) earthquakes
(20) superstitions
(21) precious stones

HOW TO PRESENT

Hand in the completed activity sheet that your teacher has given you. Your teacher may wish to check over the assignment and then have part of the class read aloud their narrowed subjects for class discussion and appraisal.

ADDITIONAL ACTIVITIES

(1) See and discuss the following video. (For address see Appendix E):

The Speech: From Preparation to Delivery (Coronet)
Five videos on the speaker's purpose, audience analysis, organizing, overcoming fear, and delivering a speech.

None of the things which are done
with intelligence are done without the
aid of speech.
—Isocrates

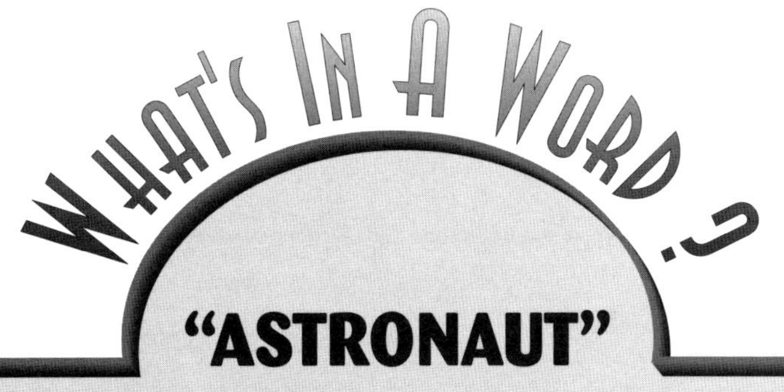

"ASTRONAUT"

Blending the idea of sea and sky, astronaut comes from the Greek: **astron**, meaning star, and **nautes**, or seaman. Hence, a sailor of the heavens.

Chapter 26

Psyche Out Your Listeners

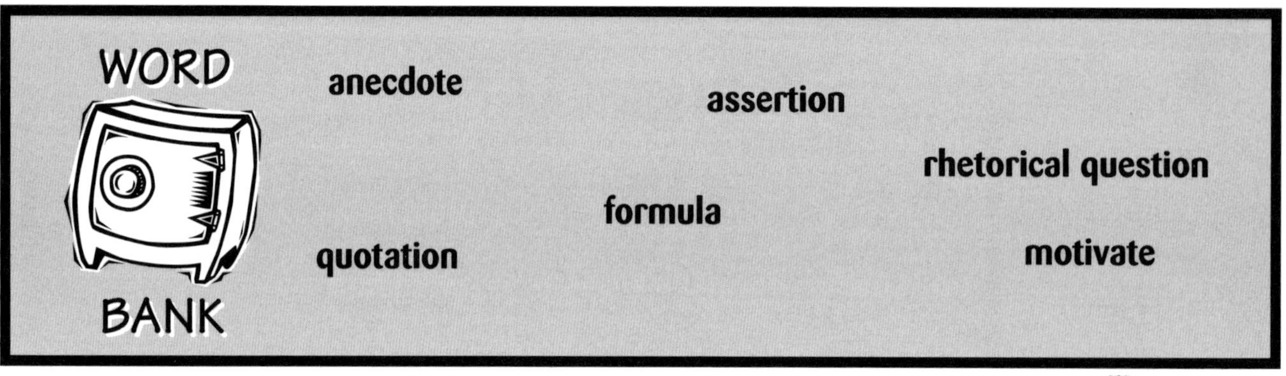

WORD
BANK
anecdote
assertion
rhetorical question
formula
quotation
motivate

Watch for these valuable words wherever you see the word bank icon. 

BRAIN TEASERS

(1) How do you organize a speech?
(2) What ways can you start a speech?
(3) How can you get an audience to listen to you?
(4) What are four methods for arranging main points in the point-support part of a speech?
(5) What are the requirements for ending a speech?

PLATFORM NOTES

Don't bore your listeners. Give them a speech they will like. How do you do that? By making your speech conform to the natural way an audience thinks.

It is true that every audience is different—different age, different background, different attitudes—and you must always account for these differences. But it is also true that every audience has a tendency to think in a uniform and predictable way.

Knowing this process, we can set up a formula for organizing speeches that meets the listeners' needs and allows you to give them a speech they'll like.

The formula is easy:

Capture ☞ Motivate ☞ Assert ☞ Preview ☞ Point-Support ☞ Action

Let us learn how to use each of these steps in organizing a speech.

Capture

Some audiences start out bored, stifling yawns. So the speaker's very first sentence must pack a punch, capturing the listeners' attention.

For example, avoid beginning a speech on cancer by saying "I am going to talk to you today about cancer, a terrible disease." Instead, say "One hundred new metal coffins will be lowered into our city's cemetery this month. Of those, at least twenty will contain cancer victims."

The following list suggests several ways to capture audience attention:

(1) *Startling statement:* an unexpected fact. See example above.

(2) *Quotation:* a famous person's words that relate to your subject.

Example: "Genius," said Tom Edison, "is one percent inspiration and 99 percent perspiration." (This quote might begin a speech on the secret of success.)

(3) *Rhetorical question:* a question the audience will silently answer in their own minds.

Example: "If you were awarded an expense free trip to any place in the world, where would you go? Would you choose a tropical island? Or a land of ice and snow? Would you seek the noisy life of a city or the pastoral scene of the country?" (You might use these questions to begin a speech on how to choose vacation spots.)

(4) *Illustration:* a short anecdote or story, which may be true or fictional and that applies to your speech. (If fictional, be sure to indicate.)

Example: "The great scientist Louis Pasteur was terrified by one thing—dogs. The sight of a dog immobilized him. Even when he heard a dog bark from blocks away, his agonized boyhood memories of friends driven crazy through the bite of a mad hound would haunt him. So at the height of his career, when doctors were pleading that he focus his attention on a dozen diseases, Pasteur limited himself to finding a vaccine for rabies. His persistent research and final triumph were possible because he had great personal feeling that aided his creativity. (So might you begin a speech that discusses how a person's strong emotions can produce inventive ideas.)

(5) *Humorous anecdote:* a story that is really funny and that directly applies to your speech.

Example: While out driving, a father and his six-year-old son passed a race track. The boy, never having seen one, asked what it was. "It's a place where people go to race dogs," the father replied. After a long thoughtful pause, the boy said, "I bet the dogs win."

Motivate

The second step in the audience's thinking process is to ask, "What's that to me?" So the speaker must motivate the audience or make them interested by showing why the subject is important to them. Tell the audience why you bring up the subject, how it affects them, how it touches on their lives. Why should the audience listen to a talk on karate? Why is your class affected because the cocoa crop is doing badly in South America? A wise speaker will answer such questions for the audience, giving them specific reasons for listening.

You can motivate or interest your listeners by using one or a combination of three approaches:

(1) *Penalty.* Through the use of fear you describe what will happen if they don't listen. An example of motivating through penalty is used when the U.S. Air Force requires each person to pack the parachute he or she will use. Failure to learn the correct way provides an obvious penalty!

Penalty examples: You will lose money.
You will endanger your health.
You will flunk the class.
You will be out of date.

(2) *Reward.* This is the preferred process because people respond more eagerly to promises than to threats.

Reward examples: You will win a prize.
You will save your life.
You will make more money.
You will increase your enjoyment.

(3) *Curiosity.* You appeal to your listener's desire to learn for the sake of learning.

Curiosity examples: "How hot is the sun? How heavy is it? How old is it? What are sunspots? These are questions that people have asked through the years."

Assert

After the audience knows why it is important to listen to the speech, the next thing they wonder about is the specific approach the speaker will use. You meet this audience need by stating your assertion or the specific purpose of your speech.

Example: "There is a correct way to hit a golf ball."
"The toy French poodle makes a good house pet."
"Many TV commercials on medicine are dishonest."

Preview

When the audience knows your specific purpose, they then wonder how you will present it. A brief initial summary or sneak preview of your main points will help them to follow easily the rest of your speech.

Example: *Assertion:* "There is a correct way to hit a golf ball."
Preview: "Let's discuss the proper stance, the grip, and the swing in order to hit that ball correctly."

Example: *Assertion:* "The toy French poodle makes a good house pet."
Preview: "The poodle is smart. It does not shed. It does not have a 'doggy' odor. Let's focus on each of these reasons in turn."

Point-Support

Your audience now wants the "meat" of your speech. They are asking themselves, "Oh, yeah?" So you must give them specific examples, instances, and proof of what you say. You will give your first main point again (the first item you listed in the preview step) and then you must support or explain it through examples, statistics, quotations. When you have covered that point completely, state your second point (the second one listed in your preview step) and support it with evidence. Continue in this manner to your third point. Notice that we mention only three main points. Three seems to be the magical number an audience can easily remember. When you use more than three, your audience will tune out. Of course, you may use only one or two main points if that gets the job done.

You may wonder in what order to place main points. It depends on your subject content and what order makes sense to you. You have a choice of four: time, space, problem-solution, and topical. If you are giving a history or a how-to-do-it speech, you will be wise to choose *Time* sequence. Begin at a certain date and move forward chronologically. For example, if you are discussing the development of television, you may talk about the 1940s, the 1950s, and the 1960s—thus using Time order. Or you may describe a step-by-step process in chronological order. For instance, if you talk about how to make pizza, your discussion may be on assembling the ingredients, preparing the dough, adding the toppings, and finally baking the pizza.

If you are discussing the layout of a building, a town, or talking about various sections of a country, place your main points in a *Space* sequence. Describe the basement of a building and work up to its top floor (or vice versa); discuss fish catches on the East coast of the United States, then move to a different geographical area, perhaps the Great Lakes, and then the Rocky Mountains, and finally the Pacific coast. Your speech order has moved in space from East to West.

When you want to present a solution to a problem, organize according to the *Problem-solution* sequence. You would have only two main points in the point-support section of your speech. The first point would state and describe the problem. The second main point would state and describe your solution.

A *Topical* arrangement is extremely useful. With it you divide the subject matter into logical topics. If you were discussing the structure of Congress, your logical topics would be the House of Representatives and the Senate, so you would have two main points. (And it wouldn't matter which you discussed first.) You might divide a speech on water pollution into its local and its national aspects, or perhaps the social, political, and economic consequences.

Your choice of which to use—time, space, problem-solution, or topical ordering of your main points—will depend on your specific purpose and your speech content. Choose the way that will be easiest for the audience to grasp.

Action

After hearing your main points and the support for each, your audience now thinks, "So what?" So at the end of your speech you must ask your audience to do something specific —something they have the power to do—that pertains to your basic idea. Join, write, vote, buy, investigate, use, remember, read, see—all of these put your speech (and audience) to work.

This action step is the conclusion of your speech, and a good conclusion has two requirements. (1) Keep it short. As the old saying goes, "Stand up. Speak up. Shut up." (2) Link the action step directly to the capture step. For example, if you begin your capture step by saying, "Shakespeare once said, 'All the world is a stage . . .'" you should end by referring to the beginning. You may say, "We've seen how the world is a stage and that you are an actor upon it. How well will you play your part?" Thus your audience has a sense of speech unity and completeness.

If you are curious about seeing this speech formula applied, turn to the platform notes in Chapter 24. That section has been written using the formula. Can you identify each step?

The following is a student speech outline using the organization formula which is identified in the margin.

(Introduction)

Capture I. This is a key to my parent's car.

A. When they want to get somewhere, they put this key into the ignition.

B. Without the key, the car stands still.

Motivate II. I have another "key" to show you.

A. This key allows you to get somewhere—not in a car but in school.

(Positive approach)
B. With this key you can earn better grades.
C. You will also save time studying.

Assert
III. Using the S-Q Three R study method will make you a better student.

Preview
IV. Let us discuss the three cuts in this key to good grades:
A. Survey.
B. Question.
C. Three R's.
1. *R*ead.
2. *R*ecite.
3. *R*eview.

(Body) (Time Sequence)

Point one & Support

I. Quickly survey the chapter or assignment.
A. Read the first and last paragraphs.
B. Read the subheadings in boldfaced print.

Point two & Support

II. Create questions that you will answer when you read.
A. Turn the chapter title into a question.
B. Turn each subheading into a question.

Point three & Support

III. Use the 3-R's.
A. Read the material to answer the questions.
B. Recite the answers to the questions until they are well in mind.
C. Review all of the chapter.
1. Do this immediately after reading it.
2. Do this again after several hours.
3. Do it again once a week.

(Conclusion)

Action

(Refer to capture step)
I. Use the S-Q Three R method each time you study.
A. You will learn faster.
B. You will have the "key" to getting somewhere in school.

ACTIVITY AND ITS PURPOSE

This will be a short written assignment. You are to begin gaining skill in using the organization formula by neatly filling out the activity sheet your teacher will give you.

HOW TO PREPARE

As you are working on the activity sheet, keep this class in mind and the audience you must reach. Formulate your answers accordingly.

HOW TO PRESENT

Hand the activity sheet to your teacher when due. After checking the material, your teacher may ask for impromptu class discussion on the material.

ADDITIONAL ACTIVITIES

(1) Find examples of television commercials that use the organization formula. Do they modify it? What steps, if any, are left out? Why?

(2) Advanced students may wish to compare the organization formula in this chapter with Monroe's Motivated Sequence in Gronbeck's *Principles and Types of Speech*, 12th ed. (Harper Collins, 1994).

I know that you believe you
understand what you think I said,
but...
I'm not sure you realize that what
you heard is not what I meant.

Chapter 27

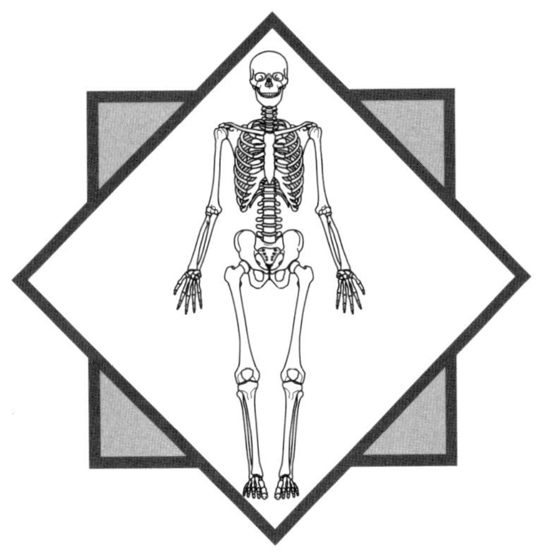

Skeleton System

Arabic numbers

consistent

indentation

Roman numerals

sub-point

Watch for these valuable words wherever you see the word bank icon. 

BRAIN TEASERS

(1) What is the importance of outlining?
(2) What are the types of outlines?
(3) What symbol pattern should you use?
(4) How do you properly indent?
(5) What are the five rules for outlining?

PLATFORM NOTES

You've got an outline inside you! Your skeleton! Like all outlines, it is extremely important, creating the "bare" form that is you. Without this network of clavicle, sternum, ribs, vertebrae, etc., your body would fall apart, a heap upon the floor.

Without an outline, your speeches will also fall apart. An outline is as important to a speaker as a skeleton is to a body, as a road map is to a motorist, or a blueprint is to a contractor. Like the map or blueprint, a speech outline tells where you are going and how to get there. And because an outline places essentials in logical order, the speaker finds it is an aid in remembering steps in the speech.

There are three types of outlines: full sentence, topic, and a combination of sentence and topic. Teachers' preferences vary as to outlines, but beginning speakers usually find a mixture of sentences and topics the most workable form, with the introduction, conclusion, and main points in complete sentences, and the sub-points in topics.

The basic rules of outlining are founded on the principle that main points must support your assertion or specific purpose, and sub-points must support, clarify, or develop your main points. Briefly, good outline form involves these rules:

(1) Use a consistent symbol pattern. Study the following sample:

I. (Roman numerals for main points)
   A. (Capital letters for main sub-points)
      1. (Arabic numerals for subordinate points)
         a. (Small letters for small divisions)
         b. ______________________________
      2. ______________________________
   B. ______________________________
   C. ______________________________

II. ______________________________

(You may also want to turn to page 118 to study the full sentence outline there.) Notice that the above outline starts with a Roman numeral, followed by a capital letter, which in turn is followed by Arabic numbers, and then small letters.

(2) Use a consistent indentation pattern called the stair-step method (because if you draw a line below each indentation, the line looks like a set of stairs). Notice in the above outline that the most important ideas (the Roman numerals) are closest to the lefthand margin. Of next importance and indented or spaced slightly to the right are the capital letters A, B, C, D, etc. Of lesser importance, and again indented even further to the right, are the 1, 2, 3, 4, etc.

Now look at the outline sample again. Notice that you can draw an uninterrupted line from Roman numeral I to Roman numeral II. These numerals are "pals" and must always contain ideas of equal importance in your speech. Notice also that you can draw an uninterrupted line between the capital letters A, B, C, etc. These in turn carry ideas that have the same importance to each other. As a further example, a study of the following outline will indicate that "Trains" and "Aircraft" have equal importance in the outline. The sub-points "Steam," "Diesel," "Electric" are of equal importance to each other and carry the same weight under "Trains" as do "Prop," "Jet," and "Rocket" carry under "Aircraft."

I. Trains have had an interesting history.
  A. Steam
    1.
      (Sub-points)
    2.
  B. Diesel
    1.
      (Sub-points)
    2.
  E. Electric

II. Aircraft now play an important role.
  A. Prop
    1.
    2.
  B. Jet
    1.
    2.
  C. Rocket

Remember always to keep the lefthand indentation clear so you can quickly see the thought relationships. In the following examples, notice that the first fails to keep the space indentation free:

wrong: I. Trains have had an
interesting history.

right: I. Trains have had an
    interesting history.

(3) Give each division adequate support, which usually involves at least two entries. Remember that sub-points clarify or divide the main idea. ("Diesel," "Steam," etc. clarify the main point, "Trains.") This means for adequate support, if you have a *I* you usually should have a *II*. If you have an *A* you probably will have a *B*. If you find you continually have main points with only an *A* or a *1* under them, it means you have not delved into the subject deeply enough; you need more material. Remember, although you want a short outline, you also need a complete one.

(4) Use only one idea for each symbol. For example,

wrong: I. Water pollution hinders recreation and wildlife.
(This is wrong because the entry has two ideas under one symbol.)

right: I. Water pollution is a serious threat.
A. It hinders recreation.
(sub-points here)
B. It hinders wildlife.
(sub-points here)

(Now each symbol has only one idea.)

(5) On your outline, write out your beginning and ending in complete sentences.

Remember, an outline is your speech's skeleton, your "road map" of where you go on the speaker's platform. Follow the above outline rules and arrive safely at your destination.

ACTIVITY AND ITS PURPOSE

This written assignment is to help you gain skill in outlining. On the activity sheet issued you is a scrambled speech outline that you are to unscramble, using the speech organization formula and correct outline symbols and indentation.

HOW TO PREPARE

Quickly review the organization formula in Chapter 26. With that in mind, as well as the outline rules in this chapter, on a scratch paper unscramble the material on the activity sheet. Decide which points fill the demand of each organization step (capture, motivate, etc.). Place in correct order. Then correctly place symbols and proper indentation to formulate an exact outline. You may renumber using Roman numeral one again for the first main point in the body of the outline. Now transfer this completed outline to the back of the activity sheet.

HOW TO PRESENT

Hand the activity sheet to your teacher when it is due. When your paper is returned, be prepared to contribute to class discussion.

ADDITIONAL ACTIVITIES

(1) See and discuss the following video. (For addresses see Appendix D):

Organizing the Speech (Insight Media)
Types of speeches and ways to organize them.

There are three sides to every story—Yours—Mine—and the Facts!

Chapter 28

Eye Spy

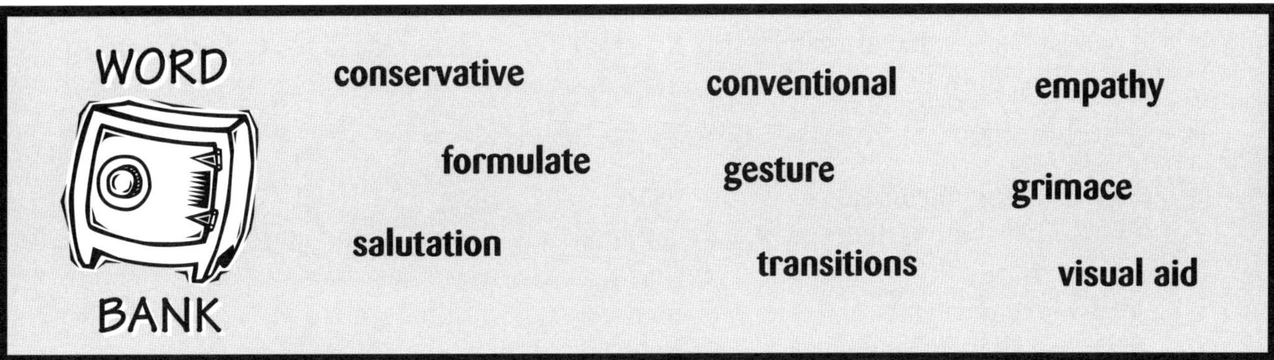

WORD
BANK
conservative
conventional
empathy
formulate
gesture
grimace
salutation
transitions
visual aid

Watch for these valuable words wherever you see the word bank icon. 

BRAIN TEASERS

(1) How can you make a good "first impression" on the audience?
(2) How should you dress for giving a speech?
(3) What is the correct way to approach the speaker's platform?
(4) What four ways should you manage your body while giving a talk?
(5) How should you leave the platform?
(6) What are visual aids?
(7) What rules apply to using visual aids?

PLATFORM NOTES

First an audience *sees* you. The way you approach the platform, the way you are dressed, the way you stand, move, and gesture give your audience its first impression. Even before you have opened your mouth, the audience has formulated an opinion of you. If your listeners like what they first see, they'll listen. If they are annoyed with what they see, they'll often "tune out."

You can control this video factor by learning how to manage your body in front of a group and by learning how to use effectively the other visual items you bring to aid your speech.

PLATFORM APPEARANCE AND BEHAVIOR

Dressing for the Speech
Your sight pattern starts at home when you dress for your speech. What you wear should be neat, clean, and appropriate for the occasion. Standard school clothes are usually acceptable for class. Dressier clothes are needed for more formal occasions. When in

doubt, be conservative. Don't hamper yourself by wearing clothes that shout louder than you do. Keep your prized "fad" togs for another time. Leave heavy, jangling jewelry at home. Remove the pencil from behind your ear. Polish and shine your shoes. Remember, what you wear should bring compliments, not competition.

Hair styling is also important. Since your face and eyes are highly expressive parts of your body, keep your hair from covering them. It may be cute to watch Fido blink between strands, but it is ludicrous to watch a speaker peek-a-boo around his or her tresses. If necessary, pin your hair back to avoid the distracting motion of brushing or blowing it out of the face.

Approaching the Speaker's Platform
As soon as you appear at your speaking destination, give the impression of being poised, confident, and friendly. Even if you feel nervous, try not to show it. Loud laughing, coughing, moving back and forth in your seat, and shuffling papers will betray you. Sit calmly and attentively. When the chairperson introduces you, react pleasantly and with poise to all of the remarks. Avoid the extremes of being aloof or making faces.

Quietly walk to the front of the group in a businesslike, confident way. There is no need to swagger or to shuffle reluctantly. Face the audience, smile (unless it is a solemn occasion when a smile would be out of place), and briefly pause, allowing time for the audience to

give you their attention. When you have their attention, begin your formal salutation by thanking the chairperson and addressing the audience. Then begin your speech. Do not state the title of your speech, for that is the chairperson's job, and do not begin with an apology. Start with your planned capture step.

On the Platform
While you are giving your speech, manage your body in the following ways:

(1) *Look alert but relaxed.* To do this you need a good posture, one that makes your body responsive but does not call attention to itself. Start by placing your feet several inches apart to give you firm control of body weight. One foot slightly in advance of the other is a comfortable position for most speakers.

With your knees unlocked and loose, keep most of your weight equally distributed on the balls of your feet. This allows you to move your body quickly in any direction, should the audience throw tomatoes, or should you need to walk for transitions. Stand tall by reaching up with the crown of your head and with your spinal column. With this action your stomach should go in and your seat tuck under. Put your shoulders back and then drop and relax them with arms and hands hanging relaxed at your sides. Keep your chin parallel to the floor. Practice this posture until it becomes natural for you. Then you'll look good both off and on the platform.

Students often ask, "May I move about in front of the audience?" The answer is "yes," as long as the movement is purposeful, helping to communicate your ideas. Aimless pacing and nervous shuffling are the "no-no's." But a good speaker adds meaning by changing position. Walk across the platform to provide transitions between major points and to emphasize certain ideas. Convey thought by shifting weight—a step forward shows interest, a step backward suggests relaxation and perhaps a change of ideas. Suit your movement to the material. The livelier your subject is, the more movement you need.

(2) *Keep your arms and hands free to gesture.* A gesture (pronounced with a soft as the initial sound in just) is movement of any part of your body to convey thought and emotion. Pointing your finger, nodding your head, raising your eyebrow, shrugging your shoulders—all are gestures. The secret of using gestures is to allow them to come naturally from your enthusiasm about the subject. They should start inside, gather force, and be activated at the right moment when you are describing something (the length of a fish, how to grip a tennis racket) or emphasizing an idea ("go away," "three strikes," "over there"). Notice that all gestures must help your speech. Unconsciously tearing your notes into bits, twisting your ring, squeezing your arms, or holding your hands waist high in front like a singer, are distractions to be avoided. Keep your hands and arms free from such nervous display by letting them hang relaxed at your side until you feel the urge to move with purpose.

While you should never plan to use a specific gesture on a certain word in your speech, you can rehearse gestures to give you a "feel" for them. Try these conventional gestures and accompanying remarks as a group in class, and then practice at home with appropriate sentences.

(a) Nodding and shaking the head.
("Yes, I will." "No, I don't believe so.")

(b) Giving and receiving: extend hands with palms up and fingers usually separated, elbow away from your side.
("Take this book." "Thank you for the gift.")

(c) Rejecting: sweeping motion with palms down.
("Get it away from me." "It can't be done." "Don't do that.")

(d) Pointing: arm extended with index finger pointing.
("Look!" "See that door." "Point one is . . .")

(e) Clinching fist: (to show anger or determination) keep fist about shoulder height.

("We'll never give up." "We'll fight if necessary.")

(f) Cautioning: hand extended about shoulder height with palm facing down.

("Now take it easy." "Don't rush to a conclusion.")

(g) Dividing: (to indicate separation of ideas) move hand from side to side with palm vertical and fingers together.

("The home boosters sit to the right; the visitors to the left.")

As you practice gestures, keep them strong and vigorous, use your whole body to carry them through (which means you must not cement your elbows to your sides) and time them to come on or slightly before the emphatic words. And, remember, the farther away your audience is, the larger your gestures must be for them to see.

Keep in mind, too, that an audience imitates the speaker's movements and gestures. This is called empathy, or a "feeling into" an experience. Observe your father watching football on TV. Does he strain as he watches the ball being carried? Does he flinch when the man is tackled? He is empathizing with what he is seeing. In like manner your audience will imitate your movements, though perhaps less noticeably. If you fidget, your listeners will inwardly feel nervousness. If you use no movement, they'll become relaxed enough to take a snooze. If you use constant action, you'll tire them. Strive for a medium amount of energetically controlled movement and your listeners will stay alert and enjoy the speech.

(3) *Look directly at the audience*. This makes them look at you and opens the communication lines. If you look at the ceiling, or out the window, or down at your shoes, you only increase your nervousness. Looking directly at various parts of the audience will ease stage fright because it makes you aware you are sharing an experience and are not a solitary figure in front of a glaring group. See the audience, get their reaction, and then adjust your speech accordingly.

(4) *Keep your face expressive*. If your ideas are happy ones, smile. If the situation you describe disgusts you, let that show on your face. Of course, you must not mechanically put on an expressive face. Like gestures, facial expression must come from the strong feeling you have inside. But if you consistently have a "deadpan" face, practice showing emotion in front of a mirror until your face naturally responds when you are in front of a group.

Two words of caution. Avoid your desire to grimace when you make a mistake. Don't advertise your errors. Carry on as though nothing had happened, and the audience will probably not notice anything wrong. Also, do not have gum in your mouth when you speak. Gum distracts your audience and interferes with your articulation.

Leaving the Platform

When your time limits are up and you have concluded your speech, pause, look at your audience, and then leave the platform with dignity. Do not say "thank you" before you leave, as this destroys the impression of your carefully planned conclusion. Neither should you heave a great sigh of relief as you return to your seat. Even though you may be glad your speech is finished, such behavior shows childishness and lack of control.

Yes, a speaker's actions are often more influential than the words. As the old Chinese proverb states, "I hear what you say, but I *see* what you do."

VISUAL AIDS

You are your best visual aid! But you can also use other visual items to reinforce or explain the ideas in your speech. Charts, diagrams, graphs, slides, pictures, working models, actual equipment, chalkboard drawings, maps, videos, and overhead projections serve the speaker as visual helpers.

Try to use at least one visual aid (other than yourself) in every speech you give, because visual aids add reality to your ideas. You can painstakingly explain where you went on vacation, but a large marked map quickly orients us. You can describe how to use a blender, but showing us with the actual article makes it clearer. You can tell us how the school divides student fees, but a pie graph immediately indicates percentages.

Whenever you use visual aids follow these suggestions:

(1) Choose aids that relate directly to your speech. If your purpose is to show the audience how to cast with a fly rod, bring the rod. It relates to your speech. Leave the trolling rod at home. It doesn't.

(2) Carefully *plan* your displays ahead of time and rehearse with them. Be sure you have everything you need and that the material is in correct sequence. If you are using electrical equipment, check to see that it works properly. Will you need an extension cord, masking tape for mounting posters, a pointer for diagrams?

(3) Keep your aids *clear and simple*. In drawing, use wide, heavy lines on large poster board. Use color when possible. Omit unnecessary details. If it takes more time to explain your aid than it would to explain your point, don't use the aid. Aids should be self-explanatory.

(4) Display your visual aids at the *proper time*. Keep them covered until you need them. Otherwise, they will prove distracting, with the audience wondering "what that thing is," instead of listening to you.

(5) When using your aid, keep it *visible*. Stand well to one side as you point to it. Choose or draw material that is large enough for all to see readily. Hold up smaller objects in such a way that your hands do not cover them.

(6) *Don't fidget* with your aids. Use them and then put them aside. Avoid holding them throughout your speech.

Some Types Of Visual Aids

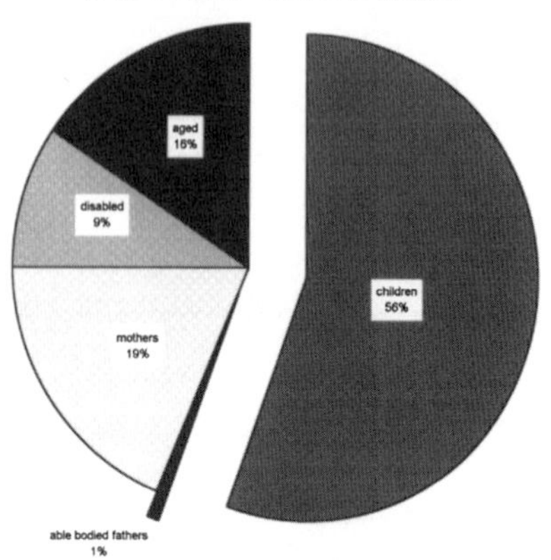

Pie Chart

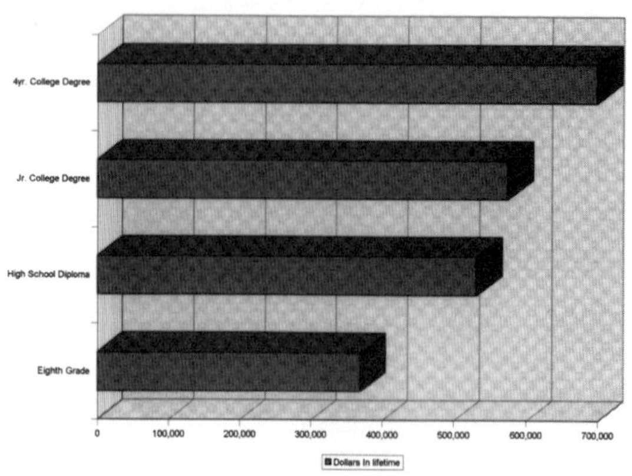

Bar Chart

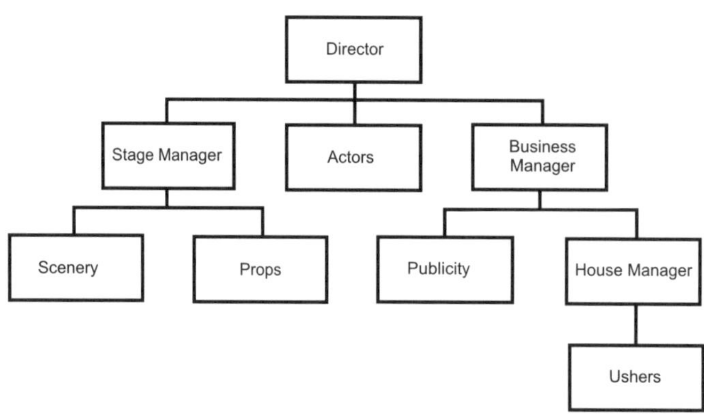

Organization Chart

Flip Chart

Audio/Visual Equipment

Remember, if you properly plan and handle it, any visual aid can be worth a thousand words!

ACTIVITY AND ITS PURPOSE

You are to present a 2 to 4 minute informative speech showing how to *do* something. As you talk, demonstrate by using body movement, gestures, and at least one visual aid. Choose a skill that uses broad actions, as suggested in the list below. Avoid demonstrating actions difficult for the audience to see, such as crocheting, knitting, or playing chess.

HOW TO PREPARE

(1) Immediately choose a simple skill to demonstrate and one that you can limit to no more than three main ideas in the body of your speech. The following are topic suggestions:

- (a) How to repair an electrical plug.
- (b) How to swing a tennis racket. (Bring and use a real tennis racket.)
- (c) How to fix a flat bicycle tire.
- (d) How to do the Heimlich maneuver.
- (e) How to juggle.
- (f) How to make chocolate chip cookies.
- (g) How to frame a picture.
- (h) How to pack a suitcase.
- (i) How to do three stretching exercises. (Have the class do them with you.)
- (j) How to do a cheerleading routine.
- (k) How to build a box kite.
- (l) How to carve a pumpkin.
- (m) How to sack groceries.
- (n) How to do three basic swimming strokes.
- (o) How to do line dancing.
- (p) How to fold one or two basic origami figures.
- (q) How to apply two or three basic arm bandages.
- (r) (Your choice, approved by your teacher.)

(2) Determine your visual aid. If your speech tells how to use a baseball bat, then use a real bat for your visual aid. Rehearse with it and take it to class for your speech. If you are giving a talk on how to iron a shirt properly, use an ironing board, an iron, and a wrinkled shirt as visual aids. If your speech is a subject such as wrestling that requires no special equipment, your visual aid could be a chart listing your main points, for example. You may also write on the chalkboard, exhibit pictures, etc.

(3) Follow the speech preparation steps listed in Chapter 25.

(4) Organize as described in Chapter 26. Be sure you break down your activity into clear, consecutive steps.

(5) Neatly outline your speech on the activity sheet your teacher will give you, labeling in

the margin the organization steps. Also fill out the source material. (See sample speech outline at the end of this chapter.)

(6) With visual aids, rehearse your speech in front of a full length mirror, practicing body movement and gestures, for they should dominate your speech. Do not memorize gestures in detail or your movements will be mechanical. Instead, be so intent on getting your ideas across to your audience that you feel compelled to use your hands and body.

After you have rehearsed a few times, invite someone to watch you and offer helpful suggestions for your improvement. Go over the checklist for use of visual aids to be sure you are handling yours correctly. Have your exhibit ready to set up quickly in class, taking no more than thirty seconds.

HOW TO PRESENT

On the day you speak, hand the class chairperson a 3 x 5 card with your name and speech title, and present your outline to your instructor. When the chairperson (see Appendix B) introduces you, go to the front of the room, following the instructions for platform behavior in this chapter. After you have quickly set up your visual aids, give your formal salutation by thanking the chairperson and addressing the audience: "Thank you, John (chairperson); Mr. Smith (teacher), and class members." Then begin your capture step. As you talk, concentrate on teaching your audience a skill. Speak enthusiastically and conversationally, as you would to a group of friends, but make your ideas clear by demonstrating. Really *show* your listener, even if it makes you short of breath from your vigorous actions!

ADDITIONAL ACTIVITIES

(1) Practice conventional gestures in class by following this procedure: the teacher begins by introducing you. Go to the front of the room, smile, pause, nod to the teacher, and say "Mr. (or Ms.) Chairperson." Then address the class: "Fellow students." Next, give one sentence and its accompanying conventional gesture. Finish by introducing the next student: "May I now present ___________," and gesture toward that student. The next student follows the same procedure but must use a different conventional gesture and a different sentence.

(2) Collect pictures from magazines that show people making effective gestures or talking with their body. Discuss in class the attitudes their bodies show.

(3) See and discuss the following videos. (For addresses see Appendix E):

Nonverbal Communication (Coronet)
Four videos on various aspects of nonverbal communication including paralanguage, problems, eye contact, kinesics.

Body Language: An Introduction to Non-Verbal Communication (Learning Seed)

SAMPLE OUTLINE FOR SPEECH TO INFORM

General Purpose: To inform
Specific Purpose: Anyone can learn to juggle.

"Even A Klutz Can Juggle"

(Introduction)

Capture I. Have you ever been in an awkward position where you need a skill?

A. You need an extra flare at a job interview to show your potential employer you have a lot on the ball.

B. You want to leave your date impressed by showing him or her that even though everything is up in the air, you are still in control.

Motivate II. By watching and listening to my speech today you will learn that skill, the skill of juggling.

A. It will help you through awkward times.

B. It will help you study more efficiently, according to Dugan Brown, former teacher of CS1 study skills.

1. Juggling uses different parts of the brain.

2. Juggling brings up the heart rate and adrenaline level which refreshes the mind.

Assert III. Authors John Cassidy and B.C. Rimbeaux in their book on juggling have diligently pointed out that anyone can juggle—even the complete Klutz.

Preview IV. There are four main steps a person learns before juggling.

A. The drop is letting the oranges drop.

B. The toss is throwing from one hand to the other.

C. The exchange is swinging to make the toss and out to make the catch.

D. The jug is bringing it all together, once.

(Body)

Point Support I. The drop (dropping the oranges) should be initially accepted as a recurring phenomenon.

A. It is important to get used to how they drop.
B. It is important to realize they will drop often.

Point Support II. The toss from hand to hand seems mundane, yet, has some important points.

A. It is important to cradle the orange in the palm of your hands, not on your fingertips.

B. It is helpful to use a relaxed throw.

C. It is necessary to keep your tosses consistent.

1. Ideally, you should be able to toss the orange from one hand to the next with your eyes closed.

2. Realistically, you will probably be one step closer to orange juice.

Point Support III. The exchange is the most important step and also the toughest.

A. You need two oranges.

B. You need to use your best toss.

C. You need to let the orange begin to descend from the top of its arc.

D. You need to perform the exchange.

1. The first part of the exchange is to "scoop toss" the cradled orange under the descending orange.

2. The second part of the exchange is to catch the descending orange.

3. This is one fluid motion.

Point Support IV. The jug is the final step.

A. You need all three oranges.

B. You put the steps together.

1. You toss.

2. You exchange.

3. You exchange again.

C. You put your jugs together and you're juggling.

(conclusion)

Action I. With practice you can become a juggler, even if you're a klutz.

A. Remember the four basic steps.

1. The drop that is inevitable.

2. The toss that is technical.

3. The exchange that is the key.

4. The jug that is the combination.

B. Don't pass up the skill that refreshes the mind and helps you get out of binds.

C. Practice these steps and learn to juggle.

Cassidy, John, and BC Rimbeaux.
Juggling for the Complete Klutz, 1984.

The word makhzan means storehouse in Arabic. Shortly after entering the English language as magazine, it began to be applied to books, or storehouses of knowledge. Only since the 18th Century has the term referred to periodicals.

Chapter 29

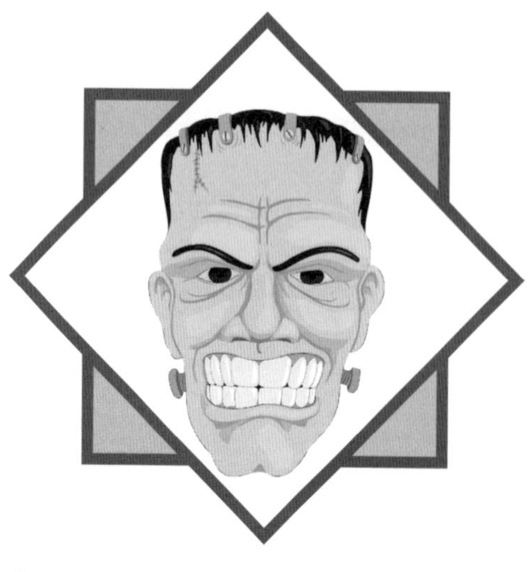

A Fearful Thing

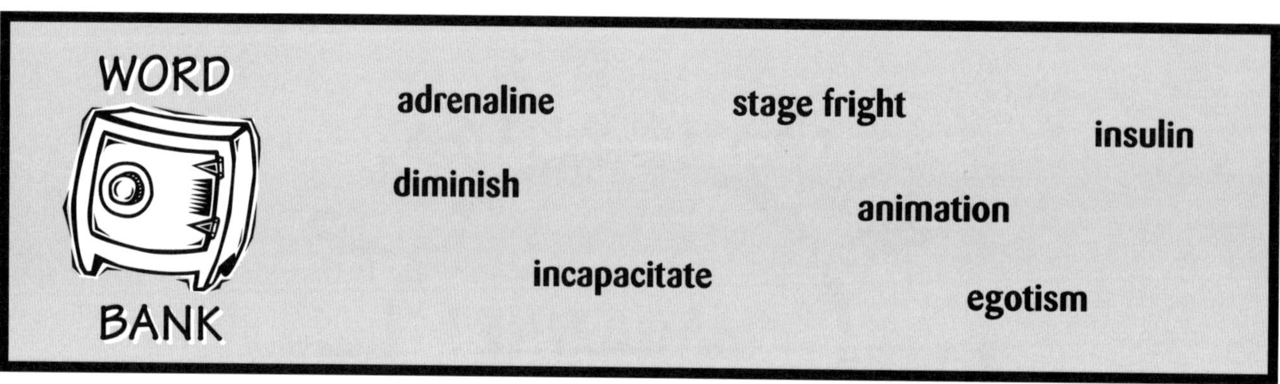

WORD
BANK
adrenaline
stage fright
insulin
diminish
animation
incapacitate
egotism

Watch for these valuable words wherever you see the word bank icon. 

BRAIN TEASERS

(1) What is stage fright?
(2) How can it work for you?
(3) How does it work against you?
(4) How can you control it?

PLATFORM NOTES

What happens to you right before you give a speech? Do you get butterflies in your stomach? Do you have shaking knees? Pounding heart? Dry throat? Sweating palms? Then you are normal, for stage fright is a universal condition that plagues almost anyone who must respond in front of a group, whether that person be acting on a stage, speaking on a platform, or playing ball on a basketball court.

Everybody gets stage fright—amateur and professional alike—for the "human mind is a wonderful thing. At birth our mind begins to work and never stops until we get up to give a speech." So if you have fear or anxiety before giving a talk (and you can undoubtedly add to the above symptoms), you are in good company.

What is stage fright (sometimes called speech anxiety)? It is nothing more than nervous energy—your body's attempt to be ready for emergency action. When you experience fear or anxiety, extra adrenaline and insulin shoot throughout your body. Breathing becomes faster and pulse rate speeds up, gearing you to respond quickly and intensely. This nervous energy is good because it is the raw material, the force that can help you become a dynamic speaker. Your challenge in this class, then, is to learn how to *control* this force, making it work for you and not against you. Properly used, stage fright gives you enthusiasm, animation, and that special "oomph" that makes the listener sit up and take notice. Controlled nervous energy puts a sparkle in your manner! But when stage fright works against you, your shaky voice, dry throat, or uneasy stomach can incapacitate, as you probably well know.

You have a choice. You can decide right now to control this menace and set about doing it in each assignment, or you can wallow in self pity and cowardliness. You *can* conquer stage fright if you are determined. Of course you'll never get rid of it entirely. Nor would you want to.

Professional speakers and actors who fail to experience *some* tension know their performance will lack zest. This knowledge induces a certain successful football coach to choose his starting lineup in the dressing room right before the game by shaking hands with each player. This particular coach selects from among those with wet palms, because he knows that since they are experiencing feelings of anxiety, they are emotionally primed for action and will play a good game.

You do need stage fright, but you must be its master. The following suggestions will help you if you apply them!

(1) *Speak in public often*. The more experience you have in speaking, the less your stage fright. So accept as many speaking engagements as you can, in clubs, in church, in school.

(2) *Pick a subject that interests you*, one that you *want* to talk about. Attention on material and not on you is your goal.

(3) *Thoroughly prepare*. This is the most important of all. When asked in a recent school survey, most students said they had stage fright because they were "scared of not doing a good job"—of making fools of themselves. The remedy for this is to prepare your speech and practice it thoroughly so that you *can* do a good job. Follow the steps on speech preparation. Do your research and create your outline. Then give your speech for the first time, not in class, but at home. Why? You should do this because people seldom do anything correctly the first time. When you learned to water ski, you probably didn't stay up the first time. It took practice. The first time you parallel parked a car, you possibly did not succeed. First times are rough times, so give your speech first by yourself in your own room. Then no one will know your mistakes. Give it over and over again

until you are pleased with the result. Then when you walk into class to give your speech you *know* you can do it. (You already have given it umpteen times.) This knowledge gives you confidence and puts you in control.

(4) *Think of your listeners.* They want you to succeed. So does your teacher. Look at these people as being your friends, and you will find the going easier. Besides, psychologists tell us that stage fright is egotism. You are thinking of yourself: "How do I sound? What grade will I get? How do I look?" Me. Me. Me. Forget yourself and think of the audience. "Do they understand? Can they hear? Did they get the point?" When you think of your listener, you forget yourself and stage fright diminishes.

(5) *Become actively involved.* Purposeful gestures and movement relieve tensions. That is one reason why actors, dancers, athletes, and smart speakers warm up before doing their "thing." Physical action uses up some of that extra energy. So take in several deep breaths before you begin to speak.

(6) *Look your best.* Worrying about your appearance throws emphasis on yourself again. If you know you look good, your confidence allows you to focus elsewhere.

(7) *Look poised.* Even though you may feel a great amount of stage fright, even though you are sure your face is red, your knees are knocking, and your pounding heart can be heard at the back of the room, even though you rate yourself as a number one specimen of fright, the audience cannot tell how scared you are! It doesn't show that much. So you can fool your listener. Now fool yourself. Stand tall and calm. Look at the audience. Act in command of the situation, and you will soon *feel* that way. Actors on stage frequently use this technique. Try it. Belief in yourself is your greatest asset!

Remember, although you'll never lose stage fright completely, you can learn to use it constructively.

ACTIVITY AND ITS PURPOSE

In this assignment you are to tell your stage fright symptoms and experiences to the class. You are to hold nothing back. Describe exactly how you feel, what your body does, and what your thoughts are when you have stage fright. If you are completely honest in your speech, you will benefit by learning that others are in the "same boat" and by getting suggestions for improvement.

HOW TO PREPARE

Fill in the activity sheet to this chapter by answering every question. Then you are through until you speak in class. This is one assignment you are not to prepare or rehearse.

HOW TO PRESENT

Since there will be no chairperson to introduce you, your teacher will probably ask for volunteers to speak. Hand your activity sheet to your instructor before speaking. When you are in front of the class, speak for 1 to 2 minutes on how you feel when you have stage fright. Speculate as to what causes your anxiety. Tell any stories on yourself that have occurred because of your tension. Be completely honest. When you are through, remain standing while class members volunteer suggestions to help you. Discuss these suggestions with them. At the end of the 1-3 minute discussion period, relate how you are feeling at that particular moment. If you have been frank in your remarks, you should feel more relaxed and in control of the situation.

ADDITIONAL ACTIVITIES

(1) Become a detective in the speech and drama section of your school and city library. Find stories about famous people or quotations by them that reveal their problems with stage fright. Give a 2-3 minute oral report in class on your findings.

(2) See and discuss the following videos. (For address, see Appendix E):

Say It Better: Fearless Public Speaking (Learning Seed)
Ways to overcome stage fright.

Delivering the Speech (Insight Media)
Defines stage fright and eight ways to overcome it.

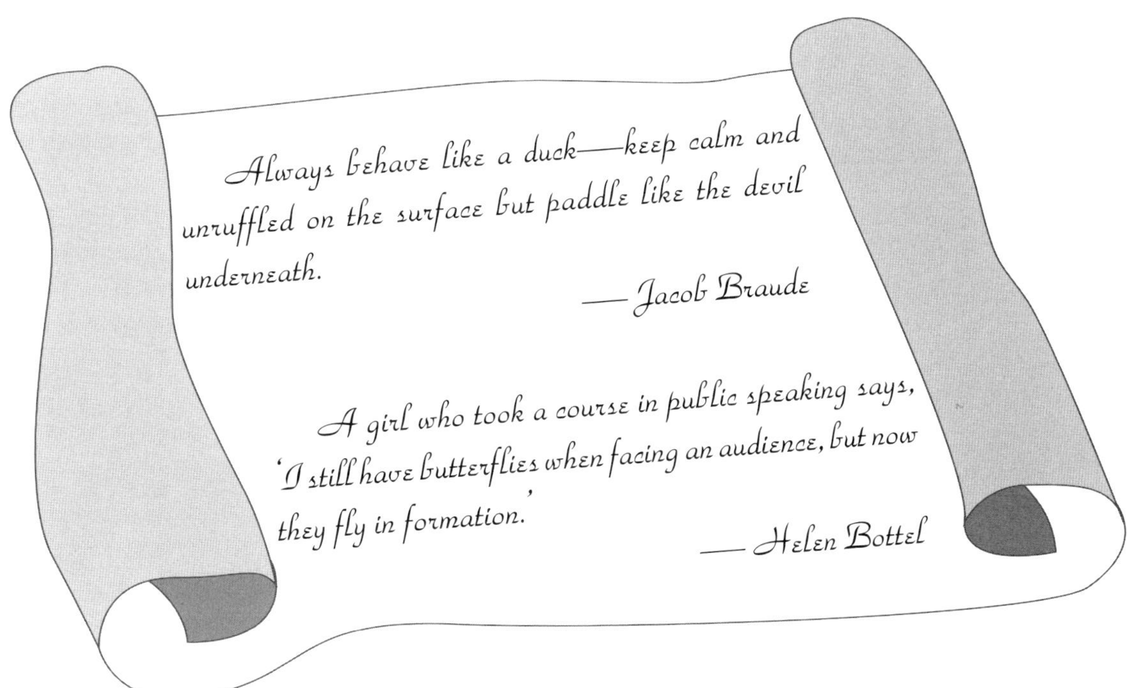

Always behave like a duck—keep calm and unruffled on the surface but paddle like the devil underneath.
— Jacob Braude
A girl who took a course in public speaking says, 'I still have butterflies when facing an audience, but now they fly in formation.'
— Helen Bottel

"FEE"

Before the Norman Conquest, **fee** meant cattle in England. Back then, a person's fortune was figured in terms of his herd: cows were literally a form of currency. Centuries later, **fee** came to mean the sum (formerly the number of cattle) that was involved in a business transaction.

Chapter 30

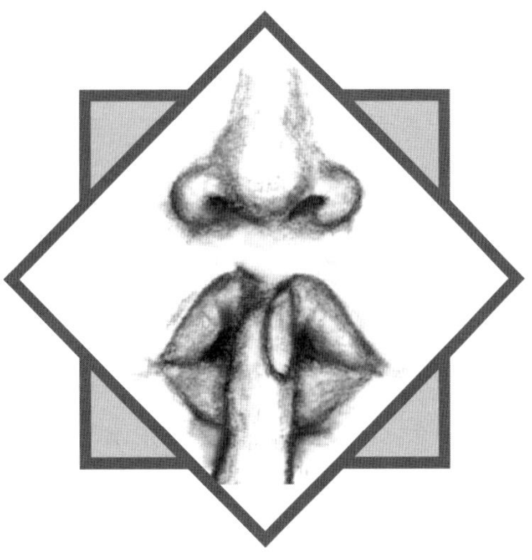

Shhh...Listen

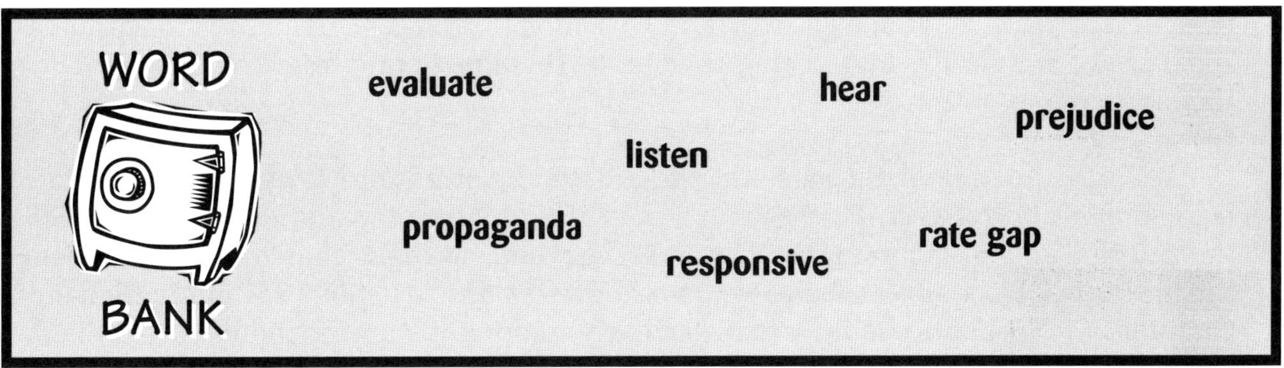

Watch for these valuable words wherever you see the word bank icon. 

BRAIN TEASERS

(1) How much time do you spend listening?
(2) Why is listening more important today than it was 100 years ago?
(3) What is the difference between hearing and listening?
(4) How can good listening help you?
(5) How can the speaker help the listener?
(6) What are your duties as listener?
(7) Why should you distrust propaganda devices?

PLATFORM NOTES

Your generation is unique. You are influenced more by what you *hear* than by what you read. This was not true of your grandparents or of people living in the last 400 years. During that time the printing press provided the major form of mass communication. Then people were greatly influenced by what they read. But today, radio, movies, and television focus on listening. Some authorities even suggest that in the future, people will not need to learn how to read, because computers will tell and show them what they want to learn.

Today you spend at least 45% of your time listening and only 30% of your time speaking! Yet have you ever been taught *how* to listen? You probably haven't, because of the prevalent idea that "anyone can listen." Not true! You may *hear*, which means that your ears receive sounds. But *listening* is an active process whereby you interpret in your brain what your ears perceive. In recent studies investigators found that most people can improve their listening ability by 75%! It is obvious that we need to study listening skills along with speaking skills. In fact, speaking and listening are partners. It takes both for communication, and throughout life you will play both roles, sometimes sending the message and sometimes receiving it.

A good listener benefits in many ways. Become a better listener and you'll hear better speeches. Why is this? Because a responsive audience stimulates the speaker to give his or her best, to go beyond the call of duty. Become a better listener, and you'll become a better speaker, for you'll be aware of what the listener needs to understand and remember. Become a better listener, and you will be in a position to protect yourself from the dishonest speakers in our society by refusing to vote for them or to buy from them or to believe them.

Who has the greater responsibility in a listening situation? It should be shared by both sender and receiver. The speaker's duty is to analyze the audience and then offer the material and examples that will interest the group. Speakers should help the audience see how the subject affects their lives, so they will *want* to listen. (See motivation step, Chapter 26.) Speakers should organize clearly, making it easy for the listener to follow the ideas.

In turn, the listener has the following duties:

Get physically prepared for listening. Sit in a comfortable but alert position where you can easily see and readily hear the speaker. If you are going to take notes, have paper and pencil handy.

Be attentive. Put all distractions and problems out of your mind. Look directly at the speaker and then show that you are listening by keeping a responsive face. A listener should be like a baseball catcher who is sending signals to the pitcher (speaker) as well as catching the ball (message). Signals will help the alert speaker, so if you agree with a statement, signal by nodding your head. Frown if you disagree. However, consideration and courtesy should prevent you from expressing boredom, contempt, or a daydreaming immobility. Become the listener you want to have when you are talking. A listener should help, not hinder, the speaker.

Use the rate gap. Have you noticed that when you listen you have extra time between words? The reason is that an average person talks 125 to 150 words a minute, but an average listener can handle at least 400 words a minute. This creates a big rate gap that the receiver should fill by actively listening to accomplish three purposes:

(1) Listen to *understand*. Approach the speech with an open mind, giving the speaker a chance to state the ideas. Even if you have strong negative opinions about the subject, be fair. Recognize your prejudices and try to understand what is being said.

(2) Listen to *remember*. Use the leftover time in the rate gap to extract the central idea of the speech. Don't worry about the details. If you outline the main ideas on paper or in your head, you'll probably remember much of the supporting material too.

(3) Listen to *evaluate*. Judge the speaker. Does he or she seem honest and in a position to know the facts? Why is the speaker speaking? Judge the material. What is the purpose of the talk? What is the evidence? Are the ideas clear? logical? relevant? truthful? Are there errors in the speaker's thinking processes? Be particularly distrustful of the following propaganda devices that some speakers use in an attempt to sway their audience by prejudice or deceit rather than by honest evidence.

(a) Name calling: making a person appear bad by associating him or her with an unpopular label such a "nerd," "pig," "radical," "communist."

(b) Glittering generalities: making a proposition sound desirable because of an approved label such as "progress," "patriotism," "thrifty."

(c) Testimonial: selling an idea or product by using famous names rather than sound evidence.

(d) Card-stacking: deceiving by giving only one-sided evidence.

(e) Half-truths: deceiving by telling only half of the truth.

(f) Band wagon: creating an impression of widespread approval by phrases such as "everybody is doing it."

(g) Plain folks: making ideas appear good or honest because they are the ideas of "common folks."

Always use your listening time effectively. *STOP* what you are doing, *LOOK* at the speaker, and *LISTEN* to understand, remember, and evaluate. Make good listening a special habit of yours. It will pay off in this world of sound.

ACTIVITY AND ITS PURPOSE

This assignment is to help you sharpen your skill at listening to instructions. In class you are to listen to instructions that a classmate gives you and then repeat them as accurately as possible.

HOW TO PREPARE

On the activity sheet to this chapter legibly write a question asking for instructions or for directions. Then answer that question in only three or four sentences. Memorize your answer. Examples of questions are:

(1) How do you correctly open a new book?
(2) How do you get to the local medical center from your house?
(3) How do you get a ketchup stain out of a blue shirt?
(4) What is the term project in history class?
(5) How do you fold whipped egg whites into a cake mixture?
(6) How should you arrange the information on this poster?
(7) How do you open this combination lock?
(8) Where is the closest bakery to the school?

HOW TO PRESENT

At the beginning of class, tear off your question from the bottom of the activity sheet, fold it in half, and place it in a container your teacher will provide. When you are called on, hand the activity sheet to your instructor and go to the front of the room. Draw a question from the container, being sure not to get your own. Read the question aloud clearly. The person who wrote the question will hand his or her sheet to the teacher and walk to the front of the room, face you, and answer the question clearly and slowly. You must listen carefully, for when he or she is through, you must repeat the answer, using as many of the speaker's exact words as you can. If the speaker decides you are not correct, the directions will be repeated and you must listen again before replying. Continue until your reply is accurate. Before returning to your desk, collect your activity sheet. Have it ready to hand to the teacher again when your question is called and you must give the instructions.

ADDITIONAL ACTIVITIES

(1) For the next speaking assignment your teacher will appoint you and another class member to focus on the same speech. In your separate listening reports, write the specific purpose of the speech, the main ideas, and the support used for each point. In class compare the two reports and discuss the findings with the speaker.

(2) Your teacher will assign listening exercises to you throughout the year, having you listen to classroom speeches and write a listening report. On your listening report list the specific purpose of the speech and each of the main headings. After the speaker finishes, he or she will read aloud the specific purpose and main ideas. Check your answers. If there is a discrepancy, discuss the cause. Is it the speaker's fault for stating them poorly, or is it the listener's fault for bad listening habits?

(3) Your teacher will assign you to listen to a political speaker on radio or television. Listen to identify any propaganda devices used. Discuss your findings in class.

(4) See and discuss the following videos. (For addresses see Appendix E):

The Art of Listening (Learning Seed)
Practical techniques using family and work situations.

Building Listening Skills (Coronet)
Three videos on the listening process, effective listening and assertive listening.

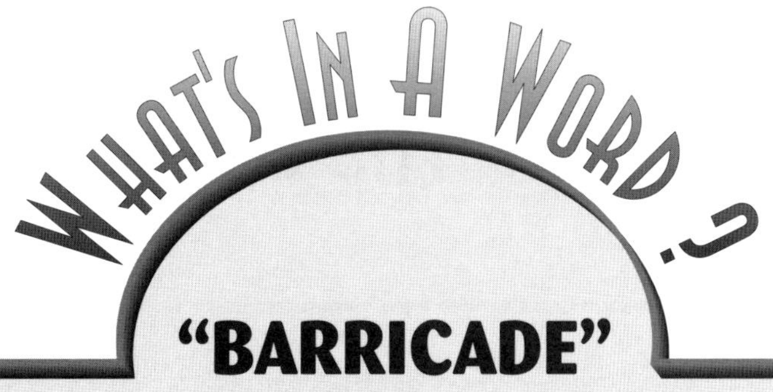

"BARRICADE"

In the streets of Paris during the religious wars of the 16th Century, crude walls made from rubble-filled barrels were a major form of "civil defense." **Barricade** comes from the French word for barrel: **barrique**.

We have two ears and one tongue in order that we may hear more and speak less.

— Diogenes

Chapter 31

Speak The Speech

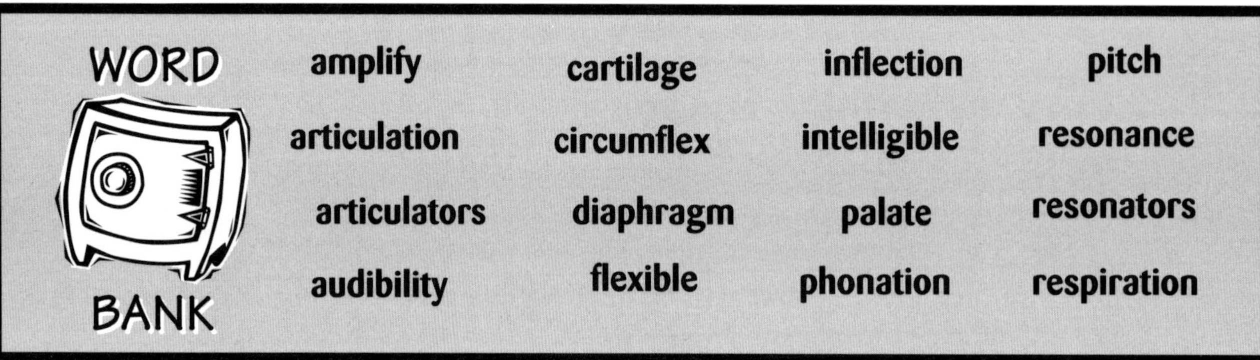

WORD BANK
amplify
cartilage
inflection
pitch
articulation
circumflex
intelligible
resonance
articulators
diaphragm
palate
resonators
audibility
flexible
phonation
respiration

Watch for these valuable words wherever you see the word bank icon. 

BRAIN TEASERS

(1) What qualities should you develop in your voice?
(2) How do you produce vocal sound?
(3) Why is diaphragmatic breathing important?
(4) What is meant by vocal quality, pitch, rate, and force?
(5) What exercises can you do to achieve flexibility in vocal quality, pitch, rate, and force?
(6) What is the cause and cure of poor articulation?
(7) What standard for pronunciation should you follow?

PLATFORM NOTES

Oh. Oh! Oh? That is about all you can do when you write the word oh. But notice the variety available when you speak that same word to sound like the attitudes printed below in parenthesis:

Oh — (That's news to me.)
Oh — (Don't be so dumb.)
Oh — (I never would have thought it possible.)
Oh — (That's a small item.)
Oh — (That hurts!)
Oh — (How beautiful.)
Oh — (How revolting.)
Oh — (I get the point.)
Oh — (What a fish story.)
Oh — (I'm so sorry.)
Oh — (Look out!)
Oh — (So you thought you could get away with it.)

By just adding the voice to a simple word, you can obtain numerous shades of meaning.

In fact, your voice is your most influential tool in a speech situation. Listeners respond more to how your voice sounds than to the truth of your statement (which says something about our listening habits). Moreover, your voice reveals your background, attitude, education, health, and personality, as we discussed in Chapter 24. Unfortunately, if you are like four out of five people, your voice reveals factors you don't want told, factors that become big blocks between you and your listener. With effort, however, you can push these blocks away by developing a voice that is easily heard, pleasant to the ears, flexible, and intelligible. Let's look at how you can make this so.

Voice Production

First, be aware of how you produce speech. When you exhale, your diaphragm (a large muscle at the bottom of your rib cavity) with the aid of other muscles, pushes the air out of your lungs and into the windpipe. In the "Adam's apple" portion of your windpipe are two cartilages that look like small lips, about one-half to three-fourths of an inch long. In breathing, they remain parted for easy airflow. In speech the exhaled air provides pressure, setting these lips or vocal cords into vibrations that create sound, much like what occurs when you strike a guitar string. But the voice sound is weak, and to be of any use it must be amplified and enriched by the resonators, which are the bones and sinus cavities in your nose, throat, and mouth. These resonators, because of their size and shape, give your voice its own distinctive sound, recognizable even to blindfolded friends. While we cannot change the "fixed resonators" (the bones and sinuses) we can change the shape, size, and tenseness of resonating chambers in the mouth and throat, and therefore make some adjustments to our voice quality. Up to now we still have "raw" sound. It becomes speech only when our articulators—the jaw, palate, lips, teeth, and tongue—create the words.

So, from exhalation to the spoken word, we have four phases: respiration (breathing), phonation (vibration of vocal folds), resonance (amplification and enrichment), and articulation (molding sound into words). Now let us discuss how we use these four phases in voice improvement.

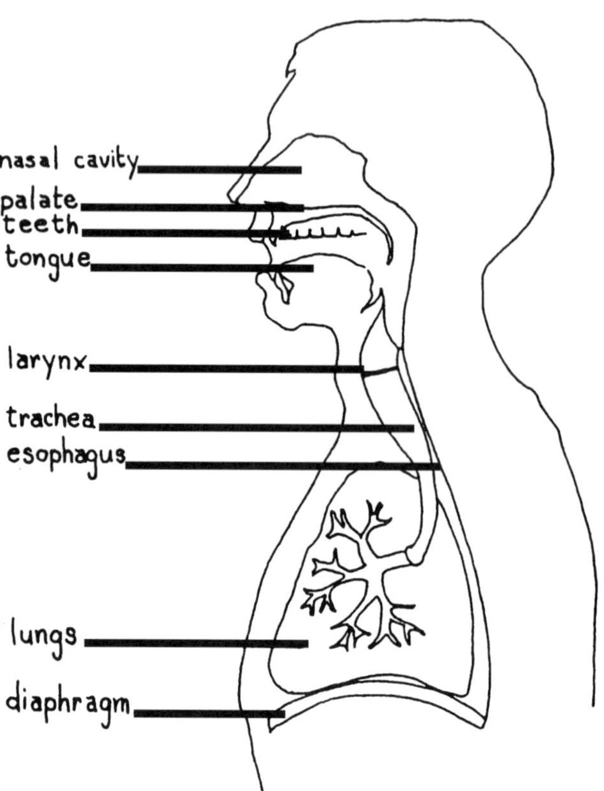

Audibility

In order to be easily heard, you need a forceful, controlled breath stream which comes from the first phase of voice production: proper breathing. While you can sustain life by breathing in any number of ways, for controlled speaking you need to breathe from the diaphragm. Check your diaphragmatic breathing with the following exercises:

(a) On the floor, lie on your back and place a book over the diaphragm area just above the waist. As you slowly inhale and exhale, the book should rise and fall. Work for this same action when you are standing up. Put your hand where the book was, and rapidly pant like a dog. Notice that your hand should move out as you inhale and in as you exhale.

(b) Standing up, place your hands just above your waistline, with the tips of the middle fingers touching each other. Slowly take a deep breath through the nose, and feel your hands being pushed outward and your fingertips gradually drawing away from each other.

(c) Inhale deeply. Hold your breath for five seconds, and then see how slowly you can exhale it through rounded lips, keeping the breath stream smooth and under control.

(d) Repeat the above exercise, but exhale with a clear "ooooh" sound, being careful not to become "breathy." Repeat with other vowels.

(e) Place a lighted candle a few inches from your mouth, and repeat the above exercise. The flame should barely flicker.

Pleasant Quality

The quality and tone of your voice speaks louder than words. Try this experiment. Using endearing words such as "sweet, cute, lovable," talk to your dog in a harsh, scolding manner and see him retreat in shame. Now reverse the procedure by using cold, hard words in a friendly, kind tone of voice and watch him happily wag his tail.

If you can create a pleasant, warm quality when talking to humans, like your dog, they'll "eat from your hand." You can improve your tone and achieve greater flexibility when you have a relaxed, open throat and when you use the resonators to full extent. For an open throat, practice the following:

(a) *Rag doll exercise*: Stand tall with your feet apart in good balance. Collapse your body from the waist with head and arms loosely hanging near the floor. Then raise the torso slowly, keeping the arms and head limp. Repeat several times.

(b) *Head roll*: In a relaxed upright position from the above exercise, slowly circle the head around to the right shoulder, back, left shoulder, and down, with the head hanging a dead weight on the chest, mouth open. Repeat in reverse direction. Keep the movement slow, smooth, continuous.

(c) *Yawn*: Put the tip of your tongue behind the lower front teeth. Yawn and inhale deeply. Then stop and notice the open, relaxed throat as the air rushes in. Repeat until you have memorized this open throat feeling. Now say "Ah" as you exhale, keeping the throat open and relaxed. Repeat with other vowels.

(d) With an open throat from the above exercise count slowly from one to twenty.

(e) With open, relaxed throat, repeat the following:

Alone, alone, all, all alone,
Alone on a wide, wide sea!
And never a saint took pity on
My soul in agony.
—Coleridge

Roll on, thou deep and dark blue ocean,
roll.
— Byron

For resonance, work on the exercises below:

(a) Do the above yawn exercise, and then slowly closing your mouth, add "mmmmmmm." Push with your diaphragm for a strong flow of air. Work until you can feel your lips vibrate.

(b) With the lips closed, hum. Place your hand on your head, then your nose, chin, chest. If you are resonating properly you should feel these areas vibrate.

While your normal vocal quality should be free of harshness, breathiness, or a nasal twang, it, of course, will vary according to thought and mood. Read the following words, changing your quality to suit their meaning.

grunt, roar, coo, crackle, bang, swish,
tinkle, wheeze, buzz, splash, gurgle,
clang, bubble

Flexibility

Variety is the spice of life, and we may add, of voice. The people we enjoy listening to are those who vary their pitch, rate, and force.

Pitch is the highness and lowness of the voice as determined by the length and tenseness of the vocal cords. Although humans have a two or three octave speaking range, too often people talk only within a four or five note variance. Such one-tone-Toms make listening a bore. Only through use of a greater pitch range can you effectively get across the full meaning and feeling of words. For example, high pitch suggests excitement, timidity, weakness, or extreme youth; low pitch reveals assurance, strength, poise, disgust, despair, and sadness.

For general speaking, you should use the lower half of your range, as a medium low tone is most pleasing to a listener. But from that level you should work toward flexibility up and down the speaking scale by using inflection and step changes. *Inflection* changes occur within syllables. Rising inflection suggests uncertainty or incomplete thought.

Falling inflection suggests finality, conviction, and completeness of thought.

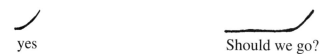

Circumflex inflection suggests those rich double meanings when we are being sarcastic, subtle, or humorous.

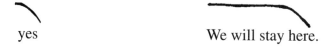

Notice the various inflectional changes you used to say the series of "Oh's" at the beginning of this chapter.

Step changes occur between words.

not It's
go
He
always
home. cold.
will

For greater pitch range, practice the following:

(a) Take a deep breath and count slowly from one to eight, saying each number on a pitch higher than the one before. Be sure you talk rather than sing the numbers. Then talk down the note scale from eight to one.

(b) Read the following phrases aloud at the pitch level designated by the meaning of every phrase:

Begin high — a little higher still — now very low — now very high —speak at a medium pitch — again very low — can you make it lower —and back to medium pitch.

(c) Read aloud the sentences below in a pitch pattern that conveys the suggested emotional meaning:

(1) I am terribly tired and discouraged.
(2) What a beautiful view.
(3) Watch out! He's got a gun.
(4) Get out of here. I hate you.
(5) Well! What do you think you're doing?
(6) I know. It's the tenth time you've told me.
(7) I am so lonely I can't stand it.
(8) My brother is the best pitcher in the league.
(9) I am so excited. We're going to Bermuda.
(10) I am absolutely positive that I sent the letter.

(d) Using the sentence: "Oh, yes, you don't say," vary the pitch according to the following notations which indicate steps – ‾ _ , and rising / , falling \ , and circumflex ∧ ∨ inflections:

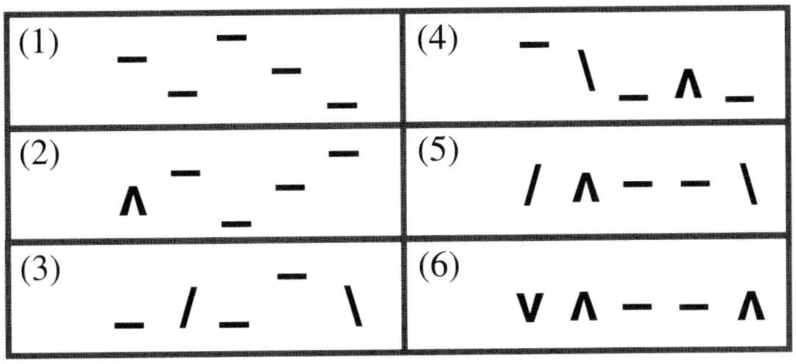

(1) – _ ‾ – _	(4) – \ _ ∧ _
(2) ∧ ‾ _ – ‾	(5) / ∧ – – \
(3) _ / _ ‾ \	(6) ∨ ∧ – – ∧

Rate means the speed of your speaking. Slow rate suggests sorrow, deliberation, reverence, doubt. A fast rate suggests excitement, anger, nervousness, happiness. Your rate will be affected by your pauses between words and the length you attach to vowel sounds. Do the following exercises for rate flexibility:

(a) Count from 1 to 20 beginning very slowly and increasing your rate until you are speaking as rapidly as you can. Then reverse: begin at a rapid rate working down to a very slow pace.

(b) While counting from 1 to 20 stretch out the vowel sounds at a slow rate but allow no pause between numbers. Repeat with short, clipped vowel sounds and long pauses between numbers. Shift between these two methods every six numbers.

(c) Say the following sentence according to the instructions below: "The snow is falling down."

(1) Use short quantity as if excited.
(2) Use long quantity as if you are sad.
(3) Use moderate rate to state a fact simply.

Force refers to volume or the energy with which you speak. We have already discussed the importance of force for audibility. Force is also varied to communicate meaning through word emphasis. Notice how meaning changes as the volume shifts to different words:

Did Steve get an A in History? (You said so, but did he really?)
Did *Steve* get an A in History? (Or was it Sam?)
Did Steve get an *A* in History? (Or was it a B?)
Did Steve get an A in *History*? (Are you sure it wasn't in math?)

(a) By emphasizing different words, how many meanings can you get from these sentences?

(1) Is Linda flying to New York this summer?
(2) Did Tim promise Dave to meet him here at 3:00?
(3) She gave him the blue book.

(b) Say the letters of the alphabet by beginning softly and increasing the force until you are nearly shouting. Then reverse the procedure.

Intelligibility
Articulation. If your family and friends frequently ask you to repeat what you have said, you may be suffering from the dread articulation disease of lazy jaw, tongue, and lips. Symptoms are many. "Jeet" for "Did you eat," "Whatjado" for "What did you do," "Harya" for "How are you," "Gunna" for "going to," and "Zwati thought" for "That is what I thought," show inexcusable sloppiness.

To conquer this disease, limber up your articulators by turning to the vocal warmup section in Appendix A and practicing the exercises daily.

Also, practice saying the following tongue twisters to help you restore precision:

(a) Open your mouth widely and say the twisters clearly, picking up speed each time:

(1) Would Wheeler woo Wanda if Woody snoozed woozily?
(2) Two teamsters tried to steal twenty-two keys.
(3) Six slim sleek saplings.
(4) A big black bear bit a big black bug.
(5) Better buy bigger rubber baby buggy bumpers.
(6) Fill the sieve with thistles; then sift the thistles through the sieve.
(7) Peter Piper picked a peck of pickled peppers.

(b) Read the following with clear articulation:

To sit in solemn silence in a dull, dark dock,
In a pestilential prison, with a lifelong lock,
Awaiting the sensation of a short, sharp shock,
From a cheap and chippy chopper on a big black block!

—Gilbert and Sullivan

(c) Enunciate the last sound in the following words:

coming	friend	singing
going	dead	past
running	across	talking

(d) Clearly articulate the following words:

gentlemen	—	(not gen'lmen)
city	—	(not cidy)
government	—	(not gov-ment)
geography	—	(not jog'phy)
twenty	—	(not twenny)
hundred	—	(not hunnard)
don't know	—	(not dunna)

Pronunciation. Many times you will be faced with the question, "What is the correct pronunciation of this word?" Although there are three definite pronunciation regions in the U.S.—Eastern (New England and natives born to New York City), Southern, and General American — our pronunciation differences are slight, compared to other countries.

Throughout the United States we pronounce about 90% of our words alike. But there are differences, and then the question comes, "Which pronunciation?" You would be wise to follow the suggestions of the national broadcasting companies in their selection of announcers: follow the pronunciation of the educated people in your community, keeping free of regional peculiarities. Then no matter where you go, you will be readily understood. How you say a word should not detract from what you say.

The following is a list of words frequently mispronounced. Learn to say them correctly, concentrating on the vowels shown in the correct and incorrect rhyme word:

Word	*Correct Rhyme*	*Incorrect Rhyme*
just	must	mist
get	bet	bit
for	ore	fur
again	pen	pin
any	penny	skinny
poor	sewer	pore
sure	sewer	per
your	sewer	per
our	hour	car
can't	pant	paint

Read the following so that a person standing fifty feet away can distinguish the two pairs of similar words:

weather - whether
formally - formerly
conscious - conscience
statue- stature
accept - except
ate - hate
precede - proceed
wandered - wondered
adapt- adopt

affect - effect
which - witch
wear - where
what - watt
win - when
ladder - latter
madder - matter
whither - wither

ACTIVITY AND ITS PURPOSE

You are to do three voice improvement exercises that hopefully will start you on a daily voice exercise program. You are to work on breath control, clear articulation, correct pronunciation, and a fusing of all of the elements discussed in this chapter.

HOW TO PREPARE

(1) Select two tongue twisters from this book or any other source. Practice saying each until you can accurately obtain good articulation at least three times at a fast rate.

(2) Choose a four line nursery rhyme such as "Mary Had a Little Lamb" or "Twinkle Twinkle Little Star." Breathing from the diaphragm practice these four lines from memory until you can recite them twice at a moderate speed on one breath. Control your breath so that it runs out as the second jingle ends.

(3) Using all ten of the words in the above "Frequently mispronounced list (just, get, for, any)" write an original paragraph of 50-80 words. Be sure you use all ten of the words. Rehearse reading your paragraph aloud, concentrating on audibility, pleasant quality, and variety in pitch, rate, volume. Pay particular attention to clear articulation and correct pronunciation of each word.

(4) Fill in the activity sheet to this chapter. Make a copy of your original paragraph to use when reading it to the class.

HOW TO PRESENT

When your teacher calls on you, turn in the activity sheet and take your copy of the paragraph to the platform. Lay it down for the moment. In a loud, flexible voice, do the exercises in the order prepared: tongue twister and nursery rhyme said from memory and original paragraph read aloud. Work to make every sound you utter, your best. Designated class members will report their findings on any slurred articulation or mispronounced words.

Note: If possible, your teacher will have you speak into a microphone for taping your presentation. Another day it will be played back and you can listen and evaluate yourself.

ADDITIONAL ACTIVITIES

(1) Carry through a self-improvement program for your voice by doing the following:

(a) Make a tape recording of your speech, and listen critically as you play it back.

(b) Get in the habit of listening to yourself as you talk; determine how you sound to others.

(c) Ask friends, family, and your teachers to describe your voice and diction.

(d) Determine your problem areas.

(e) With the help of your teacher or a speech clinician, schedule a program of improvement exercises and faithfully follow it.

(2) See and discuss the following videos. (For addresses see Appendix E):

American Tongues (High school version)
Shows how Americans' attitudes about their speech reflect cultural issues.
(New Day Films, 22-D Hollywood Avenue, Hohokus, New Jersey, 07423)

Speak for Yourself (Insight Media)
Vocal warm up exercises

(3) The following cassettes are available from Dialect Accent Specialists, Inc., P.O. Box 44, Lyndonville, Vermont, 05851

Acting With An Accent (60 minutes)
Numerous dialects. Accompanying manuals.

Speaking Without An Accent (60 minutes)
Training in non-regional American dialect.

The Sound and Style of American English (90 minutes)
Foreign accent reduction for speakers of English as a second language.

Good words are worth much and cost little.
— George Herbert
The difference between the right word and almost the right
word is the difference between lightning and the lightning bug.
— Mark Twain
Give me the right word and I will move the world.
— Joseph Conrad

"POSSE"

Despite what Western movies might suggest, **posse** is not an American original. Both the word and the thing it stands for come from ancient Rome: **posse comitatus**, or power of the county. The full term is still preserved in modern legal jargon.

Chapter 32

Information, Please

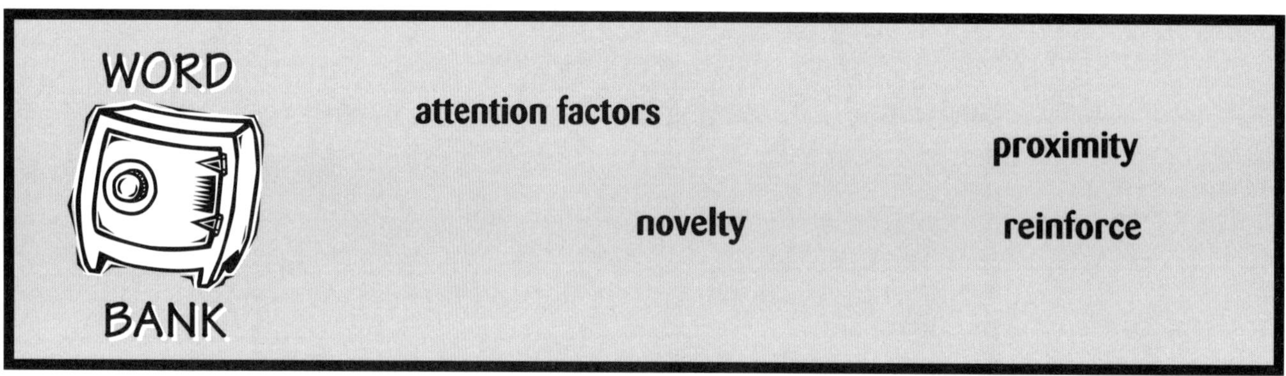

Watch for these valuable words wherever you see the word bank icon. 

BRAIN TEASERS

(1) How does teaching relate to informative speaking?
(2) What are the requirements of a speech to inform?
(3) How can you make your ideas clear?
(4) What are attention factors?

PLATFORM NOTES

Everyone is a teacher. You act that role many times a day. If a friend calls up after school asking about an assignment, your answer teaches. If a stranger stops you on the street and asks for directions to a grocery store, your reply instructs. If you give a report to the pep club, you are again serving as a teacher.

No matter what your job when you leave school, you will spend much time teaching: a doctor gives instructions to the patient, a coach explains a difficult play to the team, a scientist makes recommendations to the board of directors, a mechanic tells the customer what is wrong with the engine.

Since so much of your life is spent in teaching, you should learn to do it well. In other words, you need to study informative speaking, for that is what teaching is—giving information so the hearer can learn. Notice that when you give a speech to inform, your purpose is not to show off your knowledge, but to help others understand, remember, and apply ideas.

Think about yourself. When do you find learning the easiest? Isn't it when ideas are presented in a simple-to-follow way and when these ideas are related to material that interests you?

Carry these principles over to a speaking situation. When you give a speech to inform, your audience will learn only if the ideas are clear and interesting.

Clear
You achieve clarity in five ways:

(1) *Organize* in a step-by-step procedure. (See Chapter 26 for organization.) Let your listener know where you are going and when you get there. If necessary as you move ahead, number the points: "Point one is . . ." or "The second thing to remember is..."

(2) *Reinforce* your ideas through repetition. As the old country preacher used to say, "First I tell them what I'm going to tell them. Then I tell them. And then I tell them what I've told them." If you follow the organization formula in Chapter 26 you will succeed in this repetition by using the preview step, the point-support steps, and a summary in the action step.

(3) *Compare* the unknown to the known. If you are attempting to explain a papaya to your listeners, compare this unknown fruit to a peach, which your audience has seen and tasted and knows. Then papaya becomes understandable.

(4) *Be accurate*. Don't teach lies. Check your ideas with authorities. Look to the experts for material. Compare sources to check truthfulness.

(5) *Be specific*. Give exact examples, cite statistics, define terms, quote authorities. Use visual aids. Instead of telling about a water ski wet suit, bring one to class for all to see. Then the audience will specifically know what a wet suit is. Use concrete words. Instead of saying, "A little girl was hurt," say, "Seven year old July Walker fell from her bike yesterday on the corner of Main and Elm Street and broke her left arm two inches above her wrist." That description makes the incident clear in our mind.

Interesting
When you motivate an audience in the introduction of your speech, you are giving them reasons for being interested in your subject. You will find that certain types of material seem always to attract listeners. Throughout your

talk you can maintain audience interest by using a combination of the following *attention factors*:

(1) *Novelty*. Use materials and examples that are new, different, unusual, or contrasting. All eyes are on the extremely short girl who walks down the hall with the exceptionally tall boy, because the contrast of height is novel. In your speeches, tell the unusual aspects of your idea. Show the immensity of Alaska by listing specifically the states that could fit into it. Show how one person can lift an engine that has the power of 10,000 horses.

(2) *Proximity*. This refers to events and names that are close to the group. Mention the speech prior to yours; bring into your talk an incident that recently happened in school or in the town or in the class. All of this adds interest.

(3) *The Vital*. Hit at the basic important things that concern your audience. Give information that will affect their lives, reputations, families, freedom, possessions, or jobs. Speeches on "Seat Belts Can Save Your Life," "Drugs Kill," "How to Get a Job," appeal to vital matters.

(4) *Activity*. The more active your ideas the more interesting they are. Keep your speech moving from one point to the next. Use action verbs. "As soon as I vaulted onto the field I dynamited my way to the huddle. I felt as if I was alive with a thousand charges. I kicked the ball furiously, slamming it into the right guard's side," will keep your audience awake more than just saying, "As a replacement on the football field I hit the right guard's side when I kicked the ball hard."

(5) *Humor*. A joke always gets attention, but be sure that the joke you tell specifically relates to your speech and that it is in good taste and will not offend or embarrass anyone. Also be sure you can tell the joke fluently, remembering the punch line.

ACTIVITY AND ITS PURPOSE

Make learning for your audience an easy experience by presenting a 2 to 4 minute Chalk Talk where you inform your listener about a topic that demands you draw a sketch, diagram, graph, or map on the chalkboard in order to clarify your idea. Your drawing must be an important part of the speech. Also, you are to use the chapter suggestions for making your informative speech clear and interesting. Use at least one source for your speech and two attention factors.

HOW TO PREPARE

(1) Prepare your speech by analyzing your audience and selecting a subject of interest to them and to you. Narrow your topic so you can adequately explain

it in the 2 to 4 minute time limits. The following are suggestions for topics:

(a) A map to historical buildings around Washington, D.C.
(b) Parts of a flower.
(c) Lubrication points on an engine.
(d) Acting areas in Shakespeare's Globe Theatre.
(e) Routes of the annual migration of the Monarch butterflies.
(f) Floor plan of a jumbo jet.
(g) Charting trade wind currents.
(h) The layers of Earth.
(i) Silhouettes of ladies' fashions in the last five centuries.
(j) The heart and circulatory system of humans.
(k) The computer screen's menu.
(l) The seating arrangement of an orchestra.
(m) The parts of a side of beef.
(n) A drill team formation.
(o) (Your choice, approved by your teacher.)

(2) Gather accurate, specific material from at least one source.

(3) Clearly organize your speech according to the formula in Chapter 26. Be sure you provide a clear step-by-step pattern, that you reinforce with repetition, and compare the known to the unknown. Include in your speech content at least two specific attention factors.

(4) Copy your completed outline onto the activity sheet to this chapter. In the margin notate each step of the organization formula. Also identify in the margin each of the two attention factors you are using.

(5) Rehearse your drawing as you rehearse your speech. If you don't have a chalkboard at home, tape a large piece of wrapping paper to the wall and use a crayon for marking. Remember to draw as you talk but practice looking frequently at the audience by turning your body to them. Avoid looking at them over your shoulder. Make your drawing large, simple, and in good proportion. Anyone can do this, even if he or she isn't an artist. Practice until you can draw easily and with confidence. Label the important parts clearly. If you refer to your drawing later, step aside and use a chalkboard pointer or a yardstick to point out the parts. Give your talk and drawing to family members or friends and let them offer suggestions.

(6) Check the evaluation chart on the back of the activity sheet to see how you will be rated.

HOW TO PRESENT

Arrive in class with a confident, friendly, yet poised manner. Hand your title card to the chairperson. As you rise to speak, hand your activity sheet to your teacher. When you get to the front of the room look at your audience and get their attention before beginning your formal salutation and capture step.

As you deliver your speech, be enthusiastic. Use gestures and as much eye contact as possible. Execute your drawing as you did in rehearsal. Do not apologize for your drawing. Just do the best you can. Remember to speak slowly enough to give your audience time to catch the ideas. Stay within time limits.

ADDITIONAL ACTIVITIES

(1) Give a 1 to 3 minute speech to inform in which you tell the audience how to draw a map locating your home or a specific commercial building. Have the class draw as you talk. At the end of your speech collect the maps and see how well you gave simple instructions. Write a short estimate of your effectiveness and hand it and the maps to your teacher.

Note: This also serves as a check on listening.

(2) Give a 2 to 4 minute speech to inform called "This is the Story," relating just *one* incident in the life of a famous person.

Examples: Mother Teresa's Nobel prize.
Thomas Jefferson's construction of Monticello.
Sir Edmund Hillary's climb of Mt. Everest.
Nelson Mandela's release from prison.

(3) Give a 2 to 4 minute speech to inform called "This is the Way it Was," relating just *one* historical incident.

Examples: The Hindenburg disaster.
The founding of Disney Land.
The death of Socrates.
The construction of the Vietnam Memorial.
The Battle of Dunkirk

(4) Give a 2 to 4 minute explanation of a procedure.

Examples: How space stations function.
How CPR is correctly used.
How trees are grafted.

A good listener is not only popular everywhere, but after a while he knows something.

— *Wilson Mizner*

Chapter 33

For Example

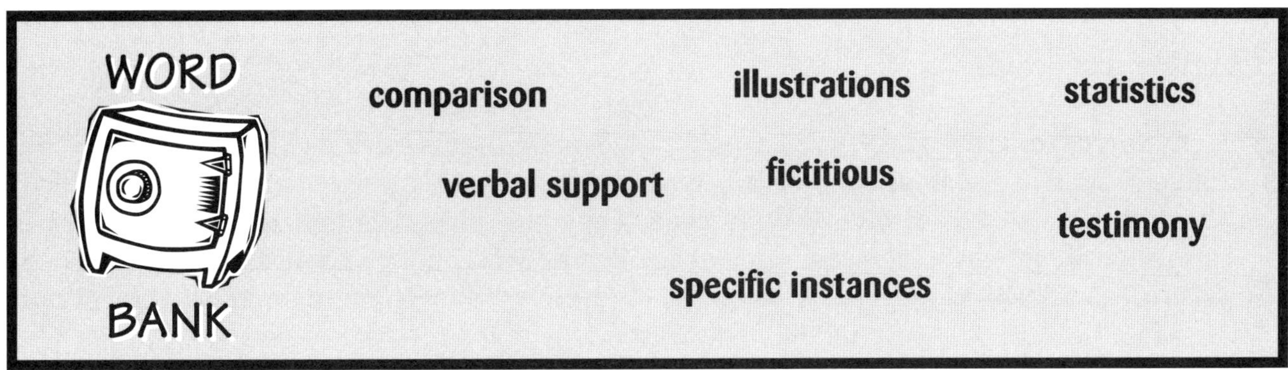

Watch for these valuable words wherever you see the word bank icon. 

BRAIN TEASERS

(1) How does verbal support help you?
(2) What are four types of verbal support?
(3) How do specific instances vary from factual illustrations?
(4) What are the requirements for use of testimony?
(5) What are the requirements for use of statistics?

PLATFORM NOTES

Your father listens to your request: "I think I should be allowed to stay out until 12:30 Friday night." He frowns. You realize that you'll not get permission unless you give him substantial reasons, unless you "support" your idea. You continue. You tell him that Friday is the final night of the school play, and as chairperson of a backstage crew your job is to assist in taking down the scenery. The play lasts until ten o'clock. The crew's work will take an hour, and after that there is a cast party until midnight. Besides, you continue, the drama coach, Miss Markham, said, "I hope all students working on the play will attend the party." Then you remind your father that this is the only curfew extension you have requested since school started three months ago. You finish your reasons by pointing out that your sister Katharine was allowed to attend late parties and since your behavior is as good as hers, you should be allowed the same privileges.

In trying to convince Dad to accept your main idea (to be out late Friday night) you have supported your statement in four ways. When you told him about the play, the set work, and the party, you used factual illustration. When you quoted your teacher's words, you used testimony. When you gave figures about the times you have asked for an extension, you used statistics. And when you talked about his policy with your sister, you used comparison.

In everyday situations, you clarify and prove your ideas only when you give reasons or support for them. In speeches you must also support your main ideas to obtain audience understanding and acceptance. Remember, a speech without support is like a tent without a pole. It collapses.

Now let's focus on four major types of *verbal support* that will keep your speech upright and strong.

Illustration is a story with a point. It can be factual (something that really has happened) or it can be fictitious (an invented story you ask the audience to suppose). Illustrations can be serious or humorous. They can also be long—telling the story in detail—or short—in which case they are called specific instances or examples. Because *specific instances* are brief facts, you need to cite several of them to make an impression.

Notice the following illustrations:

Factual illustration: (for a talk on the importance of human contact to maintain speech)

> Let me tell you a strange tale of a *Mrs.* Robinson Crusoe. In 1836 Captain Nidever was evacuating the island of San Nicolas upon orders of the Mexican government. He was to take all of the Indians there to a California mission. But just as the captain was ready to sail, one Indian woman jumped into the ocean, screaming that her child had been left behind in the confusion. The captain waited several hours, but when the woman failed to appear, he set sail, promising her friends to return for her in a short time. But that promise was broken. The ship was wrecked in a storm and the few survivors apparently forgot all about the stranded woman.
>
> In 1854 another ship's crew making an emergency stop at San Nicolas noticed footprints on the sand—footprints on a supposedly uninhabited island. A search revealed the old Indian woman, wrapped in a coat of bird feathers she had made. She was by herself, her son having been killed by wild animals the day she

went in search for him. With tears in her eyes she greeted her liberators. But to their astonishment she could speak no words. Eighteen years of solitude had robbed her of the power of speech.

Fictitious illustration: (for a talk on life saving)

Let us suppose for a moment that it is summer and you are resting by yourself on a sandy beach after a brisk swim in a cold mountain lake. Suddenly you hear screams coming from the water. A young person is obviously drowning. A quick glance around indicates that no one else is within hearing distance of the plea for help. What will you do?

Fictitious illustration in parable form: (for a talk on the power of fear)

An Arab folk tale relates that Pestilence once met a caravan upon a desert path to Baghdad.

"Why," asked the chief of the caravan, "are you in a hurry to get to the city?"

"To take 5000 lives," Pestilence replied.

Upon the way back from Baghdad, Pestilence met the caravan again.

"You lied," said the chief. "Instead of 5000 lives you took 50,000."

"No," said Pestilence. "Five thousand and not one more. It was Fear who killed the rest. "

Specific instances:

Many musicals are adapted from stage plays. For instance:

Oklahoma!, is from Rigg's *Green Grow the Lilacs.*
My Fair Lady, is from Shaw's *Pygmalion.*
Hello Dolly, is from Wilder's *The Matchmaker.*
Oliver, is from Dicken's *Oliver Twist.*
I Do! I Do!, is from Hartog's *The Four Poster.*
Where's Charley?, is from Thomas' *Charley's Aunt.*
West Side Story, is from Shakespeare's *Romeo and Juliet.*
Kiss Me Kate, is from Shakespeare's *Taming of the Shrew.*
Fantastics, is from Rostand's *The Romancers.*

Testimony means citing another person's words to support your views. The person you quote, of course, should be an authority on your subject. If you are discussing cancer research, quote a doctor, not an auto mechanic. Also make sure your audience knows why the person you quote is an expert by telling his or her qualifications: "Dr. Jacobs is a cancer specialist for the American Cancer Research Center. She says ...." Keep quotations brief. If necessary write them on a 3" x 5" card, and during your speech read from it for accuracy. While reading, establish some eye contact with the audience.

Comparison means to point out similarities between two ideas in order to make them vivid, clear, and interesting.

Examples of comparison:

> **R**eading a speech from a manuscript is like dating a girl through a high picket fence. Everything that is said can be heard, but there isn't much contact.
>
> **A** speech is like a love affair. Any fool can start it, but to end it requires considerable skill.
>
> **E**very fish has a protective coating needed to sustain its life. If you are a sportsman you throw back a fish if it is too small. But did you know your dry, rough hands can remove too much of the protective coating and kill the fish? So before grasping that catch, wet your hands. Humans are like fish in that they too have a protective coating called "pride" When the going gets rough, humans need a "wet hand" lubricant called "kindness" to sustain their self-esteem.

Statistics are numbers that show comparisons. While statistics provide strong verbal support, you should use them with care by following these suggestions:

(1) Make the statistics meaningful by putting them in terms your listener can understand. The following examples about huge sums of money do this:

> **I**f you had a million dollars and spent one thousand dollars a day, you wouldn't run out of money for three years. But if you had a billion dollars and spent one thousand a day, it would take you 3000 years to run out of money.
>
> **W**e are frequently told the importance of getting an education. But let's put it in strict dollar value. If you go through the eighth grade and then start working, your approximate average lifetime income will be $369,000. If you get a high school diploma, you'll make in your lifetime about $531,000. With a junior college degree you'll earn $574,000, and with a four year college degree you'll average $698,000. If you are wondering about not completing high school, before you quit, remember that those four high school

years will bring you at least $162,000 more during your life than if you stop school right now. That's like putting $3300 into your pocket every year for fifty years of your life—in exchange for four years of high school study.

(2) Round off numbers to an even sum. Instead of saying 4,987 1/4, say "approximately 5,000." Your listeners will better remember the statistics.

(3) Use statistics sparingly. Too many numbers either confuse or bore the listener.

(4) Check for accuracy. Remember, "figures don't lie but liars figure." Keep your statistics truthful by making sure they represent a fair sampling. To say that 1/3 of a group failed to pass the physical fitness exam is shocking unless you realize that only three took the exam and one failed.

What is misleading about the following statistics? "If you read fifteen minutes a day, you can read twenty books a year." (With this time limit, doesn't the number of books you read depend upon how fast you read and how long the books are?)

(5) Check for recency. What was true ten years ago may not be correct today. So use current figures and recent copyright dates.

ACTIVITY AND ITS PURPOSE

This assignment will give you practice in using verbal support. You will not give a complete speech. Instead, you will state one main point and adequately support it with proof in a 3-4 minute speech to convince, using at least two different kinds of verbal support.

HOW TO PREPARE

(1) From the list below choose one declarative statement that you want to prove true:

(a) The electromagnetic field of computers creates health hazards.
(b) An epidemic of ethnic hatred is sweeping the world.
(c) Humor plays an important role in wellness.
(d) Nuisance lawsuits are clogging the courts.
(e) Hospital trauma centers are facing financial and staffing crises.
(f) Trees enrich our lives in many ways.
(g) Living wills are a good idea.
(h) Loud music can impair your hearing.
(i) The elderly are today's neglected citizens.
(j) Pneumonics is an excellent aid to learning.
(k) We are being buried with rubbish and garbage.
(l) Heavy television viewing desensitizes children to violence.
(m) There are many bizarre remedies for treating illness.

(n) Suntans can kill you.
(o) It is important to become an organ donor.
(p) (Your choice, approved by your teacher.)

(2) Gather material from at least two sources by interviewing experts in the area you have chosen and reading current material at the library. Check to be sure you have at least two kinds of verbal support. Maybe you will use statistics and illustration, or comparison and illustration, or testimony and statistics. Any combination will do as long as the two supports help to prove your main idea. If possible, try to display one visual aid. Perhaps you can use a graph on the board to show statistics, or a drawing on a poster to clarify comparisons.

(3) Organize your speech in the following arrangement. Notice, for this speech only, you do not use the complete organization formula. Instead, you are developing only one point in the point-support section of the formula:

(a) State your main point.
(b) Support it with at least two types of verbal support. Be sure to state the sources of your evidence.
(c) Restate your main point in *different* words.

(4) Outline the above arrangement on the activity sheet to this chapter. Identify in the margin the type of verbal support you are using. (See the detailed speech outline at the end of this chapter.)

(5) Rehearse your speech well.

HOW TO PRESENT

Hand your activity sheet to your instructor before speaking. As you enter the room, look confident, even though you may not be. Hand the class chairperson your title card.

When you are introduced, walk with assurance to the front of the room. Pause, give your formal salutation, and then begin the speech with your topic sentence.

Show your audience your firm belief in the subject by giving your speech with enthusiasm and sincerity. If *you* don't sound convinced, your audience won't be convinced.

ADDITIONAL ACTIVITIES

(1) Read a short one or two page article in the *Reader's Digest*. On a paper to hand in to your teacher, write down the specific purpose of the article and list and give examples of each type of verbal support used.

SAMPLE OUTLINE–ONE-POINT SPEECH

General Purpose: To convince
Specific Purpose: Advances in computer technology over the last fifteen years have allowed the disabled to be more independent.

"INDEPENDENCE FOR THE DISABLED"

Factual Illustration

I. Advances in computer technology over the last fifteen years have allowed the disabled to be more independent.
    A. Kent Cullers, 39, has been blind since birth.
        1. He is a physicist with NASA's Search for Extraterrestrial Intelligence Program.
        2. He designs the complex equipment that may some day isolate intelligent signals from the random radio noise of the galaxies.
        3. He relies on a laptop computer to do his work.
            a. It automatically speaks aloud each word he types so accurately that he can hear the misspellings.
            b. It reads to him through the use of a scanner, that looks much like a copier, which transfers any document onto the computer screen.
        4. He says, "Twenty years ago I could not have held this job. Now, the fact that I'm blind is incidental."
        ("More Than Wheelchairs," *Newsweek*. April 24, 1989, p. 66)

Special Instances

    B. There are at least 1,600 products on the market today that can adapt computers into almost any form a disabled user needs.
        1. Keyboards for the disabled come in all shapes and sizes and are controlled through various means.
            a. Herman Briggman, 27, was a professional musician in New York City before he was paralyzed by viral encephalitis.
                (1) He is unable to speak or swallow.
                (2) He composes and plays music by using a head mounted spotlight that is aimed at a light sensitive keyboard.
                    (a) Each note he chooses is recorded.
                    (b) The recorded notes are sent to a music synthesizer which plays the results.
            b. John Christensen, 31, has severe cerebral palsy.
                (1) He cannot use his arms or legs.
                (2) He uses a head stick to hit the computer's keys allowing him to produce elaborate digital maps.
            c. Marc Buoniconti, 22, was paralyzed from the neck down four years ago in a football accident.
                (1) He uses a voice operated computer that manages everything from turning on the lights to answering the telephone.

Explanation

                    (a) Training the voice-recognition system takes only minutes.
                        ((1)) The program asks the user to repeat each word in the program 2 to 3 times.
                        ((2)) The software stores the vocabulary on a hard disk drive.
                    (b) After training, the computer can be operated entirely by voice.
                (2) The voice operated computer increases Marc's independence.
                ("More Than Wheelchairs," *Newsweek*, April 24, 1989, pp. 66-27)
                ("A Helping Hand," *BYTE*, December, 1989 pp. 129-1 30)

Explanation

        2. Robotic arms are being used in specially designed work stations providing greater independence for the disabled.
            a. The work station is mounted in a cubicle designed for wheelchair access.

b. The robotic arm looks like an industrial robot with a versatile, flexible arm.
   (1) It can arrange floppy discs
   (2) It can pick up books.
   (3) It can staple reports.
   (4) It can operate a copy machine.
   (5) It can move objects near the work area.
   (6) It can control the lights.
   (7) It can control the room ventilation.
   (8) It can even take a can of pop out of the refrigerator.
   ("A Helping Hand," *BYTE*, December, 1989, p. 130)
   ("More Than Wheelchairs," *Newsweek*, April 24, 1989, p. 67)

Factual Illustration

C. A 1977 diving accident paralyzed James Jotich, leaving him able to move only his arms and shoulders and raise his left wrist.
   1. Today he can write, feed himself, and even drive.
      a. His independence is possible due to experimental technology known as functional electrical stimulation - FES.
      b. This system uses low levels of electrical current to stimulate movement in paralyzed arms and legs.
         (1) A pair of microprocessors are attached to the user's wheelchair or belt.
         (2) The first microprocessor receives and deciphers the user's signal to move.
            (a) Jim sends a signal to open his hand by shrugging his shoulder.
            (b) Other systems respond to blinks or nods.
         (3) The second microprocessor relays the signal to a radio transmitter.
         (4) The transmitter sends an electric impulse down wires to electrodes planted in key muscles.
         (5) The impulses produce muscle contractions that crudely duplicate a normal grasp.

Testimony

   2. This is a big step toward independence for me." says Jatich, "My dad can put the system on me in the morning and go off to work." ("Waiting for the Bionic Man," *Forbes*, September 18, 1989, pp. 204-206)

Re–statement

II. Computer technology has combined machine intelligence, voice control, and robotic arm to provide a way for the disabled to be more independent.

Rash, Wayne. "A Helping Hand," *BYTE*, December, 1989, pp. 129-1 30.

Rogers, Michael. "More Than Wheelchairs," *Newsweek*. April 24, 1989, pp. 66-67.

Simon, Ruth. "Waiting for the Bionic Man," *Forbes*. September 1 8, 1989, pp. 204-206.

Wise men talk because they have something to say; fools, because they have to say something.
—Plato

Chapter 34

Irresistible Forces

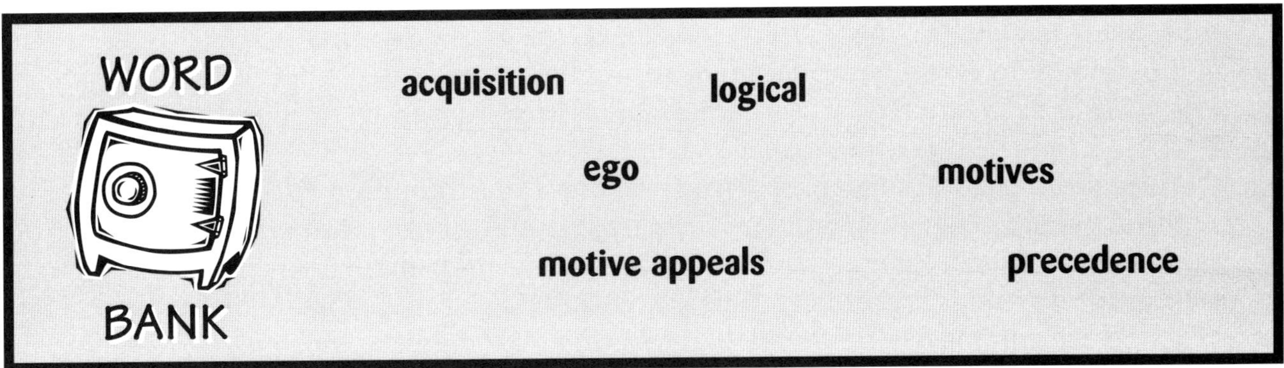

Watch for these valuable words wherever you see the word bank icon. 

BRAIN TEASERS

(1) Do people act with their heads or hearts?
(2) How can you make your ideas appeal to an audience?
(3) What are motive appeals?
(4) How should you use motive appeals in a speech?
(5) What are ten motive appeals?

PLATFORM NOTES

You have a test to study for, but instead you watch television. Why? You know you'll get hoarse, but you still shout at the game. Why? You realize that sweets are bad for your teeth, but you eat a chocolate candy bar anyway. Why?

If your answer to the above questions is "I want to," you have proven you're human! Although most of us like to believe we are governed entirely by logical reasons, much of our behavior is emotional. We are greatly influenced by our motives, desires, needs, wants, or drives.

How you act depends on which motives are the strongest. If you watch TV instead of studying, your desire for enjoyment is stronger at that moment than your motive for the personal accomplishment of good grades.

While emotions do not govern us completely, we are happiest and perform the best when we have an impelling urge to do what our minds tell us we *should* do. When logic and emotions work together, we work at peak efficiency. Our mind provides the direction, and our emotion provides the energy. For example, if we enjoy swimming and the doctor tells us we must swim daily for exercise, we'll have little trouble carrying out the orders. Head and heart are working together.

As a speaker, you can more easily obtain audience response if you relate your ideas to your listener's motives. Weight your speech with verbal support (reasons), and then show your audience how this information will help them achieve their goals or satisfy their wants (emotions).

If you have been using the organization formula (Chapter 26) in your speeches, you are already used to the motivation step where you entice your audience to listen to you. From now on, motivate your listeners throughout your entire speech by using *motive appeals*, which are images that stimulate audience desires.

Human motives are complex. People do the same thing for different reasons. Five hundred people attend a symphony concert. Why? For some, the concert satisfies their need to hear beautiful music; for others, the need of companionship is met; others attend the concert because it appeals to their motive of being seen in what they consider "high" society. Such complexity renders any index of motive appeals incomplete; however, the following is a usable list of these impelling human wants. You may later wish to add others.

MOTIVE APPEALS

(1) *Self-preservation* is the desire to survive: the need of food, clothing, shelter, oxygen, and rest. Self-preservation is usually considered the foremost motive, until it is satisfied. Then other needs take precedence. Closely associated with self-preservation is the need for security and safety—free from worries. We are responding to this motive when we lock our doors at night, get a smallpox vaccination, stop (or never start) smoking, use safety devices, take prescribed medications, or get our chest X-rayed for medical diagnosis.

Examples: "Buckle up your seat belt and live."
"If we don't stop air pollution, in twenty years man will be asphyxiated."
"Speed kills."

(2) *Pride* is self esteem or a feeling of personal worth and accomplishment. Frequently we need to strengthen our "ego," the Latin word for "I." We don't like to feel inferior or to be made fun of, so we work hard to build our morale and win approval of friends and family. We become a football player or the

editor of the school paper. We get good grades, win awards, join clubs, wear new clothes, and acquire possessions.

Examples: "If you make the honor roll, you are to be congratulated."
"Buy this new CD player, and you'll have the best one in town."
"For a real sense of accomplishment, volunteer your services at the children's hospital."

(3) *Personal enjoyment* is the desire for beauty, comfort, and recreation. "People cannot live by bread alone." They need beauty in their lives. In the dreariest of tenements you may see a tin can planted with blossoming geraniums that attests to this need. We adorn ourselves with jewelry, decorate our rooms with colorful posters, have soft over-stuffed chairs. We don't need a $200,000 home to keep out the wind and rain, but a love of fine things motivates us. We like a car with the "extras." We like food and drink that give us pleasant taste sensations. We like to own a boat for the fun of fishing and other water sports.

Examples: "Order Sullivan's ice cream for that melt-in-your-mouth smoothness of rich goodness."
"Baker's Music has an excellent selection of folk songs."
"For an evening of fun, attend the picnic at Green Park."

(4) *Love or affection* is the need to give and receive love, to have friends, to share life with others, to promote the common good. This drive motivates your parents to take out insurance for family security or to fight a war to protect loved ones. This drive spurs your donations to charity to help the less fortunate. It interests you in dating and in making friends with the opposite sex.

Examples: "People who work together build strong and lasting friendships."
"Learning to dance will make you a better dating partner."
"Send flowers to show you care."
"Take a foster child into your home and enrich both his or her life and yours."

(5) *Acquisition and Saving* is an appeal to the pocketbook, to a desire for ownership. It is often this drive that makes us work hard to earn money to buy what we want. It is this drive that entices us at the bargain table.

Examples: "Buy now and you'll save $10.00."
"Train for the job and you'll earn more money."
"Deposit by the tenth and your savings will earn interest from the first."

(6) *Adventure and curiosity* is a need for exploration. We resist boredom by participating, reading, watching, and daydreaming. We feed our hungry mind by searching for the answer to "why."

Examples: "For excitement join the Explorers in a rubber boat trip down the white water rapids."
"Why does your car have poor gas mileage? Find out."
"For a thrill every minute go to the carnival."

(7) *Loyalty* is faithfulness to nation (patriotism), school (school spirit), city (civic pride) and friends and family. You may frequently fight with your little brother, but family loyalty sends you to his assistance when an outsider picks on him. Flying the stars and stripes on holidays, bragging about your school's team, and cleaning up litter in your town stem from loyalty.

Examples: "Our club always donates to town projects."
"Attend the game and cheer for the home team."
"The Newmans are a Navy family."

(8) *Imitation* is a need to conform. This is what prompts you to "go along with the crowd" in dress, hair styles, slang, and actions. When you tell your parents "all the other kids are doing it," you are motivated by imitation. This motive also interests you in eating the breakfast cereal recommended by a football hero or buying a perfume used by a movie star.

Examples: "Smart people use Rough and Rugged Luggage for every trip."
"Try some Space Slivers, the same type food the astronauts ate on their trip to the moon."

(9) *Reverence* is a desire to "look up" to someone. This respect is manifest in three forms: (a) Hero worship, or deep admiration for people such as a star athlete, a national hero, or a person in high office; (b) Tradition, or respect for observances such as clapping after a performance, standing for the national anthem, or wearing academic caps and gowns for graduation; (c) Deity, or worship of a supreme being or universal force.

Examples: "Faith in God is our greatest strength."
"Washington and Jefferson were men of wide vision."

(10) *Creating* is the urge to invent. We get great satisfaction out of building our own ham radio set, making a dress, planting a vegetable garden, painting a picture, or organizing a political campaign. This motive is also what makes do-it-yourself kits so popular.

Examples: "Make your own original Christmas cards."
"Eat from a bowl you've made with your own hands. Take a pottery class."
"You can organize your own baby-sitting service."

In your speeches start with ideas first and then relate them to motive appeals. Choose the motive best adapted to your audience and topic. If necessary use more than one motive, but be sure they do not conflict. For example, if you use the motive of adventure, don't mention fear for safety (self preservation). Fear would defeat the adventure motive. Avoid naming the motive or calling attention to it. Your aim is subtlety.

ACTIVITY AND ITS PURPOSE

You are to gain practice in identifying and selecting motive appeals by filling out the activity sheet to this chapter. You are then to identify appeals used in magazine advertising and make a one minute report on your findings.

HOW TO PREPARE

(1) Fill out items 1-15 on the activity sheet.

(2) Search through magazines at home to select three colorful, preferably full page advertisements.

(3) Determine the motive appeals used in each of the three ads you have chosen. Identify them on the reverse side of the activity sheet.

(4) Prepare a one minute report discussing the appeals in each advertisement.

(5) Plan on showing the ads in class during your report. If possible, cut them from the magazine and mount each on construction paper.

HOW TO PRESENT

When your teacher calls on you, hand in the activity sheet and take your magazine examples to the front of the room. Show the first advertisement, holding it up high for all to see. Then discuss and point out appeals used. Repeat with advertisement two and three. Speak clearly and in a pleasant manner. Return to your desk quietly.

After everyone has given a report, determine which appeals were used the most. Perhaps a designated student will want to tabulate the appeals as each speaker talks. Discuss why these appeals are used so frequently. What do they tell about our environment, our society, and our needs?

ADDITIONAL ACTIVITIES

(1) Give a 1 to 2 minute persuasive motive appeal speech. Your subject may be either fact or fantasy, but you must use at least three different motive appeals and identify them in the margin of your speech outline. As you give your talk the class will shout aloud the name of any motive appeal they recognize. Your teacher will tabulate, giving one point for the first correct response. As a speaker you must not let the shouting

bother you. Carry on with your speech. As a listener you must quickly determine the appeal and say it aloud before someone else does.

(2) Read and report to the class on chapters assigned by your teacher from Vance Packard's two books, *Hidden Persuaders* and *Status Seekers*, in which he shows how advertisers use motives to sell.

(3) Discuss the list below of the "most persuasive words" in American usage. What words would you add, if any? What words would you leave out, if any? Why are these words persuasive? What appeals does each word use?

Persuasive word list: you, money, save, new, results, health, easy, safety, love, discovery, proven, guarantee.

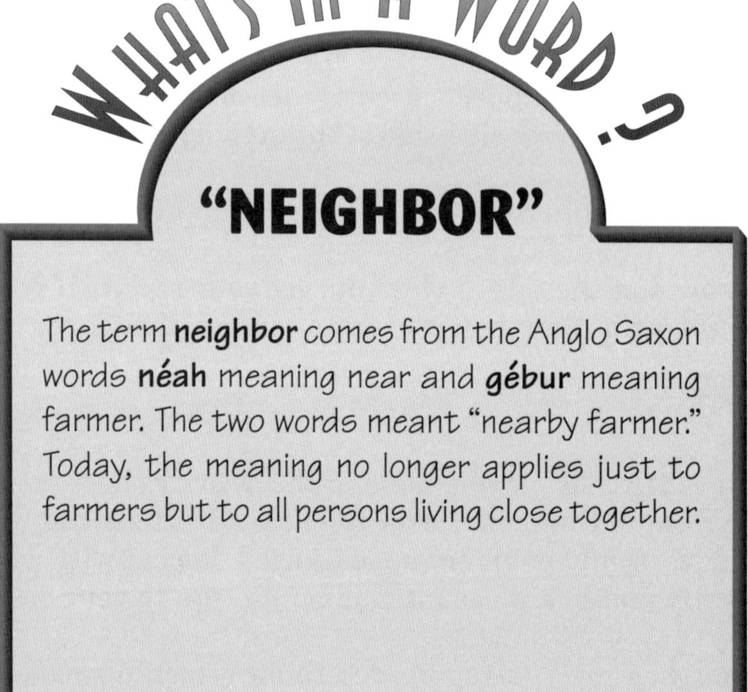

WHAT'S IN A WORD?
"NEIGHBOR"
The term **neighbor** comes from the Anglo Saxon words **néah** meaning near and **gébur** meaning farmer. The two words meant "nearby farmer." Today, the meaning no longer applies just to farmers but to all persons living close together.

Half the world is composed of people who have something to say and can't, and the other half who have nothing to say and keep on saying it.

—*Robert Frost*

Words must surely be counted among the most powerful drugs man ever invented.

—*Leo Rosten*

Chapter 35

Change Their Minds

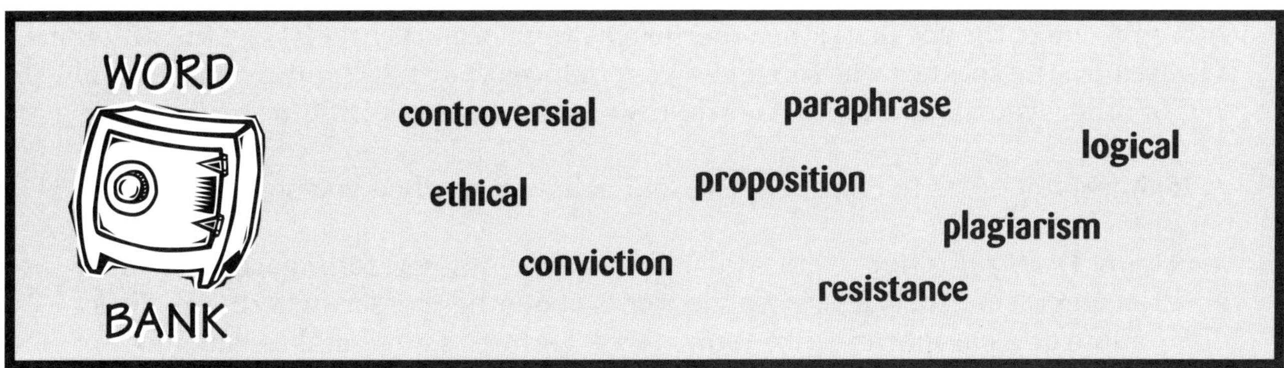

Watch for these valuable words wherever you see the word bank icon. 

BRAIN TEASERS

(1) What are the three keys that open doors to conviction?
(2) What four qualities must a speaker have to gain audience respect?
(3) How does ethical proof differ from emotional proof? From logical proof?
(4) How should you organize a speech to convince?

PLATFORM NOTES

Above are three very special keys, keys that convince people. Use them to open each of the padlocks fastened to the doors of resistance in your listeners. You probably have already noticed that whenever you ask an audience to change its beliefs, which is the purpose of a speech to convince, doors are slammed in your face, for many people are suspicious of change. To get each listener to accept your proposition you must win over his or her mind, heart, and confidence. And that is what the keys are for.

Key number one opens the door by using *logical* proof. It appeals to the *mind* of your listener with facts or the verbal support you have studied in Chapter 33. Factual illustrations, statistics, specific instances, and testimony provide the concrete evidence necessary for convincing your listener through reason.

Key number two opens the door by using *emotional* proof. It appeals to the *heart* of your listener with a combination of the motive appeals you have studied in Chapter 34. Motive appeals tie the heart strings of your audience to your proposition, making your listeners want to accept your idea because it benefits them.

Key number three opens the door with *ethical* proof. Ethical proof is that "certain something" a speaker has that *inspires confidence* within the audience. For example, two different speakers try to convince you on a controversial subject. Both use basically the same evidence and the same motive appeals. Yet you are strongly moved to agree with only one of the speakers; the other leaves you absolutely cold. Why the difference? It is because the speaker who convinces you, induces your trust and seems believable to you. In other words, ethical proof is what the audience thinks of the speaker.

If your audience is to respect, trust, and believe you when you speak, you must

(1) *Be Truthful*. Give facts and evidence. Avoid stretching the truth or exaggerating. Also, if you use the words of another person, whether in direct quote or a paraphrase, give your source. Failure to do so makes you guilty of plagiarism, an untruthful act. Present your case in such a way that even those who still disagree will say, "Spoken with honesty."

Adopt as your code that standard expressed by Adlai Stevenson on the eve of the 1952 presidential election in which he was running. "I have said what I meant and meant what I said. I have not done as well as I should like to have done, but I have done my best, frankly and forthrightly; no man can do more, and you are entitled to no less."

(2) *Be Well Informed*. Through your research and your personal experiences, show — without boasting— that you know what you are talking about. Use statements such as "While I was on a fishing trip with my Dad last summer, we discovered ...." "Last year my grades weren't good, so I decided to find out what the experts recommend for improving grades. Let me share my findings with you."

(3) *Be Friendly*. Establish a common ground between yourself and the audience by showing genuine goodwill and respect for them. Choose words that will tactfully persuade without giving offense. Identify yourself with the audience. Instead of saying "You have not done your duty," say, "We are all guilty of ..."

(4) *Be Sincere*. Honestly believe in what you are saying. An audience never respects a speaker who uses hot air, bluff, and gimmicks. In addition to believing your message, you must have the skill to communicate your sincerity. As you speak, look your audience in the eye, let your strong feelings activate gestures and an alert posture, keep your voice varied and forceful, select exact words that crystallize your ideas, and then tie this all together with genuine enthusiasm.

Whenever you speak to convince, use your key chain of logical, emotional, and ethical proofs. The doors to audience acceptance will open!

ACTIVITY AND ITS PURPOSE

You are to give a 3 to 5 minute speech to convince using all three proofs as described above. This assignment will give you practice in persuasive speaking and will strengthen skills that you can use in political meetings, business encounters, social gatherings, and debates.

You are to have at least two sources for your speech and must outline the talk on the activity sheet to this chapter. You may use visual aids if you wish.

HOW TO PREPARE

(1) Select for your specific purpose a controversial proposition that describes a course of action you want taken. The topic should be of interest to you and your audience, and it should be one on which you can easily obtain source material. Be sure your proposition is controversial. Avoid a topic that your audience already agrees on such as "We should all drive safely." Instead, choose a debatable statement such as "National requirements for driver's licenses should be established," or "Thirteen-year-olds should be allowed night driver's licenses." State your proposition so that it contains the word "should," meaning the course of action you favor "ought to be" done.

The following is a list of sample propositions (assertions). Notice that you can take the reverse side of the topic if you wish.

(a) Adopted children should be allowed to search for their birth parents.
(b) All cars should have safety air bags.
(c) Newspapers should be required to use recycled paper.
(d) Mandatory gun-safety classes should be taught at the middle school level.
(e) Cleanup of old hazardous waste sites must be expedited.
(f) Astroturf should be removed from all playing fields.
(g) Term limits should be imposed on all members of congress.
(h) Prescription drug ads should be illegal.
(i) Bicyclists should be required by law to wear helmets.
(j) Physician assisted suicides should be legally allowed.
(k) (Your choice on a controversial issue approved by your teacher.)

(2) Do research by interviewing authorities, making your own observations, analyzing a television news documentary, and reading magazines and books on your topic. Get specific examples, illustrations, statistics, and testimony. Research until you are well informed, using at least two sources.

(3) Organize your material by including the following information in your basic organization formula:

(Introduction)

(a) *Capture*: immediately focus audience attention on some aspect of your proposition.

(b) *Motivate*: Make your audience want to listen by describing *a problem that exists* and how this problem directly affects them. Speak from the viewpoint of the audience. Show how the problem endangers them. Tell its size and implications.

(c) *Assert*: briefly state your exact proposition, which is the *solution* to the problem you have just described.

(d) *Preview*: give an initial summary of your main points, indicating to your audience the ideas for which they should listen.

(Body)

(e) Point one and support: if necessary, discuss the problem more. If not, *give details* of your solution. What specifically is the plan? What are the rules? Who will administer them? Use concrete verbal support.

(f) Point two and support: show that this plan is *practical*, that it will work. Has it worked in other places? Specifically give examples. Are there safeguards for making it work? Tell them. Will it do what you say it will do? Give examples, testimony, and statistics.

(g) Point three and support: show that this plan is *desirable*, that it will benefit the audience. Here you can effectively use motive appeals in addition to verbal support.

(Conclusion)

(h) Action: tell the audience what they can *do* to promote the plan: such as write their congressman, or subscribe, amend, give, clean up, organize, volunteer.

If you happen to be talking against a proposition, follow the same steps but show how the plan is not needed, not practical, and not desirable. (See sample speech at the end of this chapter. Notice that the problem is expanded in the body before discussing the solutions. This creates four main points.)

(4) Outline your speech on the activity sheet to this chapter. Keep your main

points short and direct. Use catchy words. List concrete support for each main point. State your sources for this evidence.

(5) Rehearse your speech aloud. Practice it many times until you are sure of your material and until you are effectively getting it across to your listeners. If you use notes, put them on 3" x 5" cards. Do not write your whole speech on them. Use only key words, statistics, and exact quotes on the cards. When using notes, practice holding the cards high enough to see. Make no attempt to hide them.

HOW TO PRESENT

Have your activity sheet ready to hand to your teacher when you are called upon. As you enter the room give your chairperson a note card with your name and speech title.

Sit poised and quiet in your seat until the chairperson introduces you. Walk with assurance to the platform, pause, give a formal salutation, and then begin your capture step.

Show your audience that you are convinced by making your voice back up your words with varied force and enthusiasm, by making your body back up your words with strong, purposeful gestures and movements. Be friendly but firm in your delivery. Really try to convince your listeners that your proposition is the best for them and society.

After you have spoken and returned to your desk, class members (previously appointed by your teacher) will write an evaluation of your speech, using one of the forms your teacher will give you. Evaluators are to make one rating in the proper box for each quality listed and then to write suggestions for improvement on the bottom of the sheet. They will sign their name, which your teacher will cut off after he or she has read the evaluations. You will receive these nameless evaluations at a later date.

ADDITIONAL ACTIVITIES

(1) You and a partner are to give a 3-5 minute speech to convince on a controversial subject. One partner will take the affirmative side of the issue and the other partner will take the negative side. For example, the affirmative issue may be “We should have government control of firearms,” and the negative side may be “We should not have government control of firearms.” Each partner may research and prepare separately. On presentation, the two partners will sit at a table in front of the room. The affirmative will speak first and then the negative. After both speeches the chairman will allow 1-3 minutes for the partners to question each other. For an additional 1-3 minutes he will entertain questions from the class specifically directed towards either of the speakers.

(2) See and study the following (for addresses see Appendix E):

Powers of Persuasion (Coronet)
Four tapes on how to speak persuasively.

Persuasive Speaking (15 minutes.) (Educational Video)

SAMPLE OUTLINE FOR SPEECH TO CONVINCE

General Purpose: To convince
Specific Purpose: "Three strikes and you're out" bill should be passed.

PASSAGE OF "THREE STRIKES AND YOU'RE OUT" BILL

(Introduction)

(Capture) ***Analogy***
I. Strike one, strike two, strike three and you're out.
  A. This is a familiar sound in the world of baseball.
  B. This will be a familiar sound to the habitual offender.

Definition
    1. Those who commit violent crimes will hear this phrase.
    2. Those who commit many crimes will hear this phrase.

(Motivate) ***Statistic***
II. Seven percent of today's criminals commit about seventy percent of the crimes. ("Posturing About Crime is Always Easier Than Doing Something," *The Washington Times,* January 29, 1994, p. A17)
  A. We need to do what we can to get these habitual offenders off our streets.

Assert
III. House bill H.R. 3981, better known as "Three strikes and you're out," should be passed to keep this type of criminal off the streets.

Preview
IV. I will answer these questions.
  A. What's the severity of the problem with habitual offenders?
  B. What does H.R. 3981 bill entail?
  C. If H.R. 3981 passes, what will be the effects?
  D. How does the American citizen feel about H.R. 3981?

(Body)

(Point Supports)
I. What's the severity of the problem with habitual offenders?

Statistics *(notice that the speaker expands the problem in this point)*
  A. Seven percent of today's criminals commit about seventy percent of the crimes. ("Posturing About Crime is Always Easier Than Doing Something," *The Washington Times*, January 29, 1994, p. A17)
  B. Habitual criminals are generally arrested five or more times before the age of eighteen. ("What to do About Crime," *U.S. News and World Report*, November 8, 1993)
  C. Reported violent crime has escalated.
    1. In 1970, violent crime was a bit more than half a million.

2. In 1992, violent crime was nearing two million.
   a. Seventeen percent of those arrested for violent crimes have charges pending on other crimes.
   b. Thirteen percent of those arrested for violent crimes are/ were on parole, probation, etc... ("Violence in America," *U.S. News and World Report*, January 17, 1994, p. 28)

Factual Illustrations *(or Examples)*

D. Here are some examples.
1. Leslie Williams had a long criminal record.
   a. In 1992, he confessed to the murder of four teenage girls.
   b. He confessed to at least four sexual assaults including a nine year old girl.
2. James Porter was a former priest.
   a. He has admitted to molesting 50 to 100 children over 30 years, in parishes from River Fall, Mass. to Las Vegas, Nevada.
   b. In 1992, he was convicted in Minnesota of molesting his own children's babysitter in 1987. ("The Incorrigibles," *Newsweek*, January 18, 1993, p. 49)
3. If the H.R. 3981 bill had been in effect then, these people would not have been free to commit as many crimes as they did.

(Point Support)

II. What exactly does the H.R. 3981 bill contain?

A. H.R. 3981 is "a bill to provide mandatory life imprisonment for persons convicted of a third violent felony." (*H.R. 3981*, Charles E. Schumer, March 6, 1994)

Definition

1. A violent felony would be defined as murder, aggravated sexual assault, sexual assault, the use of guns during drug deals, kidnapping, arson, extortion, and assault with the intent to commit murder and/or rape. ("Senate Swing at Felons is Wider than Clinton's 'Three Strikes' Plan," *Atlanta Journal and Constitution*, March 2, 1994, p. A5) (*H.R. 3981*, Charles E. Schumer, March 8, 1994)

Definition

Testimony

B. Deputy Attorney General Philip B. Heymann said that the law requires life in prison without parole without exceptions.
1. "The whole purpose is to send a clear signal to potential offenders." ("Bar President Swings at 'Three Strikes' Crime Provision," *The Los Anqeles Times*, January 27, 1994, p. 12)

(Point Support)

III. If H.R. 3981 passes, what will be the effects?

A. A potential three-timer, Randy Berg, is a crack addict serving seven years in Minnesota for his second violent assault.

Factual Illustration

1. He said, "I know that if this goes through there is no chance..."
2. His voice fades.
3. Then he adds, "If I was on the streets and had my rights, I would vote for this law." ("Lock 'Em Up," *Time*, February 7, 1994)

B. Earl Shriner is 43 years old and a habitual offender for 24 years. ("The Incorrigibles," *Newsweek*, January 18, 1993, p.48)
1. In 1966, he was apprehended for choking a seven year old girl.
   a. He led police also to the body of a fifteen year old girl.
   b. She was strangled and tied to a tree.
2. He later served ten years for abducting and assaulting two sixteen year old girls.

3. In 1987, he served 66 days for stabbing a sixteen year old boy.
4. In 1989, he attacked a seven year old boy near the boy's home in Tacoma, Washington.
    a. He stabbed the boy in the back.
    b. He tried to strangle the boy with a cord.
    c. The boy survived and testified.
    d. Because Washington had recently passed the "Three Strikes and You're out" bill, Earl Shriner will serve 131 years without parole. ("The Incorrigibles," *Newsweek*, January 18, 1993, p. 48)

(Point Support)

Specific Instances

IV. How does the American public feel about H.R. 3981?
  A. At least 30 states are considering this bill, with some states, like Georgia, proposing stricter laws. ("Lock 'Em Up," *Time*, February 7, 1994)
  B. Right now Californians are attempting to get a measure on the ballot for this November.
    1. 15,000 people are signing petitions for the measure each day. ("Slamming the Prison Door," *People*, February 7, 1994, p. 52)
  C. Washington voters voted 3 to 1 for the "Three Strikes" measure despite the cost to build and operate the prisons. ("The Voters' Cry for Help," *U.S. News and World Report*, November 15, 1993)

(Conclusion)

(Action)

Analogy

I. No longer will the American people sit back and play T-Ball with these habitual offenders.
  A. It's time for hardball and we're up to bat.
  B. So let your government representatives know how you swing the bat at these criminals.
  C. Let's put them out for good.

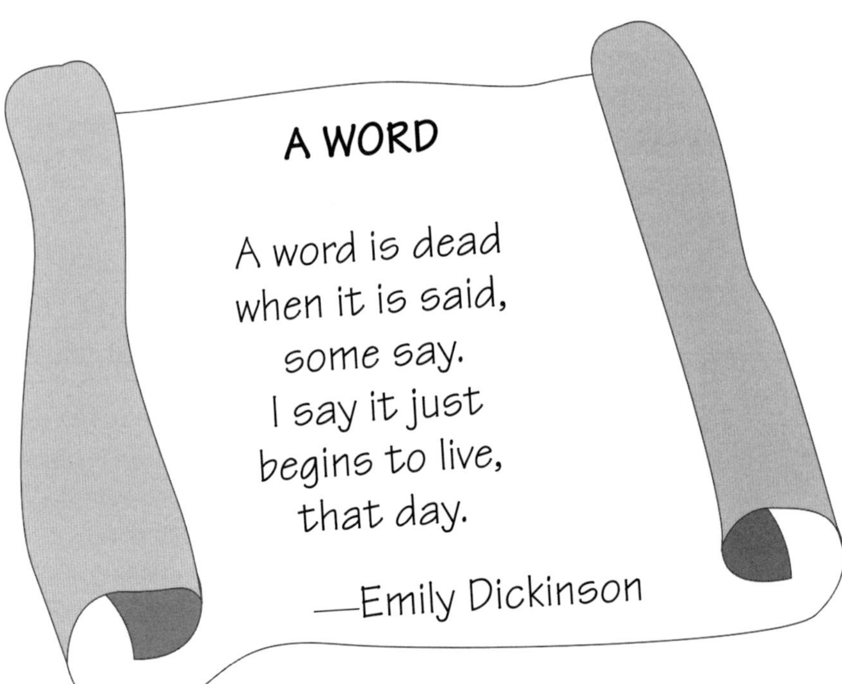

A WORD
A word is dead
when it is said,
some say.
I say it just
begins to live,
that day.
—Emily Dickinson

What's In A Word?

"CURFEW"

It was a law in the Middle Ages for peasants to cover or put out their fires at a certain time each evening. The time was announced by the ringing of a bell called couvre-feu (cover fire) from the French. The Norman French used this term in England where it evolved into curfew meaning the hour for people or children to go to their homes.

Chapter 36

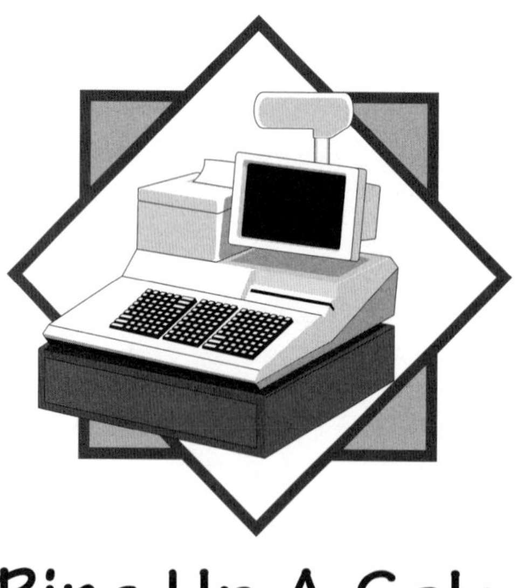

Ring Up A Sale

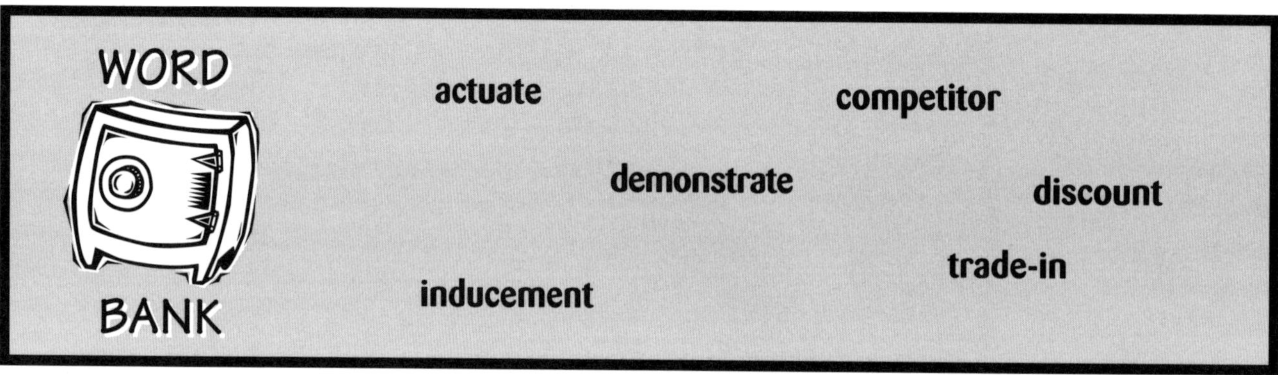

Watch for these valuable words wherever you see the word bank icon. 

BRAIN TEASERS

(1) What is the general purpose of a sales speech?
(2) Why must you believe in your product?
(3) How can you get your audience to want your product?
(4) Why should you demonstrate the product?
(5) How do you handle questions from the audience?

PLATFORM NOTES

"Who will gimme ten, ten, no ten? Then whowillgimme five, justafive, heresafive, nowaten, gimmeten, gimmeten heresaten andits sold tothe gentlemaninthebrowncoat." Thus the auctioneer clinches another sale.

While none of you may ever be an auctioneer, you quite possibly will be in a situation where you must sell a product to a group of people. Perhaps as a student body officer you will attempt to sell a certain school ring to your class. As a representative of a service club you may speak to local organizations in hopes of selling candles to assist the needy during the holidays. As a future employee of a business you may sell your firm's product at a convention meeting attended by dozens of potential customers.

Your general purpose in a sales speech is to persuade—to actuate your audience into buying the product now. To do this you must make your listeners *want* your product so much that they will pay money to obtain it.

You ring the cash register by doing the following things:

(1) *Believe in your product.* To sell an audience, you must first be sold on the product yourself. If *you* think it is great, it is easier to convince your listeners. Sincerity in selling is a must. If you can't stand crunchy peanut butter, don't try to sell it. Your distaste will show through.

(2) *Tell your audience why they need the product.* Use motive appeals. What can the product do for them? How can they use it? Why will life be better for them because of this product? Will the water jet cut down on their tooth cavities? Can they give the fruitcake to Grandmother? Will the safety bindings prevent them from ski injuries?

(3) *Know your product thoroughly.* How does it work? Of what is it made? In what color does it come? What are its special features? Is there a guarantee? What is the cost? Can it be repaired? Why is it better than a similar product manufactured by a different company? Be careful, though, when talking about your competitor. Never tear down the "other" company's product. Just show how you think yours is better. Be truthful by presenting the facts. Avoid dishonest claims.

(4) *Demonstrate your product.* If you are selling electric scissors, cut different fabrics with them in front of the group. If you are selling a trash compactor, fill it with empty cans, old shoes, bones, and turn it on. Then show the compacted results. Throw unbreakable tempered glass on the floor to prove it doesn't break. Pass around samples of the fudge so the audience knows it is delicious.

(5) *Make it easy to buy.* State the price and where the audience can buy your commodity. Is there a down payment? Installment plan? Can they get a discount on a trade-in? Is there an inducement such as a special price or a free gift? Can they buy right now the article you are demonstrating? Can they give you an order?

ACTIVITY AND ITS PURPOSE

For this speech you are to sell a product that you can demonstrate to your classmates. This 3-4 minute speech is to be an actual selling effort. If someone wants to buy your product, you must part with it at the stated price, or tell the customer where to purchase it, or take orders that you will fill within the week. After you have concluded the speech, you will be allowed two minutes to ask for and answer questions from the audience regarding the product.

HOW TO PREPARE

(1) Choose an article that you believe in, one that your audience can use, and one that you can demonstrate. If you have something at home that you want to use as a demonstration model but do not actually wish to sell, be sure the article is still available for purchase and know where the audience may buy it. If your teacher suggests that you borrow a product from a local store, your parents must sign for it, and you (not your teacher or school) will be held responsible for returning it promptly in new condition.

The following are suggestions for products to sell and demonstrate:

(a) Home food processor: plug it in, cube potatoes, slice carrots, chop cabbage.

(b) Portable video camera: show how it works, take pictures of the class, and display them on a monitor.

(c) Cordless telephone: show its features and demonstrate its use.

(d) Kerosene heater: show how to fill it, turn it on, show its safety features, have the class feel the heat emitting.

(e) Insulated picnic basket: tell how to protect food from summer heat; place items in it to show its capacity.

(f) Portable computer for student use: show how you can take, store and retrieve classroom notes.

(g) Hand tool.

(h) Decorator item.

(i) Sporting equipment.

(j) Kitchen gadget.

(k) Toy.

(l) Jewelry.

(m) Hand-crafted items.

(n) Small appliance.

(o) Clothing.

(p) Garden supplies.

(q) (Your choice, approved by your teacher.)

(2) Learn all about the product from at least two sources. Read the instructions that come with it. Talk to clerks who sell it, to people who already own one. Be sure your demonstration article is in good working order and that you learn how to demonstrate it effectively.

(3) Using the organization formula, outline your speech on the activity sheet at the end of this chapter.

Capture audience attention in your own clever way. Do not use TV or radio commercials. Make this original.

Motivate by telling your audience why they need this product. In this step introduce yourself, the company you represent, and your product. Use motive appeals. (See Chapter 34.)

Assert by telling your audience specifically how your product will satisfy their needs.

Preview your main points.

Point-Support should give clear details about the features, advantages, dependability, and beauty of your product. Point out factors you can demonstrate. Try to anticipate and answer all objections or questions that the audience may have.

Action asks your audience to buy. State price, terms, where they can purchase it. Tie up your final idea with your capture step.

(4) Rehearse aloud both your speech and demonstration. Be sure to talk while you are demonstrating, telling what you are doing. Use varied and descriptive words. Don't be like the student who used the adjective "nice" eighteen times to describe her product. Think of other words that more vividly entice the audience.

(5) Check to be sure you have all necessary equipment to take to class—your product, an extension cord if necessary, materials needed for the demonstration, any other visual aids, an order pad if you are going to have to take orders. Have everything prepared so you can easily set up your demonstration materials on a table within 30 seconds.

HOW TO PRESENT

On the day you are to speak, take special care with your appearance, looking neat and businesslike. Your teacher may even require that you "dress up" for the speech.

Tear out the activity sheet to hand to your teacher. As you walk to the front of the room, do so in a mature, confident way. Quickly and quietly set up your materials. Resist the urge to mutter under your breath or to sound off with a wisecrack. This just shows nervousness. When everything is in order, pause, smile, and look at your audience. Then begin your speech.

Keep your attitude friendly and conversational, trying to put your audience at ease and to win them over to your product.

After you have completed your speech, remain standing and ask if there are any questions. Your classmates *will* ask questions, as this is part of the assignment. Repeat the question, and then answer it to the best of your ability. If you do not know the answer, politely state so and tell the questioner where the information may be found or say that you will find it and report back within a day or two. Be courteous. Questions from an audience usually mean that you have created audience interest, and this is what you want. During the question period you may want to hand out samples, take money, or take orders.

When there are no more questions or when the two minute question period is over, state one or two sentences to finalize your speech in which you ask the audience to try or buy your product. Pause, quickly gather your materials, and quietly go to your desk.

ADDITIONAL ACTIVITIES

(1) See and study the following video. (For address see Appendix E):

First Impressions: The Sales Connections (Insight Media)
Discusses the sales person's image and ways to improve with language.

"PERIL"

In the sixth century B.C. the Sicilian tyrant Phiaris ordered an inventor named Perilus to build a hollow torture chamber shaped like a bull. Victims were placed inside the metal bull and roasted to death. To this day to be in peril means to be in grave danger.

Chapter 37

Tickle The Funny Bone

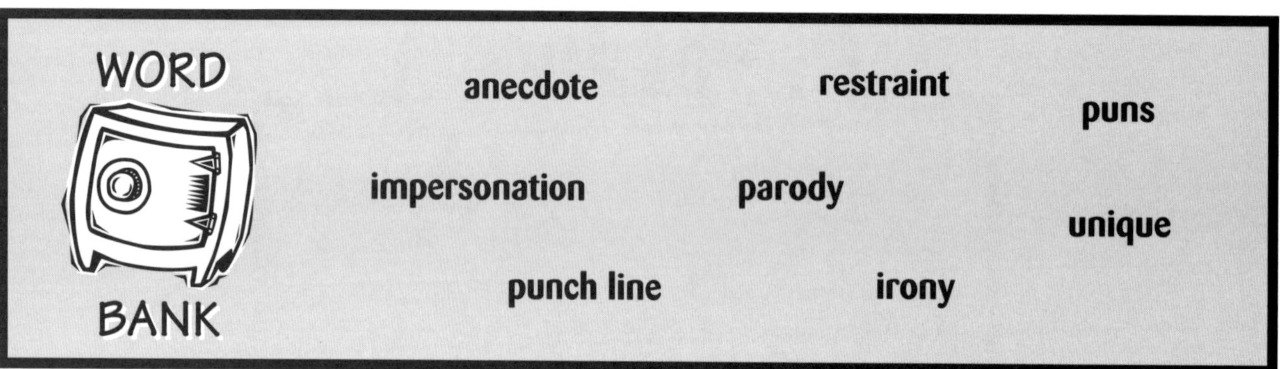

WORD
BANK
anecdote
restraint
puns
impersonation
parody
unique
punch line
irony

Watch for these valuable words wherever you see the word bank icon. 

BRAIN TEASERS

(1) What is the purpose of a speech to entertain?
(2) Besides humor, what other material can be used in a speech to entertain?
(3) What holds together a speech to entertain?
(4) What requirements must humor meet in a speech to entertain?
(5) What are some of the types of humor?
(6) How do you introduce jokes in a speech?
(7) When an audience laughs at a joke, what do you do?

PLATFORM NOTES

Everybody likes to be amused. That is why speeches to entertain have great popularity at dinners, parties, and lighthearted meetings.

While most speeches to entertain appeal to the audience's sense of humor, entertainment can also be provided by novel or unique information, anecdotes on unusual people, or an exciting dramatic description of events. The basic requirement is that the speaker holds audience attention in a pleasant way.

False is the idea that entertainment speeches must make the listeners roll down the aisles with hearty laughter. Effective speeches can produce numerous responses—from an inner smile to a loud guffaw.

Also false is the idea that speeches to entertain consist only of a series of jokes. While jokes may be used, the entertainment speech should progress from an underlying serious theme, always there but never dominating. Unique stories, verses, and anecdotes weave in and around the central theme—frolicking, sometimes peeking around corners, but constantly catching the audience's attention and maintaining their interest in an enjoyable though not necessarily humorous manner.

Humor, of course, is the favorite vehicle. When you use it, be sure it (1) relates to your subject and (2) is in good taste. Never offend any member of the audience by telling off-color jokes. The supply of funny and clean stories is extensive. If you can't find them, it means you haven't bothered to look. Keep in mind, too, that it is not necessary to use "canned" material from books or magazines. Original humor—funny things that have happened to you or your friends, or humor you make up—is usually the most entertaining of all material. Remember, the magic lies in treatment, not in subject matter. Almost anything can be presented entertainingly if you approach it with a different viewpoint and spice it with human interest.

When you want to evoke laughter, try the following methods:

(1) *Exaggeration* or overstatement: Tall tales and "Texas" jokes fit in this category.

> Example: A group of golfers were telling tall stories. "Once," said a golfer, "I drove a ball, accidentally of course, through a cottage window. The ball knocked over a candle and the place caught on fire."
>
> "What did you do?" asked his friends.
>
> "Oh," said the golfer, "I immediately teed another ball, took careful aim, and hit the fire alarm on Main Street. That brought out the fire trucks before any damage was done."

(2) *Surprise turns*: Start out by saying the normal thing and end up by saying something unexpected.

> Example: If at first you don't succeed, you are about average.
>
> Example: Roses are red, Violets are blue, Orchids are $16.95, Will dandelions do?

Example: "Do you know the difference between an elephant and a loaf of bread?

"No. "

"I'd hate to send you to the grocery store."

(3) *Irony*: Say something so that the opposite meaning is implied.

Example: After a long evening the tired host insisted on accompanying his guest downstairs. "Please don't bother," said the guest. "Don't trouble to see me to the door."

"It's no trouble," said the host. "It's a pleasure."

Example: A gushy society matron was talking to a famous author at a party. "Oh," she exclaimed, "yesterday I walked right past your house."

"Thank you so much, madame," said the relieved author.

(4) *Parody*: Treat serious material absurdly and trivial material seriously.

Example: Beware of calling yourself an expert. One definition of expert is that an "ex" is a has-been and a "spurt" is a drip under pressure.

(5) *Pun*: Use words with double meanings or those which sound like words of different meanings.

Example: A Long Island potato married an Idaho potato, and eventually they had a little sweet potato. The little one flourished, and in due time announced to its parents that it wanted to marry a certain television reporter. "But you can't marry that TV reporter," declared the parents. "He's just a commentator."

Example: It is easy for people to make monkeys of themselves just by carrying tales.

Example: Confucius say: Salesman who cover chair instead of territory always on bottom.

Example: During a recent near-hurricane in New York, a business man looked out of his window and remarked, "It's raining cats and dogs today."

"I know," said his partner, "I just stepped into a poodle."

Other methods of achieving humor are to tell a joke on yourself, or in a spirit of good fellowship to tell a story on someone in the audience.

ACTIVITY AND ITS PURPOSE

Present in class a 2 to 4 minute speech to entertain that will maintain audience attention and amuse them. One source is required, but you may use more. Avoid using note cards if possible. Outline your speech on the activity sheet to this chapter.

HOW TO PREPARE

(1) After considering your audience and the type of humor they will like, quickly select a topic. Your subject may be commonplace as long as you treat it in a novel manner and with a light touch. Remember, this is to be a speech, not a humorous reading or an impersonation. Look primarily to personal experience, unique or unusual happenings in life, interesting jobs you have had, or unusual people you have met. Spend your time in preparation, not in selection. The following are suggested topics:

(a) Dogs and people they own.
(b) The joys of city living.
(c) Nearsighted people have troubles.
(d) Vacations, who needs them?
(e) How to attract attention effectively.
(f) Chewing gum: a national menace.
(g) Ice skating (skiing, etc.) in one easy lesson.
(h) Shopping: the weekly hazard.
(i) The art of eating pizza.
(j) The fish that got away.
(k) How to be a howling success.
(l) Words don't mean what they say.
(m) Baby sitting—the domestic battlefield.
(n) Silence is not always golden.
(o) My life with a computer.
(p) The born loser.
(q) A look at modern art.

(2) Determine the point you want to make—your specific purpose that is the serious line of thought around which all of your speech will romp.

(3) Gather your material or create your own original humor that grows out of your experience and observation.

(4) Organize your speech using the following pattern that deletes the preview step of the organization formula:

(a) Capture and motivate: use a clever story that sets the right mood.
(b) Assert: touch briefly on the essential idea your introduction expresses and around which you will unify your speech.

(c) Point-Support: reinforce your main idea with additional incidents, stories, short poems, jokes, and anecdotes. Keep your speech moving ahead by giving just enough concrete detail to stimulate audience imagination. Build to a climax, keeping the audience in suspense until the punch line. Work also on clear and clever transitions. Never advertise your humor by saying such things as "You'll laugh at this one," or "This reminds me of a story." Instead, provide smooth transitions to enable the story to sneak up on the listeners and happily surprise them because it is unannounced.

(d) Action: restate with a story, verse, or quote.

Write your outline on the activity sheet to this chapter.

(5) Rehearse aloud. This step is very important. Material, to be amusing, must be given effortlessly and fluently. As you rehearse learn the correct sequence of ideas. Nothing is more aggravating than a speaker who stops in the middle of a story and announces, "Oh, I forgot to tell you something you need to know before I continue."

Also, practice saying the punch lines of jokes clearly and slowly so your audience will catch them.

As you rehearse, use gestures, facial expression, and pantomime. Entertainment speeches more than others lend themselves to open body movement. Also consider the use of visual aids such as posters, articles, and costume pieces to add interest.

HOW TO PRESENT

Hand your activity sheet to your teacher before speaking. When the chairman introduces you, rise quietly and walk to the platform. Pause and look pleasantly at your audience before beginning. If you want your audience to enjoy themselves, you must keep your manner lively, pleasant, and confident. Stick to your prepared speech, but if you can add something impromptu that fits the occasion, do so.

It is usually best not to laugh at your own jokes. If you do laugh, keep it restrained and let your laughter follow rather than precede that of the audience. If the audience laughs loudly at a joke, avoid continuing your speech until the laughter starts to diminish. Then continue. Whatever you do, keep a spirit of goodwill and playfulness about you.

ADDITIONAL ACTIVITIES

(1) Present a "Hat Speech" to entertain. Prepare as you did for the above assignment, but choose a hat that pertains in some way to your topic. The hat may be as imaginative and unique as you wish. Bring it to class and wear it while giving your speech.

(2) Present a travelogue that has entertainment as its general purpose. If you have traveled to other states, national parks, or foreign countries, you can use some of your own experiences, supplemented with reading to refresh your memory and point out details you may have missed. As you talk, keep audience attention on the unique and picturesque aspects of the place or country you describe. Use visual aids such as pictures, posters, maps, and articles to stimulate interest.

(3) Present a humorous after-dinner speech preceded by either a mock or real banquet. Appoint a class member to welcome the group and briefly and humorously introduce each speaker. Speeches will follow the same outline as that described in this chapter, but should definitely use humorous material. If a real banquet is planned, class members should organize into committees (menu and reservations, decorations, finance) to insure smooth functioning of the event.

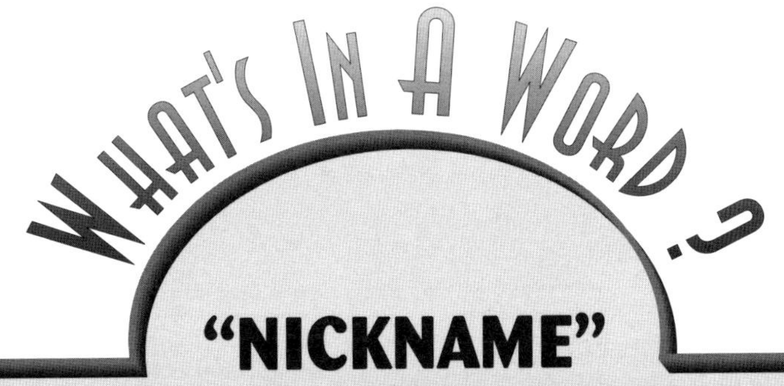

"NICKNAME"

Babies who are given long names are often called by shorter terms. William becomes Bill, James becomes Jim, Thomas becomes Tom.

In Saxon times these short names were called **eke-name**, for the Saxon word eke meant "also." The slurring that occurs with usage produced **nekename** and finally nickname.

PEANUTS® by Charles M. Schulz

Chapter 38

Mixed Bag

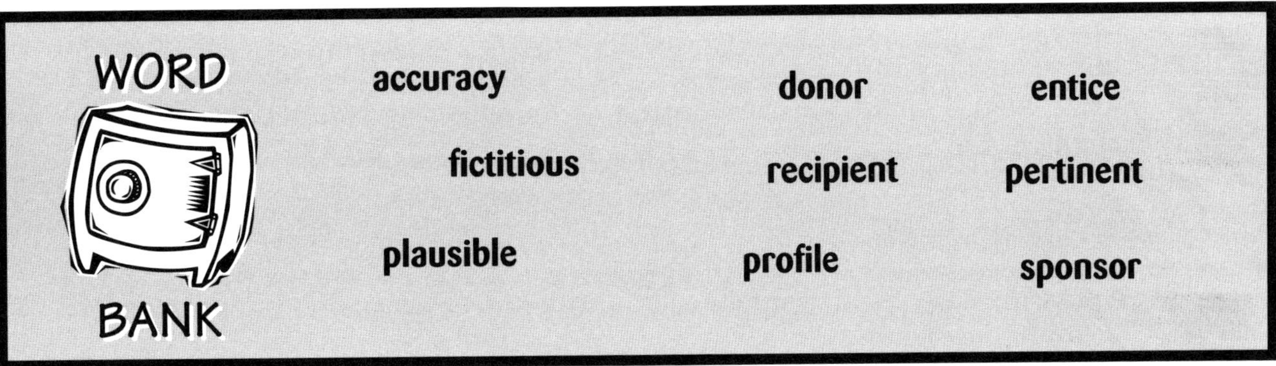

WORD
BANK
accuracy
donor
entice
fictitious
recipient
pertinent
plausible
profile
sponsor

Watch for these valuable words wherever you see the word bank icon. 

BRAIN TEASERS

(1) What qualities should an announcement have?
(2) What is the purpose of an introduction speech?
(3) What should you emphasize in a presentation speech?
(4) How can you accept an award without sounding boastful?

PLATFORM NOTES

Good things come in small packages. This "mixed bag" chapter contains four small packages to help you gain experience in four sure-to-happen-to-you speaking situations. Practicing each of these types will give you confidence when you are asked to present one outside of class.

MAKING AN ANNOUNCEMENT

Announcements are probably the most frequently given mini-speeches and often the most poorly done. The purpose of an announcement is to give information that is

(1) accurate: be correct about the time, cost, and place.

(2) complete: include everything the listener must know—who, what, when, where, why, and how.

(3) clear: arrange the information to help the listeners easily follow and understand it.

(4) short: give only necessary facts.

ACTIVITY AND ITS PURPOSE

Within a 1 to 2 minute time limit, give two or three announcements on either real or imaginary events. Fill out the correct activity half-sheet (labeled ANNOUNCEMENT) to this chapter.

HOW TO PREPARE

(1) If possible, select real events to announce or invent plausible ones. Suggested topics follow:

(a) an all school play
(b) new hours for the library to be open
(c) a cooked food sale
(d) a class picnic
(e) a pancake supper
(f) an archery tournament
(g) a school dance
(h) a swimming meet
(i) an awards assembly
(j) auditions for a talent show
(k) a ski race
(l) yearbook picture appointments

(2) Gather necessary information, checking for accuracy and any last minute changes.

(3) Organize each announcement according to the following plan:

(a) catch attention (capture).

(b) entice the audience to listen (motivate) by showing that the event (the what) has value for them (the why).

(c) clearly state the other *w's* and *h*:
who the sponsor is
when the event takes place, date and time
where it is, location or place
how much the tickets are, how to get them, how to find the location, how to register, how to participate.

(d) summarize the basic information and ask for audience participation (action).

(4) Write facts on a 3" x 5" note card for use during your presentation. Fill out the correct activity half-sheet to this chapter.

(5) Loudly and clearly rehearse the announcement, standing tall with good posture.

HOW TO PRESENT

When called on to speak, hand the activity half-sheet to your teacher and walk with poise to the front of the room, taking your note card. Pause, stand in an alert manner, and look directly at your audience before beginning to speak.

Make your voice clear and loud as you give the announcements, being sure that everyone in the audience can readily hear. Do not read constantly from your notes, but look at them when you want to check accuracy. Hold your notes medium high when you read from them, so your voice will be thrown out to the listeners and not down to the floor. Return to your desk in a businesslike manner.

INTRODUCTIONS

If you have served as class chairperson, you have already gained some experience in introducing speakers. A more intensive assignment is helpful, however, to prepare you for giving a speech of introduction outside of class.

The purpose of an introductory speech is to "break the ice" between audience and speaker. In the introduction you should:

(1) give the speaker's qualifications so the audience will listen with interest and respect,

(2) make the speaker feel at ease in approaching the group,

(3) briefly state the speaker's subject,

(4) pronounce the speaker's name correctly and audibly.

After the introduction you should become the model listener, paying close attention and responding to the speech.

ACTIVITY AND ITS PURPOSE

To gain additional experience, present a 1 to 3 minute speech of introduction using a real or imaginary speaker, and labeling your class as any type audience you wish. Fill out the correct activity half-sheet to this chapter.

HOW TO PREPARE

(1) Select either a real or imaginary person. Avoid choosing a classmate, however. Decide what audience you want the class to be. The following are topic suggestions for introductions:

(a) a famous scientist to your science class
(b) the governor to a school assembly
(c) a foreign student to the Honors Society
(d) a war hero to a civic group
(e) a missionary to your church group
(f) an actress to your drama club
(g) an athlete to a school service organization
(h) a news commentator to the journalism class
(i) an experienced mountain climber to a scout conference
(j) the mayor to an ecology group
(k) an airline pilot for a career day program
(l) your state senator to the student body

(2) Collect accurate information about the speaker's background, special training, positions held, speaker's title, books written, travels taken, honors received. Learn to pronounce the name correctly. Invent details for an imaginary person.

(3) Using the following organization plan, outline your speech:

(a) Capture audience attention with interesting material that relates to the speaker or subject.

(b) Present a brief objective description of the speaker's career, giving pertinent facts but not embarrassing him or her by too personal information or too lengthy a description. Whatever you say, aim at making the audience and speaker feel comfortable about each other.

(c) Give a statement about the subject, but not a speech on it. Stress the importance of the subject to the listeners.

(d) Clearly introduce the speaker's name and speech title.

(4) Rehearse aloud your introduction, working on speaking clearly and sincerely. Time your speech to insure that it meets the time limits.

HOW TO PRESENT

Have your outline in readiness for your teacher. When it is your turn to speak, go to the front of the room. Stand tall, with equal weight on both feet. Pause and look at your audience. Then properly address them: Ladies and Gentlemen, Members of the PTA, etc. Give your speech as rehearsed, with enthusiasm and sincerity.

PRESENTATION OF A GIFT OR AWARD

The occasions for presenting gifts and awards are so numerous that at some time you will undoubtedly be in a position either to make a presentation or to receive an honor.

When you make a presentation, your purpose is to praise the recipient sincerely and make the audience feel admiration for that person. To accomplish this, carefully adapt your speech to the occasion and award. At a sports banquet, humor and an informal touch are appropriate. Presentation of an honor at commencement demands dignity. Announcing the winner of a much sought after prize requires great tact since rivalry produces strong emotions.

All presentations should be brief, identifying the group making the award or gift, the reason it is being given, and the nature of the award. Avoid flowery language and overpraise. Emphasis should be on the honor, not on the value of the gift.

Note: the following two speeches may be done as one assignment, with one partner giving the presentation and one the acceptance speech.

ACTIVITY AND ITS PURPOSE

Your teacher will assign you a partner. One of you will present a real or fictitious award, and the other will receive it (see Acceptance of an Award later in this chapter). The presentation should be 1- 2 minutes. Use an actual article for the award or gift. Fill out the correct activity half-sheet to this chapter that your teacher will give you.

HOW TO PREPARE

(1) Meet with your partner to determine a real or imaginary occasion and award for presentation. The following are suggestions:

(a) a silver emblem to the student chosen for a citizenship award
(b) an award to a retiring school official
(c) a trophy to an outstanding athlete
(d) a money prize for first place in a poetry writing contest

(e) a bouquet of flowers to a guest performer
(f) a scholarship to a summer music workshop
(g) money for a swimming pool for the city
(h) an achievement certificate to the student with the highest grade point
(i) a gift to a favorite teacher who is leaving
(j) a gavel to an outgoing student body president
(k) an engraved plaque for the teacher of the year award
(l) a trophy to a winning bowling team

(2) Gather accurate information on a real presentation or make up material for a fictional one.

(3) Outline your speech on the activity half-sheet by including the following:

(a) Greet the audience with remarks appropriate to the occasion.
(b) State the reason for the award and identify the group or person donating it.
(c) Briefly describe why the recipient deserves this award.
(d) Explain the award and its purpose, indicating that it is only a remembrance of the great appreciation or esteem felt for the recipient.
(e) Call the recipient forward and make the actual presentation by summarizing the reasons for it.

(4) Rehearse your speech with a clock to be sure you stay within the time limits. Practice with the article that is the "mock" award or gift you will use in class.

HOW TO PRESENT

Hand the activity sheet to your teacher immediately before you speak. Walk confidently to the front of the room with the award.

Place the award on the table, pause, stand tall, and look directly at the audience. Then give your speech loudly in a pleasant manner that fits the occasion.

When you are ready to present the gift, call the recipient to the platform. Pick up the award and hold it so all can see. Wait until the recipient arrives and then again address that person by name. Present the award as rehearsed. Give it to the awardee by using your hand farthest away from the audience (upstage hand). If you must pin on a medal, stand profile to the audience as you pin. If the object to be given is large, such as a picture on an easel, it should be covered until the actual presentation and then unveiled.

Await the recipient's acceptance speech before sitting down.

ACCEPTANCE OF A GIFT OR AWARD

When you accept a gift or an award you need to say thank you and show sincere appreciation for the honor. This you must do in a friendly, modest way that impresses the donors with your worthiness and makes them happy with their choice.

When awards are surprises, the acceptance will be impromptu—without preparation. But if you are forewarned or suspect an award, prepare a short speech ahead of time.

ACTIVITY AND ITS PURPOSE

Present a one minute acceptance speech that coordinates with your partner's presentation speech. Fill out the correct activity half-sheet to this chapter.

HOW TO PREPARE

(1) Meet with your partner to determine the occasion and the award.

(2) Outline your speech by including the following:

(a) Sincerely express your gratitude. Do not apologize for winning. Do not state that you are unworthy.

(b) Modestly share the credit with those who assisted you in any way. Praise them for their help and cooperation.

(c) Describe your appreciation for the significance or beauty of the award, without exaggerating your praises. Never show disappointment. If you are accepting the award for a group, tell why your club did the service and relate its continuing policy.

(d) Conclude by stating your plans for the future if they are connected to the award. Repeat your thanks.

(3) Rehearse your speech aloud in front of a full length mirror.

HOW TO PRESENT

Hand your activity sheet to your teacher before the presentation speech. When you are called to the front, walk up confidently but without arrogance. Stand near the donor, but avoid standing in front of the award. Never look anxiously around, wondering where your gift is.

Accept the award with the hand farthest from the audience. Hold the award for a few seconds in full view, or stand to the side if it is a large article that must be unveiled.

Give your speech clearly and loudly while standing tall with your weight equally distributed on both feet. Be friendly and enthusiastic. Don't be afraid to show emotion; just keep it under control.

As you sit down, avoid stuffing your award into your pocket. Carry it to your desk with dignity, in a manner that shows you value it.

Chapter 39

Instant Speech

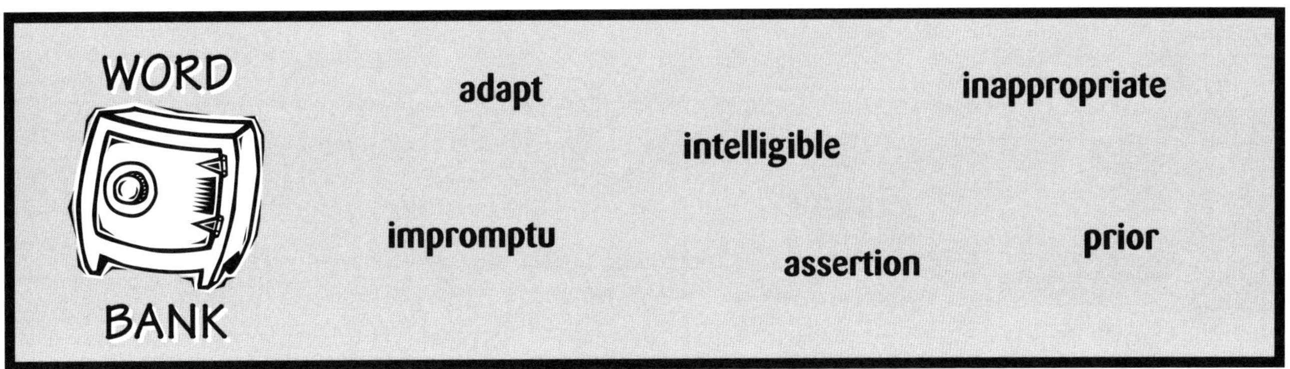

Watch for these valuable words wherever you see the word bank icon. 

BRAIN TEASERS

(1) What is the difference between an extemporaneous and an impromptu speech?
(2) How can you prepare for an emergency speech situation?
(3) How should you organize an impromptu speech?

PLATFORM NOTES

Impromptu means emergency—a spur-of-the-moment speech—a situation that demands you talk without prior notice. It occurs in meetings, conferences, and social gatherings where you are involved and enjoying yourself until the chairperson suddenly calls your name and says, "Would you stand up and say a few words?" That is impromptu. It is also frightening, except to those who know the impromptu secret. And that secret is: you can be *prepared* for an emergency speech. Let's see how.

Once there was a man who claimed he had made an exciting discovery. In an age that had instant coffee and tea, cocoa and punch, he had invented the ultimate: instant water. His directions were simple. Into a glass add one heaping teaspoon of this special powder, fill with water, and presto: H_20.

The same situation exists with impromptu speaking. You can have what looks like instant speech (but isn't quite) by adding the right ingredients. Not water this time, but a *prepared method of attack* that meets any emergency speech situation. Presto! You concoct an impromptu speech that really isn't. Remember, if you know you have to give a speech, prepare it. Impromptu is for emergencies only. Now here is the way to do them.

(1) *Outguess impromptu situations* by analyzing the occasion to see if there is a likelihood that you will be asked to speak. For example, if your mother is being honored at a banquet, and the family is there, chances are that each of you will be invited to give a few remarks.

Remember, in most situations you'll not be asked to do an impromptu unless you have some knowledge about the subject. Otherwise, there would be no reason to ask you to speak.

(2) *Listen carefully* to what is said at the gathering you attend. Then if you are asked to talk, you can at least discuss your views as they relate to what has been going on.

(3) *Memorize an organization pattern* that you can pull from your brain at a moment's notice and adapt to any subject. If in previous assignments you have been using the organization formula discussed in Chapter 26, you are already prepared for this step. All you need do is simplify.

In the few seconds you have between being called on and rising to speak, quickly relate the topic to your experience. Then determine your assertion—the one key point you want to make. Decide how best you can organize the material in the body of your speech. Will you use Time, Space, Problem-Solution, or Topical? Choose one and stay with it. Then rapidly think of a capture sentence to begin the speech. Now you are ready to talk.

Your instantly organized impromptu speech should follow this pattern:

(a) Capture audience attention with a dynamic sentence.

(b) Motivate by relating the subject to your audience.

(c) Assert with your one main point.

(d) Now using either Time, Space, Problem-Solution, or Topical, support your assertion. (See Chapter 26 on organization.) Use specific illustrations—something that has happened to you or that you have read.

(e) Restate your main point to conclude and if possible tie it up with the beginning capture step.

(4) Remain calm. If you push the panic button, all is lost. So keep poised no matter how surprised you are at being asked to talk. It may help to remind yourself that you are not frightened when you participate in conversations, although they too are impromptu situations. Also remember that the audience is on your side. They want you to succeed.

(5) Don't apologize for being unprepared. Naturally you are "unprepared" in an impromptu speech. If anyone should apologize, it should be the people who asked you without advance notice. So begin your speech with a capture step and not with an apology.

ACTIVITY AND ITS PURPOSE

You are to give a one minute impromptu speech on one of three topics you will draw. The purpose of this assignment is to encourage you to think on your feet, giving you confidence to meet impromptu situations outside of speech class.

HOW TO PREPARE

(1) On the activity sheet to this chapter, list three topics that can be used for impromptu speeches in class. Take care that the topics you list are of general interest to your classmates so that they can readily talk on them. Don't choose silly or difficult topics. The following are suggestions:

dogs	home safety	first aid
manners	diets	outdoor cooking
airplane travel	charity drives	my favorite sport
popular music	dentists	my greatest disappointment
superstitions	foreign cars	women's purses
vacations	my hobby	parades
TV commercials	my favorite food	video games

Tear out the three slips of paper plus the evaluation sheet your teacher will give you.

(2) If you have not already done so, memorize the organization formula discussed in this chapter.

HOW TO PRESENT

At the beginning of class, hand the teacher your three slips of paper with a general topic written on each. He or she will quickly approve them, throwing away any inappropriate ones. All topics will be put into a container (a hat, box, basket), mixed up, and placed on a side table with a chair by it.

The first student to speak will draw three topics, select one, return the others to the container again, and sit on the chair by the topic table. That student will have one minute to prepare thoughts. As he or she goes up to talk, the second speaker will draw three topics, select one, put back the others, and sit by the topic table. While speaker one is talking for one minute, speaker two will be preparing thoughts. This same procedure will be used until all have spoken.

As you sit in class, awaiting your turn, don't fidget in your seat. When it is time to draw, quietly do so, without remarks. Quickly choose one of the three topics that suits you best, again without speaking, and sit to prepare.

As you go to the front to speak, leave your topic paper. If you carry it up with you, it will prove a distraction. Announce to the class your topic and the organization pattern you intend to follow (Time, Space, Problem-Solution, or Topical) and begin your capture step. You must talk for one minute, ending your speech only after the one minute time card has been flashed. Since people under pressure usually talk fast, try to slow your rate to an intelligible pace. When you see the time card, don't stop in mid-sentence. Finish your speech with an appropriate concluding statement before you sit down.

The class may quickly discuss whether or not you followed your announced organization pattern and if you observed the other rules of maintaining poise and not apologizing.

If your teacher wishes, the class can list in order the five best impromptu speakers of the day. A tally can be made and class discussion follow as to the results. Why did some students rate consistently high? Why are there variations?

ADDITIONAL ACTIVITIES

(1) Using the above speech situation, increase your speaking time to two minutes and finally an impromptu speech in which you are talking three minutes.

(2) Bring an object to class (a marble, a hammer, a brush, etc.) concealed in a paper bag, *but approved by the teacher*. Without choosing the one you brought, select a concealed parcel. Unwrap it and take one minute to prepare before talking about that article or making up a story about it.

(3) Bring a teacher-approved picture. It may be an art print or a picture taken from a magazine—just so it is large and lends itself to a good story. Lay the pictures on a table and select one on which you wish to give an impromptu speech. You will have 1- 2 minutes to prepare. Before beginning your speech, place the picture on an easel in front of the class for all to see.

(4) Speak impromptu from a general topic assigned you by the teacher.

Impromptu Speech

In 1762, an English nobleman found his card game so engrossing that he refused to take time out for a meal. After sending a servant to bring him a snack, John Montague, Earl of Sandwich, received the first in a long-line of concoctions which have borne his title ever since.

Chapter 40

Person To Person

appropriate | interviewer | interviewee
classified ad | mannerisms | simulated
conservatively | extemporaneous | predetermined | tactful

Watch for these valuable words wherever you see the word bank icon. 

BRAIN TEASERS

(1) How does an interview differ from a conversation?
(2) In making an interview appointment by phone, what do you say?
(3) What is the difference between an open-ended and a closed question?
(4) How do you properly conduct an interview?

HELP WANTED: Student for part time stockroom work on Sats. at Miller's Dept. Store. Must be dependable. Call for interview appointment 784-9631.

This classified newspaper ad catches your eye, for you need a job to earn extra spending money. You dial the number, explain your purpose, and obtain an appointment to be interviewed.

Do you get the job? That depends almost entirely on how you conduct yourself during this person-to-person situation—what you say and what you do. This chapter will help you prepare for many types of interviews, whether as interviewee or interviewer.

Purpose. In an interview two people are involved: the interviewer who asks the bulk of the questions and the interviewee who gives the information. Unlike conversations where rambling is permissible, an interview seeks information by working straight towards a predetermined goal, avoiding sidetracks and trivial details. In an interview, for example, a personnel manager's aim may be to decide if the job applicant can do the work satisfactorily. A doctor's interview may dwell on finding out why the patient is sick. A teacher's interview may be to discover the pupil's problem. A journalist's interview may be to gather specific information for a newspaper story.

Preparing to Interview. As an interviewer, first, make an appointment, usually by telephone. Be sure you are talking to the person you are to interview and then identify yourself. State the purpose of the interview and the approximate time it will take. Ask when it would be convenient to meet. Agree on a definite time and place. Before hanging up, leave a phone number where you can be contacted if necessary.

Second, word and memorize the questions you will ask:

(a) Keep the questions brief.
(b) Use open-ended questions that allow the interviewee to respond with as much information as he or she wishes. Avoid closed questions that ask for only a single answer or a yes or no response.

Closed Questions	**Open Questions**
"Which team do you want to win?"	"What are your reactions to . . ."
"Do you want ...."	"How could this be solved?"

(c) Use tactful wording. Avoid embarrassing questions and those with loaded words.

Bad	**Better**
"How often do I get a raise?"	"What is your company's salary schedule?"
"Why should you be elected?"	"What are your qualifications for this office?"
"Did your last boss fire you?"	"Why did you leave your last job?"

Conducting. Whether you are the interviewee or the interviewer, follow the suggestions below:

(1) Dress neatly and conservatively. (This is especially important if you are being interviewed for a job where first impressions are usually the only impressions.)
(2) Arrive at least five minutes before the interview.
(3) Have necessary materials such as paper and pencil at hand. You may need to write down some answers to remember them.
(4) Be friendly and courteous; the person in authority should take special

care to put the other person at ease.

(5) Avoid arguing, even though opinions differ.

(6) Keep the interview on the right track, moving toward the goal with planned questions.

(7) Let the other person do some of the talking.

(8) Avoid nervous or discourteous mannerisms such as looking constantly at your watch, tapping the table, chewing gum.

(9) Listen carefully and respond to the other person.

(10) Keep the interview short—within the set time limits.

ACTIVITY AND ITS PURPOSE

This is to be a 3 to 4 minute "role-playing" or simulated interview. With your teacher's approval, you and a partner will select a situation and role from which you will conduct an interview. Fill in the activity sheet to this chapter.

HOW TO PREPARE

(1) Select a partner and a situation. Determine who will be the interviewer and the interviewee. The following are suggestions, with the person underlined being the "authority."

	Interviewer	*Interviewee*	*Situation*
(a)	newspaper reporter	<u>candidate</u> running for mayor	to learn the candidate's views on a new water system for the town
(b)	<u>personnel manager</u> of a manufacturing company	job applicant	to decide if applicant can do the work
(c)	<u>teacher</u>	parent	to learn why the student never has the homework done
(d)	<u>lawyer</u>	client	to learn the details of the client's car wreck
(e)	<u>supervisor</u>	surgical nurse	to learn why the nurse is uncooperative on the job
(f)	president of a local service group	<u>police sergeant</u>	to learn how the police department is organized
(g)	employee of a department store	<u>manager</u> of that store	to ask for a raise
(h)	Radio Newscaster	<u>opera singer</u>	to discover the singer's key to success
(i)	high school thespian	<u>director</u> of a university theatre	to learn requirements for acting in the group
(j)	<u>college dean</u> of students	high school graduate	to determine if the student deserves a scholarship

(2) Working alone, the interviewer should write on the activity sheet the questions to be asked. The interviewee should anticipate what questions will be posed and plan the answers accordingly. Both parties may have to do some research within the area selected, to determine the issues for questioning. The interview must be conducted extemporaneously, as in actual situations. If both know in advance the other's questions and answers, the assignment is not being fulfilled.

(3) If you are the interviewer, rehearse your questions and commit them to memory. If you are the interviewee plan your character's or company's background on the back of the activity sheet, so you can readily answer the questions. The party holding the authority in the interview (the employer, the famous person, etc.) must plan the setting (placement of desk, chairs, tables) for the interview. If costume pieces such as hats, suits, briefcases will help your interview, plan on using them. Review the suggestions in the Platform Notes in preparation for conducting the interview.

HOW TO PRESENT

Have your activity sheet in readiness to hand to your teacher before your interview.

The "authority" will set the stage with necessary furniture, being sure that the faces of both partners can be easily seen by the class. When the stage is set, the "authority" should stand in front of the class and briefly explain his or her role and that of the partner, the purpose of the interview, and the setting.

Conduct the interview as true to life as possible, following the material presented in this chapter. Speak loudly so all can hear. At the opening of the interview the two parties should greet each other in a friendly, polite manner. The "authority" should ask the other person to sit down. The interviewer should then state the purpose of the interview and ask the first question, using memorized questions and any other appropriate ones that come to mind during the session. Both should keep the interview moving towards its goal. Remember, the interviewee may ask questions too. Keep within your role and character. Don't mumble, feel embarrassed, or start giggling. Also, don't let your partner do all of the talking. You both have a part to play and a job to do, so push ahead in a dynamic way.

When the interviewer has the facts needed, he or she should indicate the end of the interview by saying something like, "I believe I have all of the information I need. Thank you very much." Good-byes should then be said and a prompt departure made.

ADDITIONAL ACTIVITIES

(1) You and a partner conduct a simulated job interview by using actual job openings that are listed in the classified ads of your local newspaper. With your teacher's approval, choose the ad, decide who will be the interviewer and who will be the applicant. Play the interview as though it were real.

(2) With a partner, improvise a scene where the interviewer is conducting a poll on an important political question. He or she knocks at the door of a house and must carry on a scene with the person who answers and says one of the following:

(a) "Why do you want to interview me? My opinions aren't worth much."
(b) "I'm busy. Go away."
(c) "Who are you and what do you want?"
(d) "If you are trying to sell me something, I don't want any."

(3) With your teacher's approval, actually interview a business or professional person in town—someone you do not know and to whom you are not related. Decide the purpose of your interview (what information you want to gather). Phone for an appointment, plan questions, and then actually do the interview. Your teacher will send a rating sheet with you. You are to give the interviewee the rating sheet and a stamped, addressed business envelope that you supply. When you have left, that person will rate you on how you conducted the interview, the quality of your questions, your appearance, attitude, voice, and behavior. This rating sheet will be sent to your teacher. As a follow up, you will give a 2-4 minute oral report in class on the interview and the information you gathered.

(4) See and study the following video. (For addresses see Appendix E):

Sell Yourself: Successful Job Interviewing (Insight Media)
With humor, demonstrates some interviews that are a disaster and those that are a success. Examines the correct technique.

Chapter 41

Pooling Ideas

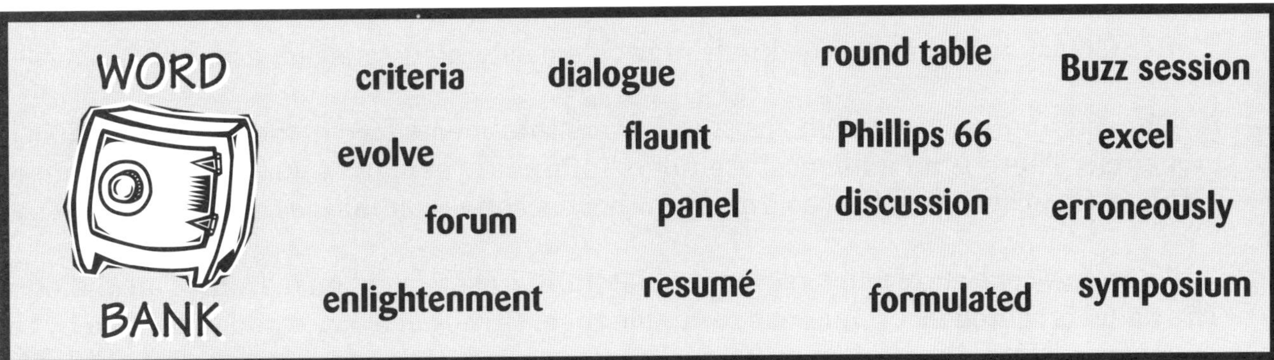

WORD
BANK
criteria
dialogue
round table
Buzz session
evolve
flaunt
Phillips 66
excel
forum
panel
discussion
erroneously
enlightenment
resumé
formulated
symposium

Watch for these valuable words wherever you see the word bank icon. 

BRAIN TEASERS

(1) How does group discussion differ from conversation and debate?
(2) What are the specific characteristics of each of the six types of problem solving groups?
(3) What are your duties as a participant in group discussion?
(4) What are your duties as a chairperson in group discussion?
(5) How should a subject problem be phrased?
(6) What are the five steps in the problem solving process?

PLATFORM NOTES

All of your life you will be faced with problems. Sometimes you can solve them by consulting an authority, such as by asking a doctor what medicine to take. Sometimes your problem is solved when you collect information. Learning that the average yearly temperature in Mexico City is 72° degrees, will solve your problem of what to wear when you go there on vacation. But if you have a problem that concerns many people, one of the best ways of solving it is through group discussion.

Group discussion is a democratic, cooperative method whereby several individuals under the guidance of a leader contribute ideas, opinions, and facts aimed at solving a problem or bringing enlightenment to the group. It differs from conversation in that it follows a plan and has a specific purpose. It differs from debate in that its method is to search for an answer rather than to win support for a course of action already formulated.

Study groups are those that explore a subject for the sake of understanding it. Problem solving groups are those that try to find a workable answer to a problem. In this chapter we will be concerned with problem solving groups.

Although it takes considerable time for people working together to evolve a solution, the benefits are great. Better thinking usually comes from a group than from one individual because there is a pooling of knowledge. Then, too, when people have a part in making a decision, they are more likely to abide by it.

TYPES OF PROBLEM SOLVING GROUPS

Let us look into the various kinds of problem solving discussion groups.

The *round table* discussion is a small group that meets face to face around a table or in a circle. There is no audience. Members informally explore a subject or delve into a problem. City councils, school boards, and other executive committees employ this method.

The *panel* consists of four to seven people who discuss a problem in front of an audience. The panel is seated in a semicircle to enable them to see each other and to be seen by the spectators. No prepared speeches are given, as is sometimes erroneously thought. Informal, spontaneous discussion based on previous study takes place.

The *dialogue* is a public discussion between two people. One asks the questions, and one (usually an expert) answers them.

The *symposium* consists of three to six members who each present a prepared speech on a single subject before an audience. One of two methods is employed. Each speaker may talk on a different aspect of the problem. For example, if the question is "How can we best solve the problem of litter?" one speaker may describe the nature of the problem, another may tell what city and county government can do, another may concentrate on how the private citizen can help. The second method uses speakers who are experts with diverse backgrounds and opinions. They present their personal views on the entire subject, telling the conditions and causes and suggesting remedies.

The *forum* is an audience questioning session that follows a panel, dialogue, symposium, speech, or film. To prepare the audience for the forum, at the beginning of the meeting the chairperson should state that there will be a question period after the discussion. When the discussion has concluded, the chairperson should call for questions that pertain to the subject and indicate whether they are to be directed to individual members or to the group as a whole. The chairperson should point out that questions, not speeches, are in order. Or if speeches are to be allowed, they should be no longer than one minute. (Sometimes written questions are submitted to the chairperson who decides which are to be used.)

When an audience is large, questioners should stand to be easily seen and heard. In a small group they may remain seated. If the audience is slow to respond with questions, the chairman should lead off with one or two.

When you handle questions either as a discussion member or as a chairperson, you should be alert and friendly. If you do not understand the question, ask for it to be restated. If you can't answer it, admit it, although if you know your subject well you should be able to answer most questions. Respond to hecklers politely but firmly. Don't engage in debate. Just go on to the next question. If the question is off the subject, point this out, and if you are not prepared to answer it, say so.

A forum usually lasts about thirty minutes. Approximately three minutes before the end of the forum the chairman should announce that there is time for just one more question. After it is answered, the session is concluded by thanking the audience for their interest.

The *Phillips 66 Buzz* session is a method named after its originator and employs six people who discuss a topic for six minutes—hence "66." These buzz sessions are good for involving a large audience in a limited time. The session starts with the chairperson who gives a short lecture or who leads the audience in a brief discussion that stimulates their thinking and gives them background on the topic. The audience is then asked to move their chairs around or stand in groups of six members where for six minutes they are to discuss the problem. The chairperson should announce whether they are to find a solution, make a recommendation, or formulate a question to be later discussed. After six minutes, one member from each group reports for one minute or less on the group's contribution. The chairperson summarizes the findings, pointing out similarities and differences. Then the chairperson leads the whole group in a discussion of the proposed solutions or recommendations. If there are submitted questions, they should be answered.

GROUP RESPONSIBILITIES

Discussion does not just happen. Effort is required to solve the problem. Before you participate you must understand the procedure of group discussion and determine to carry your share of the responsibility. The following suggestions will help you become an effective participant:

(1) *Investigate the problem*. In good detective fashion thoroughly collect the facts so you will have concrete information to discuss. Remember, the group's method is to pool knowledge, not ignorance.

(2) *Follow in order the five steps in the "problem solving process" during the discussion.* They are:

(a) Describe—define the terms, state the symptoms and the size.
(b) Determine the causes of the problem and the criteria or standards that solutions must meet.
(c) Suggest several possible solutions with the strengths and weaknesses of each one.
(d) Select the "best" solution—the one that seems to excel.
(e) Prescribe definite ways to carry out the "best" solution.

(3) *Participate with enthusiasm.* The group needs your contribution. Don't dominate the discussion, but assume your share of the responsibility. Think before you speak, but do speak.

(4) *Listen carefully to what the others say.* Listen to understand and evaluate, not to attack.

(5) *Be receptive to ideas.* A person who says, "My mind is made up; don't bother me with the facts," has no place in a group discussion. Keep your mind open. Expect new ideas to evolve as each member contributes knowledge. Avoid identifying yourself with your ideas. Stay objective, with your emotions under control. Remember, your purpose is not to win an argument or flaunt your knowledge. You are to help find the best solution to the problem. Of course, differences of opinion will occur but handle them with respect and courtesy.

CHAIRPERSON OR GROUP LEADER DUTIES

When you serve as chairperson or group leader, it is your duty to help the discussion group achieve the best of which it is capable. You do this by leading and guiding, not dictating or shoving. You must assume all of the group responsibilities listed above as well as specifically carry out the following duties as leader.

(1) *Study the problem thoroughly.* Without this preparation you will be unable to guide intelligently and organize the group's thinking.

(2) *Prepare a series of leading questions for each step of the problem solving process.* (See item two under group responsibilities.) Questions should stimulate group thinking along a definite pattern. Avoid questions that can be answered by a "yes" or "no." Learn to use the following openers for different types of answers:

Start with "what" to learn an individuals' reaction.
Start with "why" to gather facts and reasons.
Start with "who" to discover sources and authorities.
Start with "how" to determine solutions.

(3) *Open the discussion.* If there is an audience, introduce group members and the subject problem. Explain the purpose of the group and the procedure and time limits involved. Create audience interest in the subject by relating the problem to their lives. Then turn to the group and with a series of questions suggest the starting point of the discussion. For example, you might say, "We are all aware of this problem, but how does it affect us here in this school? How are we specifically involved?"

(4) *Guide group thinking along the problem solving process.* When one step has been adequately discussed, provide a summary of the points agreed upon and move forward with a transition to the next step.

(5) *Help the group to think "straight."* Ask for specific examples and support. Probe for sources. Insist that material relate to the subject problem and be logically presented. Questions such as "Can you give the group an example? Who said this? What other evidence is there to support this idea?" help to keep the group's thinking valid.

(6) *Secure the participation of everyone.* A friendly, courteous attitude will encourage most members. If there are shy individuals, don't embarrass them with a pointed question that they may not be able to answer. Instead, say something like, "I believe John had some experiences along this line last summer. What are your reactions, John?" If another group member monopolizes the discussion, firmly break in as he or she takes a breath and say, "Now we need to hear from someone else on this subject." If there is an argument, intervene with, "You two have definite feelings on this point. Now let's see how someone else reacts."

(7) *Close the discussion.* Summarize the agreements reached and if necessary indicate further aspects to investigate.

THE SUBJECT PROBLEM

Choose a subject for discussion that involves a real problem important to your group. It should also be one that involves a policy (something that should or should not be done) rather than one that deals with fact or value.

Clearly phrase the subject as a question that helps the group focus on the problem that needs solving and that invites all possible solutions. A question that reads "Should we have a talent show?" is not well phrased because it dismisses all solutions except talent show. A better subject problem would be worded "How can we best earn money for our class project?" This phrasing is effective because it does not limit the solution.

An acceptable pattern to follow in phrasing discussion questions is "How can we best deal with (name the problem)?"

ACTIVITY AND ITS PURPOSE

You are to serve on a classroom panel whose purpose is to solve a problem that is important to the group. The panel will first meet in a closed planning session. Depending on class time, the actual discussion (thirty minutes or more) will occur during one class period or will be divided into two meetings with the first covering steps one through three in the problem solving process. The second discussion meeting will cover steps four and five.

HOW TO PREPARE

(1) Your teacher will divide you into groups of 5 to 7, appoint one of the group to be group leader, and will announce the number of meetings you will have, their time limit, and exact date.

(2) Meet with your group in closed planning session (no audience) to pick a subject that meets the requirements discussed in this chapter. Be sure it is a subject everyone in your group is interested in and is capable of discussing. Phrase your subject problem "How can we best (state the problem)?" The following are suggestions:

How can we best

(a) improve our school's assembly programs?
(b) eliminate cheating in our classrooms?
(c) improve our scholarship in school?
(d) improve our school paper?
(e) eliminate congestion in the lunchroom during the noon hour?
(f) obtain better attendance at school dances?
(g) help our community deal with litter pollution?
(h) handle drug abuse in our school?
(i) improve school spirit?
(j) provide a student service to the community?
(k) increase learning opportunities for our students?

(3) Working individually outside of class do research on your problem. Read literature and interview authorities. Gather as much information as possible.

(4) On the activity sheet to this chapter follow the problem solving steps to outline the information you have obtained. In each outline entry include material and its source.

Note: If you are a chairperson, on the activity sheet write three or four leading questions for each of the problem solving steps. Outline your introductory remarks on a separate page.

Your teacher may ask for your completed activity sheet several days before your discussion. It will be returned so you may refer to it if necessary during your discussion.

(5) Memorize the steps in the problem solving process and follow them when contributing to group thinking.

(6) Review the responsibilities of participants and group leaders in preparation to accept your specific duties. Also see the rating sheet your teacher will distribute.

HOW TO PRESENT

Hand your evaluation sheet to the teacher before your group begins. Take your activity sheet or notes to use in the discussion.

The group leader should place chairs in a semicircle around a table, insuring that all members can see each other and also be seen by the class audience. The leader should sit with participants on each side.

He or she will give introductory remarks and then point to the beginning of the discussion (step one) with specific questions. As you spontaneously participate, speak loudly and clearly for all to hear. Be courteous, open-minded, and eager to discover the facts. Carry out your duties as listed in this chapter.

At the end of the discussion the leader will summarize the group's effort.

Note: If the discussion covers more than one meeting, at the next session the leader should give a brief resumé of the previous meeting before posing the starting questions.

ADDITIONAL ACTIVITIES

(1) In class hold a symposium-forum where each member speaks on a related aspect of a large problem. The chairperson should state the problem, give a brief history of it, give reasons for its discussion and indicate its importance to the audience. He or she will introduce the speakers and their topics and will tell how the symposium-forum will be conducted. After the symposium the meeting will be opened to audience questions.

(2) Hold a lecture-forum in which the class invites an expert to lecture in his or her field. Following the lecture, the chairperson will invite questions from the audience directed to the speaker. Suggested subjects: crime rate, drugs and the teenager, honesty in advertising, etiquette while on a date, defensive driving, summer jobs.

Note: An alternate assignment is to have class members do extensive research and present a speech to inform (see Chapter 32, "Teaching Tale"). After the conclusion, a chairperson will conduct a forum with class questions directed to the student speakers.

(3) Watch a panel discussion on television and write a report as to its goal, its procedure, the behavior of the participants and chairperson, and the outcome.

(4) Conduct a Phillips 66 Buzz session in class in order to obtain ideas quickly for solving a school problem.

(5) Hold a film-forum in which your class sees a film, video, or film strip and then discusses it afterwards. A leader and a committee appointed by your teacher will preview the film and carefully plan questions to discuss. Before the film is shown to the class, the leader should briefly introduce its subject and indicate what the viewers should look for. If possible, list these areas on the chalkboard. After the film the leader will lead a discussion of each question.

(6) Rent and show the following videos. (For addresses see Appendix E):

Group Discussion Series (Insight Media)
Seven videos on forms of discussion, solving the problem, the discussion group, and leader.

Effective Decision Making In Groups (Insight Media)
Stages of the group process including diagnosing the problem, searching for solutions, and making decisions.

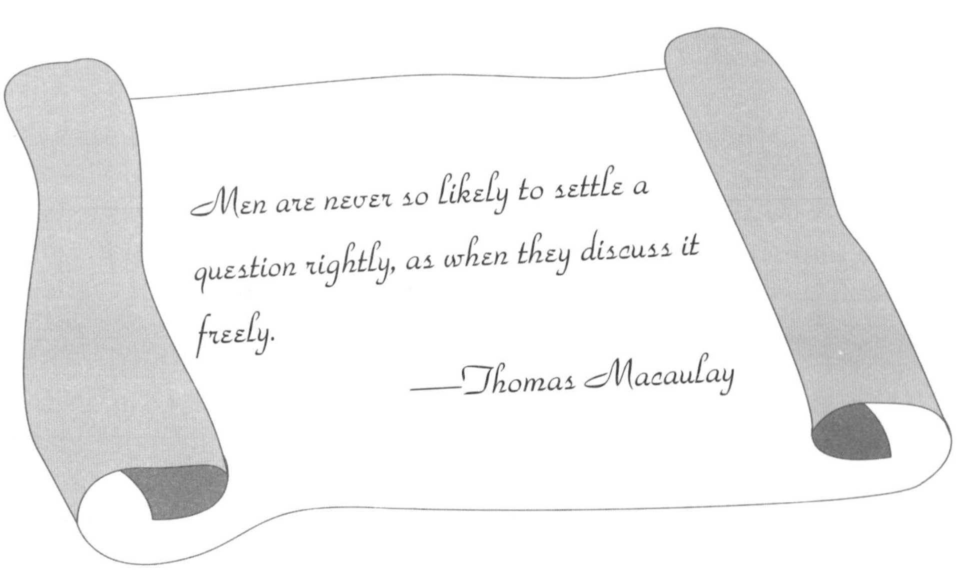

Men are never so likely to settle a question rightly, as when they discuss it freely.
—Thomas Macaulay

"COMPANION"

In ancient times it was an unwritten Roman law that a family must graciously welcome any traveler who needed food and lodging. Even though it might be only a once-in-a-lifetime encounter, men who broke bread together were by custom bound in friendship.

The word **companion** literally comes from the Latin **come** (together) plus **panis** (bread). Companion therefore came to mean lifelong friend.

Chapter 42

Defend Your Side

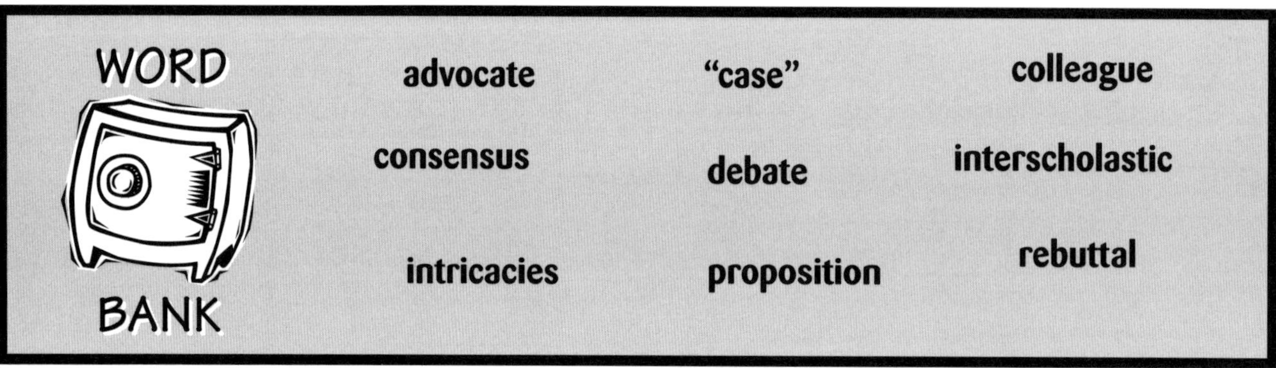

WORD
BANK
advocate
"case"
colleague
consensus
debate
interscholastic
intricacies
proposition
rebuttal

Watch for these valuable words wherever you see the word bank icon. 

BRAIN TEASERS

(1) How does debate differ from group discussion?
(2) What is the traditional order of speakers?
(3) What should you consider in choosing a debate proposition?
(4) How should the proposition be worded?
(5) What should the affirmative prove in its constructive speeches?
(6) What should the negative do in its constructive speeches?
(7) What is the correct way for doing research on a debate question?
(8) What is the purpose of a rebuttal?
(9) On what qualities is a debate judged?

PLATFORM NOTES

American history is marked with famous debates. Men like James Madison and Alexander Hamilton who helped form the United States Constitution engaged in dynamic debate concerning the type of government proposed for the new nation. Later the country grew excited over debates by Webster and Hayne and by Lincoln and Douglas. In modern times presidential candidates debate face to face on television.

Every year in high schools and colleges, debate is a popular activity in which teams participate in interscholastic competition. This chapter will provide you with an introduction to debate's stimulating mental process. As you continue in school you may wish to learn more of the intricacies of this discipline.

Debate is a special type of argument in which two or more speakers present opposing propositions in an attempt to win the audience to their sides. The teams are not concerned with convincing each other. Their purpose is to try to alter audience thinking by presenting the issues honestly with reliable evidence.

Debate differs from group discussion that you studied in the previous chapter. The list below presents a comparison:

Debate	Discussion
(1) competitive (judges vote to determine a winner)	(1) cooperative (consensus reached by the group)
(2) participants take an affirmative or negative stand that does not change throughout	(2) participants retain an open mind, often changing their opinions when facts call for it.
(3) starts with a proposal	(3) starts with a problem
(4) aims at winning advocates to a side	(4) aims at finding the "best" solution to fix the problem
(5) set rules used for time limits and order of speakers	(5) flexible time and participation
(6) persuasive style	(6) conversational style

Many values come from your debating. Because you usually debate current issues, it helps you to gain an interest in public affairs. It helps you to analyze problems, to reinforce your statements with proof, to express your ideas clearly and with confidence, and to think quickly while on your feet.

TRADITIONAL PROCEDURE

A debate team usually consists of two members for each side, although one person teams can also be used. Each member presents one constructive speech that develops a carefully documented plan, and one rebuttal that refutes the opponent's case (the stand he or she takes). There are many forms of debates, but the traditional one follows this set speaking order.

Constructive speeches:	*Rebuttals:*
First affirmative	First negative
First negative	First affirmative
Second affirmative	Second negative
Second negative	Second affirmative

Notice that the affirmative team always begins and ends the debate. They are given this favored position because they have the most difficult job. The affirmative always proposes a change, and human nature generally resists change, thereby leaning towards the negative side.

In traditional contest debating, the time limits are generally ten minutes for each constructive speech and five minutes for each rebuttal speech. But in the classroom, of course, time may be changed to suit the situation.

DEBATE QUESTION

In debate, the subject is called a proposition and is stated as a formal declarative resolution, not as a question. Each debate subject begins with the words: "Resolved that __________." The proposition is worded so that the affirmative is for the change and the negative is against it. The topic should be interesting, timely, and appropriate to the debating group. It should contain only one proposal, and it should definitely be debatable. Don't choose something that is already settled. "Resolved that the voting age limit be lowered to eighteen in the U.S." is no longer a debatable question.

CONSTRUCTIVE SPEECHES

Preparing your constructive speech takes thorough research. Most topics will necessitate library work, starting with the *Reader's Guide*, the index to source material in magazines. Or use a computer database. Some libraries and schools have the popular InfoTrac computerized index CD ROM which can search for general interest, magazine articles, and newspapers. As you read, accurately record the facts for both sides of the issue on 4" x 6" note cards, labeling them according to topic divisions such as history of the problem, present situation, and causes. Write down the material you need and the author, magazine title, publication date, and page number. Also write down why the author is an authority on the subject. See Chapter 25 for correct procedure in note taking.

Your constructive speech is basically a speech to convince. You will want to load it with evidence —facts, examples, statistics, and testimony—that supports your stand on the question (see Chapter 33 on verbal support). Be sure that you check your sources. As you read ask yourself, "Who says so? Is he or she an authority in the field? Competent? How do I know? Impartial? Are the facts up to date?" Don't skip this checking process. Your facts are only as good as your sources!

If you are on the affirmative side, you must prove three things to win. You must prove that your proposition is *needed*, that it is *practical*, and that it is *desirable*.

In contest debate the negative has a choice of several courses of action, but in this class we will be concerned only with the most basic which is to attack the affirmative's issues directly.

Each side equally divides its case between the two partners who respond to the previous speaker's attacks before continuing their planned outline.

A sample of the contents and sequence of each debater's constructive speech is shown below:

First Affirmative's Constructive Speech

I. Introduce the proposition.
  - A. Clearly state it.
  - B. Define the words that may be unclear.
  - C. Give a brief history or background of the proposition.

II. State the affirmative's position.

III. Prove that your proposition is needed.
(Use examples, statistics, testimony, specific instances.)

IV. Summarize your stand.

First Negative's Constructive Speech

I. Introduce your position.
  - A. Recognize the affirmative's plan.
  - B. Accept or substitute the definition of terms.
  - C. State the negative's position.

II. Attack and question the affirmative's idea that the change they advocate is needed.
(Give proof that there is no need for a change.)

III. Conclude.
  - A. Summarize your statements.
  - B. Ask the second affirmative to reply to your questions.

Second Affirmative's Constructive Speech

I. Reply to the attack of the first negative.

II. Attack the negative's case.

III. Repeat the affirmative's position and the need.

IV. Prove that your plan is practical (that it will work).

V. Prove that your plan is desirable (that it will produce many benefits).

VI. Conclude.
  - A. Summarize the entire case.
  - B. Strongly ask the audience to accept your proposal.

Second Negative's Constructive Speech

I. Reply to the second affirmative's attack.

II. Restate the negative's position.

III. Attack the affirmative's case.
- A. Prove that it is not practical.
- B. Prove that it is not desirable.

IV. Conclude.
- A. Summarize the case.
- B. Urge the audience to reject the proposition.

THE REBUTTAL

During your rebuttal speech you point out the weaknesses in your opponent's reasoning and defend your own case. Your success in the rebuttal will depend on how well you have listened to and taken notes on the debate, how quickly you can reestablish proof, and how convincing you are. Don't waste time refuting small details. Concentrate on the important issues. If you cut down a big branch, the little branches go with it.

In attacking you may try to prove that your opponent's evidence is weak, or the sources unacceptable. You may show that his or her reasoning is faulty, the plan is unclear, or that basic issues were evaded.

In answering accusations you may admit the weakness but show how it does not basically harm your case, or you may prove that your opponent's argument does not relate to your plan. You may also match the attack with one of your own that is equally strong against his or her stand.

Below is a sample outline for a rebuttal speech:

Basic Rebuttal Outline

I. Reply to any major attacks.
- A. Tell what you are refuting by exactly quoting, if possible, your opponent's words.
- B. Disprove the attack with exact evidence and facts.
- C. Show how your opponent now has no case against you.

II. Advance the arguments against your opponent's case, step-by-step. (Note that in the rebuttal the first affirmative will reply to the second negative's constructive speech as well as to the first negative's rebuttal speech. The last speaker of each rebuttal should urge acceptance of the plan.)

JUDGING DEBATES

Debates are judged on the speaker's effectiveness, not on the judge's personal bias about the proposition. The judge will consider your analysis of the problem, your evidence, your organization, refutation, and delivery.

ACTIVITY AND ITS PURPOSE

This assignment will give you practice in classroom debating. You and a partner will debate an opposing team of classmates. The traditional form will be used with shorter time limits which your teacher will set. If possible two debates will be held each class period. Suggested times are 3 to 5 minutes for each constructive speech and 2 to 3 minutes for each rebuttal.

HOW TO PREPARE

(1) When your teacher assigns you a partner, confer with your opponents to determine a suitable debate question. One team is to be the affirmative and uphold the change. The other team is to be the negative and argue against the proposition. Be sure the proposition you choose interests all of you and that it meets the requirements discussed in this chapter. After serious thought select your topic. Don't waste time in trivial disagreement. While it is desirable to debate on the side that you personally agree with, it is not necessary. Contest debaters learn to debate either side effectively. If you and your partner do not agree on a topic, your teacher will assign one and appoint you as an affirmative or negative speaker. The following are suggestions:

Resolved that:

(a) All high school students should be required to take a computer class.
(b) All polystyrene packaging should be banned.
(c) The government should give top priority to funding money for AIDS research.
(d) All oil tankers should be required to be double-hulled.
(e) Convicted murderers should never be paroled.
(f) All cars should be required by law to have standardized instrument panels.
(g) The national minimum hourly wage should be increased by fifty percent.
(h) All television beer commercials should be banned.
(i) Drug testing should be mandatory for all drivers in public transportation.
(j) Parental consent should be required for all abortions on minors.
(k) There should be a moratorium on adding to the endangered species list.
(l) Colleges should require all entering students to have fulfilled a two-year foreign language requirement.
(m) Prayer should be allowed in public schools.
(n) (Your choice of any controversial current issue approved by your instructor.)

(2) You and your partner should decide who will speak first.

(3) Individually do research on material for your whole case. Later you and your partner may exchange the information each needs for your constructive

speech. As you research, look for your opponent's view. You must be familiar with his or her side if you are to conduct a successful rebuttal.

(4) After material is collected, outline your constructive speech on the activity sheet to this chapter, pooling your information with that of your partner. Adapt your case to the sample constructive speech outline in the chapter, selecting the sample for your side and speaking order (second negative, etc.). If possible, you and your partner should work together on developing both constructive speeches.

(5) Rehearse your speech outside of class until you have it so well in mind you need refer to notes only occasionally for specific data. Then rehearse with your partner who should offer helpful suggestions. Remember, you are a team and must work together and support each other.

HOW TO PRESENT

Before your debate begins, hand your activity sheet to your teacher and your rating sheet to the judge. Both teams will face the audience as they sit at tables on opposite sides in front of the class. The chairperson should sit on the front row with the timekeeper.

Your teacher may serve as judge, or may invite one or three people from outside of the class to judge. After the debate and without consultation, the judges will write their decision which the chairperson collects. The judges will rate each debater individually. Turn to the rating sheet now to see how you will be judged.

The chairperson will start the debate by reading the question aloud and introducing the speakers, judges, and timekeeper. After the debate the judges' decision as to the winning team will be announced.

When you debate, greet the audience, judges, and your opponents. Refer to the latter as "my opponents," or "the first speaker for the affirmative," etc. Refer to your partner not by name but as "my colleague." Discuss the case as "our position," or "we contend."

Communicate an attitude of confidence, without appearing snobbish. Be poised, friendly, and courteous. Even in a heated clash, never stoop to sarcasm or shouting. Be sincerely aroused, yes! But keep in control.

When you speak, rise. It should be determined beforehand whether you speak from your position behind the table or walk to the center and speak from behind a lectern. Maintain an alert posture. Avoid leaning on the table or lectern. Speak loudly and clearly. Be intent but don't preach or "ham" it up.

After the debate is finished, teams traditionally rise, meet in the center, and shake their opponents' hands.

ADDITIONAL ACTIVITIES

(1) In class, conduct an informal debate (no decision as to winner and more relaxed rules) on a proposition of value or on a light or humorous topic. Suggested topics: Resolved that dogs make better pets than cats, that it is more desirable to own a __________ car than a _________ car, that men are better cooks than women, that today's clothing styles are more attractive than those of the past five years.

(2) See and discuss the following videos:

Debate and Forensic Speeches.
Shows current 50 minute high school debates. Also 10 minute speeches in persuasion, information, interpretations, etc. (Forensics Suite, University of Northern Iowa, Cedar Falls, Iowa 50614.)

Chapter 43

Tune In

WORD BANK

adhere "dissolve" monitor
"cut" media video tape
influential transmitted
studio camera shot control room
boom mike distort diverse

Watch for these valuable words wherever you see the word bank icon. 

BRAIN TEASERS

(1) What are the unique qualities of radio and television?
(2) What microphone techniques should you use in radio speaking?
(3) What hand signals must you learn for radio and television?
(4) What rules should you follow in writing a speech for radio?
(5) How do camera shots create a television story?
(6) What camera techniques should you use in television speaking?

PLATFORM NOTES

Radio and television speaking offer you a special challenge. When you work with these electronic media, you are involved with the most far-reaching, varied, and influential tools ever known in the history of communication. These two media stretch your environment to include the whole world. Instantly you can hear and see news being made in lands on which you may never set foot. Instantly you have a choice of programs that extends from horse racing to ballet, from situation comedies to parlor games. A special interest broadcast alone can reach millions of people at one time. And because radio and television are instant background companions to many of you, their continuous messages, commercials, and views sway your thinking and behavior. Truly, radio and television have changed people's lives. Can you think of specific examples to show this change?

Radio and television have two other unique qualities. While the audience is immense, it is divided into small groups—usually family units. Since these individuals generally receive the transmission in their home or car, they are easily distracted. They have no hesitation about turning off a program that disinterests them. They would rather "switch it" than "fight it."

When you perform on radio and television, you must adjust to these conditions by retaining a friendly conversational manner appropriate to small groups. You must also have material that immediately catches and holds their attention.

Let us now focus on these media individually. If possible, visit radio and television studios in your area for additional information.

RADIO

When you broadcast over radio, you will probably do so from a small soundproof studio that is separated from the control room by a large glass window through which the engineer will give you hand signals. You will read your typed and exactly timed manuscript in front of a stand or table microphone. Although you are reading, your aim is to achieve the spontaneity and liveliness of conversation. To create this intimacy you should imagine that you are talking to just one or two friends. Since a radio audience receives only sound, your voice is the sole communicator of images, ideas, and emotion. To be effective you will need to use all of the techniques of oral interpretation (see Chapters 44-46).

MICROPHONE TECHNIQUES

The microphone is your only contact with the audience, so you must learn how to use it. Below are listed basic "mike" techniques.

(1) *Don't touch the studio microphone*. It is a sensitive and expensive piece of equipment that should be handled only by an experienced engineer.

(2) *Keep your volume constant*. Don't fade at the end of sentences and blast out at the beginning. Before you go on the air the engineer will test your voice over the "mike" and will tell you the basic volume to maintain and the distance to stay from the instrument.

(3) *Consistently stay the same distance from the microphone.* Weaving to and fro and back and forth distorts the volume and presents problems for the sound engineer.

(4) *Clearly articulate your words.* If the audience can't understand you, they'll shut you off.

(5) *Use a medium pitched voice.* A high sounding voice is particularly unpleasant over the air. To avoid shrillness keep your throat relaxed by doing body and vocal warmups before performing.

(6) *Don't rush your speaking rate.* A normal rate is about 140 words a minute. In rehearsal exactly time your script. A leeway of only ten seconds is allowed, so you must strictly adhere to time limits.

(7) *Handle your script quietly.* The microphone amplifies paper rustling. Don't clip pages together. After reading each page, carefully drop it on the floor or quietly place it under the rest of your script.

(8) *Use gestures and facial expressions.* They won't be seen, but they will be heard! Physical response with its muscular tension and relaxation affects the sound of your voice. Proper gestures will give your voice "believability."

(9) Avoid sneezing, coughing, or throat clearing when using a microphone. Even breathe silently!

HAND SIGNALS

When you are on the air, learn to watch the control room for any hand signals the director or engineer may give you. Following are the basic hand signals universally used by radio personnel (and sometimes used by television directors).

standby
arm raised above the head.

you're on
arm dropped and hand pointed to the person who starts the show.

speed up
hands rotating around each other.

slow down
hands moved slowly away from each other.

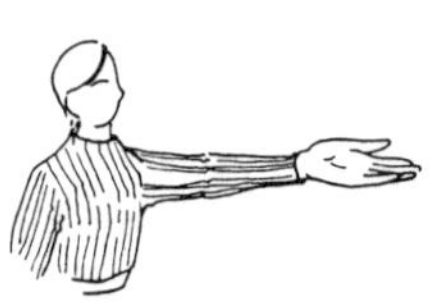

more volume
hand extended with palm upward.

less volume
hand extended with palm down.

move closer to "mike"
hand in front of face with palm toward nose.

move away from "mike"
hand in front of face with palm away from nose.

"cut" or stop
move index finger across throat.

everything is ok
Hand extended with circle made with thumb and index finger

SCRIPTS

All fundamentals of speech composition apply to radio and television speeches too. Use a simple-to-follow organization, orally numbering your points if necessary. Use frequent summaries to help those who have just tuned in. For ease in listening, keep your sentences short. No more than twenty words per sentence is the rule used by some professionals. Use attention factors throughout, to keep your audience from turning the dial (see Chapter 32 for attention factors). Also, avoid frequent use of words with sibilant sounds (s,z,ch,sh), for the microphone seems always to distort them.

TELEVISION

Television studios are usually large rooms crowded with cameras and their attached lengths of cable, boom microphones, batteries of strong lights, and diverse scenery and properties. For easy moving, cameras are attached to tripods on wheels, or in large studios they are mounted on cranes that can move about the set. Each camera has a small light in front that gleams red when it is taking a picture. Cameras are run by cameramen who wear earphones that pick up the instructions given by the director in the control room.

Unlike the stationary position of microphones in radio, television microphones are usually mounted on a long overhead mobile boom that the "boom man" can lengthen or shorten to follow the performer.

In the control room is a monitor (small television set) for each camera. The director studies the picture on each monitor and decides which he or she wants to use. When the corresponding button is pushed that camera's picture is aired. A master monitor shows exactly what is being transmitted.

CAMERA SHOTS

Through this selection of camera pictures called "shots" the director creates a story. A shot is the continuous portion of an action that one camera picks up. Actors may move during the shots and the cameras follow them. A new shot occurs when a different camera is used with a different perspective.

Suppose a portion of the story being created on television is to show a man arriving for dinner at the home of his date. Camera one may picture a close-up of a lighted match igniting a candle. Camera two may have a long shot of a woman moving away from a candle lit dinner table set for two. Camera three may picture a car moving up a driveway in front of a large house. A well dressed man gets out. Camera one pictures that man knocking at a front door. These four shots called by the director in proper sequence create the story.

Transitions between shots are usually created by a "cut" which is a quick change from one shot to another and by a "dissolve" which is a fade out on one shot as another comes in on top of it.

CAMERA TECHNIQUE

When you appear on a television show, whether it is a live broadcast (aired at the same time of production) or a video taped program (sound and picture recorded on tape for later showing) you must know how to behave in front of the cameras, for the visual dimension throws emphasis on what you do and on how you look. The suggestions below should be helpful:

(1) *Adjust your eye focus to the program situation.* If you are giving a speech, an oral reading, or a direct commentary, you want to appear to be looking right at the audience, so look into the camera where the red light beams. In a television play or during most interviews look at the participants and not at the camera.

(2) *Never sneak a look at yourself on the studio monitor.* This will be noticeable to the audience and will be a distraction for you.

(3) *Let the visual element dominate.* If the audience can *see* it, they don't want to be *told* it.

(4) *Keep your voice conversational for general television work.* Imagine yourself talking to only two or three individuals gathered in their home.

(5) *Keep your gestures close to your body.* Large ones may reach outside of camera range. Avoid unexpected moves. Remember, the camera must follow you.

(6) *Keep your facial expressions subtle.* Television magnifies action. A little goes a long way.

(7) *Sit and stand closely together within the camera's range when you are in a group.*

(8) *Project your voice to the microphone.* Unlike radio where the microphone is immediately in front of you, on TV it is usually above you, out of camera range. You must use volume to reach it.

(9) *Wear proper clothes and makeup for the station's equipment.* Camera types and available lighting must be considered. Check with the television director. Always avoid flashy jewelry that picks up light.

ACTIVITY AND ITS PURPOSE

With a group of classmates you are to write, rehearse, and broadcast a ten minute radio program (plus a station break and sign-off). You must use a set format. The project will take approximately two weeks of class time. You may use sound effects and music if necessary on your show.

HOW TO PREPARE

(1) Your teacher will divide the class into groups of 7-9 and assign you a presentation date. Each group will prepare a radio program following the same format but using different material. Below is the format which your teacher may vary.

RADIO PRESENTATION FORMAT

(10 sec.)	*Station break*	Announce the time Identify the station call numbers Identify the city
(1 min.)	*Public Service Announcement (Do only one.)*	Give to charity drives (United Fund, Heart, Cancer) Support community groups (Join YFCA, lead a Scout troop, teach a Campfire group) Vote at the election Attend community functions (school activities, community symphony, community theatre)
(1 min.)	*Commercial*	*(Use two voices if possible and one sound effect.)*
(2 min.)	*News–Use all of the following:*	International, national, state, local.
(2 min.)	*Sport news*	International, national, state, local.
(1 min.)	*Weather report and forecast*	
(30 sec.)	*Commercial*	
(2 min 30 sec.) ..	*Feature program*	*(Do only one. You may use sound effects.)* Interview with celebrity or authority Children's story time Homemakers' Corner (recipes, household hints) History Highlights (You are there.) Farm Journal Special Entertainment (dramatization, musical talent)
(10 sec.)	*Sign off*	

(2) Your teacher may assign you a job, or may allow you and your group to confer and decide which role each will have. The student who does the station break should also do the sign off and have one more speaking part. Another student should serve as the group's director, tying the program together. If possible, the first commercial should use two or more voices and sound effects. Individual students may do the other portions of the format. The feature section may utilize any number of students.

(3) Write or adapt your own material. For the news and sportscast you may obtain used material from your local radio station or you may revise newspaper accounts. Each announcer will be responsible for their own material and sound effects.

(4) Write or type your entire script, double spaced, on the activity sheet to this chapter. This must be handed to your teacher for approval at least three days before you give your show. Your script will be returned so you may use

it as a script during rehearsal and performance.

(5) Time your portion to fit the exact time limits! Cut or add as necessary.

(6) Rehearse with a tape recorder if possible. Play back the tape to see what improvements you must make. Have a friend listen and offer helpful suggestions.

(7) When individual portions are ready, rehearse the whole show in class with music and sound effects. Work toward smooth transitions. Incorporate all the microphone techniques discussed in the chapter.

HOW TO PRESENT

If possible, your group should broadcast in front of a live microphone in one room while the rest of the class serves as audience to the loudspeaker in another room. If this is not feasible, the group may privately tape their show and replay it to the class. Or the cast may perform in the classroom behind a screen or curtain that hides them from the audience.

Your teacher will rate your rehearsal behavior and performance skill according to the chart distributed to you. Read it to see how you will be evaluated.

ADDITIONAL ACTIVITIES

(1) If your school has a video camera, create a three-minute television demonstration program in which you use at least two visual aids. Incorporate the camera techniques listed in this chapter. As you present your one-person show in extemporaneous style, you will be videotaped. You and your teacher will observe the rerun at a later time, discussing effective aspects as well as areas for improvement. The following are suggestions for demonstration: making a stencil, tying knots, cutting a dress pattern, kneading bread, tying flies.

(2) Divide into groups of six and prepare a ten-minute radio or television news broadcast from actual events. One student should serve as general announcer, signing on and off and adding any necessary human interest "fill" at the end. Different students should give international news, national news, state and local news, sports, and weather. Determine how many minutes each newscaster has. This complete show should run exactly ten minutes.

(3) Conduct a study group which explores in a discussion the specific ways that television has changed our lives, or its great influence on us, or standards to use as a guide in selecting television programs to see.

(4) Check with your local television station for presenting a special program on

its public service time. The purpose of the program should be to show to the community some of your school activities. For example, show a speech class with students giving speeches, present scenes from a play, hold a panel discussion, present a choral reading program, do a Readers Theatre show. Before using copyrighted material (plays, poems, short stories, novels) check clearance with the publisher.

(5) Prepare a four minute "as it happens" radio program in which you broadcast as though describing an actual event that is occurring. Prepare an introduction about the event, where it is, and names. Then use your imagination and knowledge to "ad-lib" the event as it proceeds. The following are suggestions: sports events, a fire, parade, fashion show, launching of a ship, a rocket blast off.

(6) Create an original one minute television commercial using at least two visual aids. Use your own ideas; do not copy something you have seen. Trim the commercial to the exact time. Memorize it and present it to the class in front of a video camera, using correct camera technique.

(7) Cast, rehearse, and broadcast a radio play. Find scripts in your local library or send for some of the following (see publishers' addresses in Appendix D):

Hamlett, Christina. *Famous Film Parodies.* Contemporary Drama Service.
Three comedy spoofs for radio show taping.

Robert, Donna. *Comedy Plays for Taping #2*. Contemporary Drama Service.
Six condensed comedy satires for broadcast. Each is a spoof of a familiar movie, book, or story.

Sheeley, Stuart. *Radio Plays for Taping #1.* Contemporary Drama Service.
Ten comedy scripts.

Sheeley, Stuart. *Radio Plays for Taping #3.* Contemporary Drama Service.
Ten satirical takeoffs on the various types of old-fashioned radio shows.

Sodaro, Craig. *No Chance of Error.* Contemporary Drama Service.
An award-winning radio script of a suspense thriller. Solid characterizations, sound effects and music.

(8) See the following Videos. (For addresses see appendix E)

News Production (Insight Media)
Shows the creation of an evening newscast for television.

Radio News (Insight Media)
An in-depth view of the production of radio news programs.

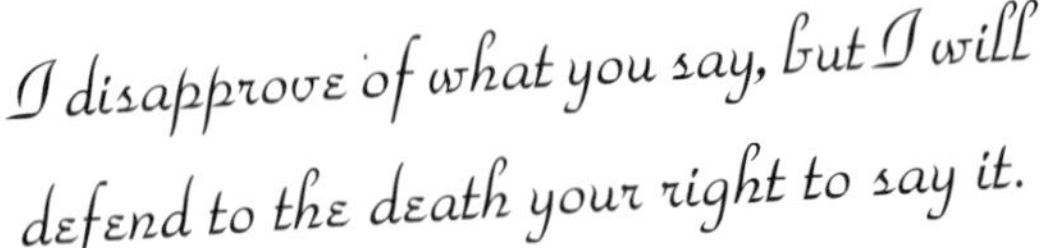

I disapprove of what you say, but I will defend to the death your right to say it.

—Voltaire in a letter to Madame du Deffand

"BONFIRE"

Because of war and disease in the Middle Ages, it was necessary to burn rather than bury the dead. These funeral pyres were called "Bonefires" (fires of bone). Later the term was used for fires that burned witches, and finally for any open air fire.

UNIT III

Oral Interpretation

Chapter 44

Share Your Find

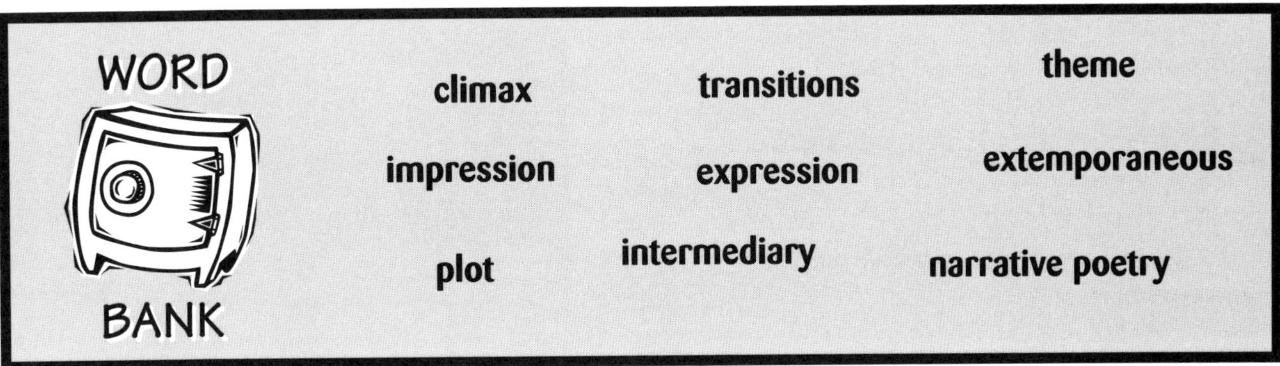

Watch for these valuable words wherever you see the word bank icon. 

BRAIN TEASERS

(1) What is the aim of an oral interpreter?
(2) Why is an oral interpreter called an intermediary?
(3) As an oral interpreter how can you be faithful to the author's purpose?
(4) What information should you seek in analyzing the material?
(5) Why can expression never exceed impression?
(6) What information should you include in your introduction?
(7) How should you hold your manuscript?

PLATFORM NOTES

"Listen to this," you eagerly say to friends as you focus on a newspaper or magazine article and read a short portion of it aloud. Whether or not they catch your enthusiasm depends primarily on the way that you read the material. If they yawn in your face, you've failed. If their eyes sparkle and they give an appropriate response, you've succeeded with your oral reading.

Reading aloud well is an art worth developing, for throughout your life you will be called upon to read orally. Business people read reports aloud to their boards; secretaries read minutes to the club; parents read stories to small children; teachers read material to pupils; news commentators report aloud to radio and television viewers; and professional interpreters read orally to audiences.

Everyone seems to read aloud, but not everyone reads aloud well. Many voices are dull and lifeless, stumbling through the selection with cold monotony. But you needn't bore people when you read orally. You can learn to be effective in the oral interpretation of all types of literature—prose, poetry, and drama—if you apply the fundamentals in this unit.

Just what is your role as an oral reader or oral interpreter? Since you do not read your own words but those of another, you serve as an intermediary between author and audience. Your purpose is to use your voice and body with such skill that your listeners imaginatively experience the ideas and feelings which inspired the author. For example, if the author has written about an exciting first airplane ride, when you are through reading the selection aloud, your audience must imaginatively sense an exhilaration over this experience. If the author describes defiance over accepting the death of a friend, you should lead your listeners also to feel this rebellion.

To achieve the goal of *sharing* experience in oral reading, you must pay careful attention to what the author intended, being as faithful as possible to his or her aim. This means that you must thoroughly understand what you are reading. Of course there is no absolute meaning in literature. As in all art, you interpret the material according to your own background. If your background is limited, you may find it difficult to share the author's experience. However, through adequate research, you, as a reader, should be able to arrive at an interpretation similar to that of others who have studied it.

ANALYSIS

If your mind and heart are to be as one with the author, you must carefully analyze the selection you have chosen to read orally. Study it until you can answer the following questions:

(1) *What do the unfamiliar words mean?* Look up in the dictionary each word you do not know. Learn both its meaning and its correct pronunciation. Don't try to "fake" through this. Perhaps the word you do not know will give you the key to understanding the whole selection.

(2) *Who is speaking?* Is it the author? Is it a main character? Is it a minor character? Is it an objective viewer rather than someone within the story?

(3) *Who is listening?* Is the selection geared to a general audience or is there a specific listener in mind? Is the person speaking to a son, an enemy, a sweetheart?

(4) *Where and when does the action take place?* Does it happen on the beach, in a forest, in a dungeon? Does it occur in the 1880's, today, in future times? Are there changes in time and place within the selection? If so, where do these transitions come?

(5) *What happens?* What action (plot) occurs? Do the main characters kidnap a small boy and then wait unsuccessfully for ransom? Do two young people from rival families meet, fall in love, and marry secretly?

(6) *When does the climax occur?* The climax is the most exciting part or the highest emotional peak in the selection. Identify the exact lines.

(7) *What is the basic mood in the selection?* Is it primarily one of sadness, bitterness, joyfulness, fright, sarcasm, playfulness, defiance, wistfulness? How is the mood achieved?

(8) *What is the theme?* Theme means the basic idea that the author is suggesting and that runs underneath the action.

(9) *How does this selection keep you in touch with life right now?* What in your background gives you a feeling or an appreciation for this literature?

Such careful study should give you a working command of the material. As you rehearse aloud it is from this *impression* that you will build meaningful *expression* in your voice and body.

INTRODUCTION

Before you read your selection to an audience, you need to give a brief (approximately 1 minute) extemporaneous introduction. Extemporaneous means that you carefully prepare what you are going to say, but that you do not memorize it word for word.

In the introduction, which should catch the audience's attention, include the following information—though not necessarily in the following order:

(1) Name of selection.
(2) Author of selection.
(3) Background information about the material that will help the audience to understand it better. Perhaps you'll have to define a keyword, or tell why the

author wrote the selection, or explain how it relates to life today. Do not, however, interpret or summarize the selection. Your reading should take care of those aspects.

Be sure your introduction sets the proper mood of the selection. It would be misleading to use humor in introducing heavy, serious material and vice versa.

ACTIVITY AND ITS PURPOSE

You are to prepare and read aloud a short 1 to 3 minute poem that tells a story. It should be a poem that you really like—one that you have a feeling for and that will be of interest to your classmates.

HOW TO PREPARE

(1) Select a 1 to 3 minute narrative poem (one that tells a story). It may be one completely new to you, or it may be an old friend. In either case pick one you are excited about. The following are suggestions:

"The Death Of The Hired Man," by Robert Frost
"Badger," by John Clark
"The Ghost That Jim Saw," by Bret Harte
"Mr. Flood's Party," by Edwin Arlington Robinson
"Lord Randall," a traditional ballad
"The Creation," by James Weldon Johnson
"Patterns," by Amy Lowell
"Bredon Hill," by A. E. Housman
"Annabel Lee," by Edgar Allan Poe
"Incident of the French Camp," by Robert Browning
"Casey At The Bat," by Ernest Thayer
"The Blind Men and The Elephant," by John Saxe
"Danny Deever," by Rudyard Kipling

(2) Silently read the poem completely through and respond to its story, mood, and style.

(3) Study the selection to answer the questions listed in the above analysis.

(4) Fill out the analysis form on the activity sheet to this chapter. Be sure to do this, since you will not be allowed to read without having the analysis completed.

(5) If possible, type the poem, double spaced, using sheets measuring 5 1/2" by 8 1/2" (half the regular typing size). Insert these in a small stiff notebook. This size and weight is easy for an oral interpreter to hold and provides a less distracting manuscript than when you use a large heavy book.

(6) Prepare a short introduction as discussed above.

(7) Rehearse aloud your introduction and poem. Stand up tall and give your introduction in a conversational style, talking directly to the audience. Pause and then read your poem. Hold your script in one hand, with the other lightly placed on the open book. This hand is then free for gesturing. Rehearse orally at least ten times. You should become so familiar with the selection that you can frequently lift your eyes from the page and establish eye contact with the audience. Hold your manuscript high enough for easy reading without having to bob your head up and down as you look from audience to book.

Put yourself wholeheartedly into what you are reading. Be alert and animated and let this interest show in your face, voice, and body.

HOW TO PRESENT

When you are called upon, hand the activity sheet to your teacher and walk quietly to the front with your manuscript. Pause, look at the audience, and then give your introduction. Communicate the attitude that you are prepared, that you are interested in what you are going to read, and that the audience will also find it interesting.

After your introduction, pause, open your notebook, and read your poem as you rehearsed it. Clearly pronounce the words and read slowly enough to be readily understood. Many beginners have the tendency to rush through their selection, leaving the audience puzzled and panting.

When you are through, quietly close your book. Don't destroy the mood you have created by startling the audience with a big bang of the manuscript.

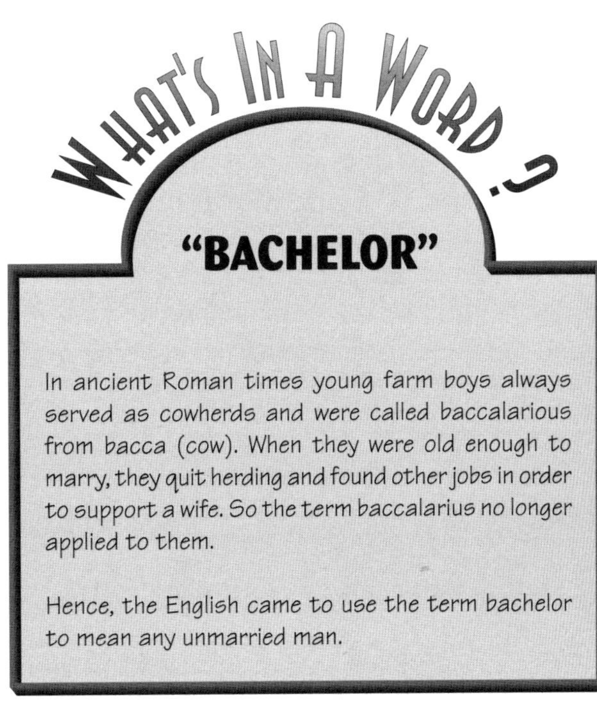

WHAT'S IN A WORD?
"BACHELOR"
In ancient Roman times young farm boys always served as cowherds and were called baccalarious from bacca (cow). When they were old enough to marry, they quit herding and found other jobs in order to support a wife. So the term baccalarius no longer applied to them.
Hence, the English came to use the term bachelor to mean any unmarried man.

Chapter 45

A Telling Time

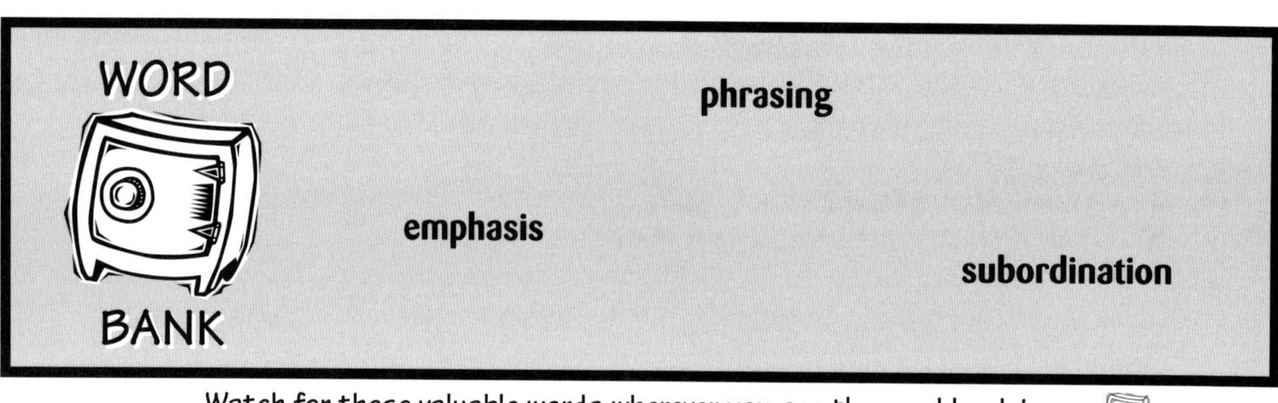

Watch for these valuable words wherever you see the word bank icon. 

BRAIN TEASERS

(1) As an oral interpreter how can you achieve effective phrasing?
(2) What determines the length of pauses in oral reading?
(3) What ideas need emphasis in oral reading?
(4) How can you achieve emphasis?
(5) What words need subordination?
(6) How can you achieve subordination?
(7) In marking a script what symbols should you use?

PLATFORM NOTES

Here's a puzzle for you. Try to read the following so that it makes sense:

"Woman without her man would be miserable."

If you were alert, you found at least two meanings: "Woman! *Without* her, *man* would be miserable." "*Woman* without her *man*, would be *miserable*." The interpretation that you would use in an oral reading of this line, of course, would depend upon the focus of the material.

The above puzzle illustrates two techniques the oral reader must develop in order to get the meaning of the selection across to the audience. These two techniques are phrasing and emphasis.

Phrasing means that you group together all of the words necessary to convey an idea. Instead of pausing after each single word in a sentence such as "the—little—brown—dog—ate—the—big—bone," place these words in groups to create meaningful thought units. In this example you would probably need two phrases: "The little brown dog—ate the big bone." It should be evident that in order to phrase the words according to their proper relationships, you must understand the meaning of the sentence. You cannot always rely on written punctuation to help you with the meaning. Sometimes punctuation is misleading, particularly in poetry. Therefore, let the *meaning* indicate phrasing.

Between thought units, you use a *pause* to provide oral punctuation. Every phrase, then, is separated with a pause. The length of the pause is determined by the importance of the transition. When ideas are closely related or easily grasped, your pauses between phrases should be short. In the following examples, short pauses are signified by one diagonal line.

"I went home / and painted the garage."

When there is a major shift in thought, place, or time, your pauses must be longer and may be signified by two diagonal lines:

"It had been a wonderful evening. // Later that week / Jack rode back to the same place."

Also, when an idea has great importance, you must give the audience time to let it "sink in," by making your pause duration longer:

"They had fifteen children, // four girls and eleven boys."

When the approaching idea is of great interest, a long pause *before* it creates necessary suspense to gain audience attention:

"I was alone late at night / in the house. / I heard something pound at the window. // Cautiously I approached / and there staring at me was a // horse!"

In the examples below, notice how different word groupings create different meanings:

(1) What do you think? I'll let you hear my new CD!
What! Do you think I'll let you hear my new CD?

(2) The principal says the teacher is correct.
"The principal," says the teacher, "is correct."

(3) A man called, while you were out to eat with your wife.
A man called, while you were out, to eat with your wife.

(4) "You hope," he said, "too much."
You hope he said too much.

In poetry, word groupings are particularly catchy, for the end of the poetic line does not necessarily mean the end of an idea. Sometimes the thought is carried over into the next line. You must group the words accordingly. See if you can meaningfully phrase the words in the following poem:

I saw a peacock with a fiery tail
I saw a blazing comet pour down hail
I saw a cloud all wrapt with ivy round
I saw a lofty oak creep on the ground
I saw a beetle swallow up a whale
I saw a foaming sea brimful of ale
I saw a pewter cup sixteen feet deep
I saw a well full of men's tears that weep
I saw wet eyes in flames of living fire
I saw a house as high as the moon and higher
I saw the glorious sun at deep midnight
I saw the man who saw this wondrous sight . . .[1]

If you discovered that the thought continues through the end of the line and ends in the middle, you phrased the above poem according to meaning.

Besides phrasing to communicate meaning, you need to learn what words to emphasize and what words to subordinate. *Emphasis* means that you stress a word by giving it more force, more time, and a pitch change. You should emphasize words that have the following functions:

(1) Words that carry the main idea in the sentence.
"His team had *lost*."

(2) Words that carry new ideas in the paragraph.
"There were suitcases stacked all over the room
when the delivery man brought the *trunk*."

(3) Words that are compared or contrasted.
"*Mary*, not *Jane*, has the mumps."

[1] From *Reading Aloud*, 3d ed. by Wayland Maxfield Parrigh, 1953, The Ronald Press Co. Reprinted by permission of John Wiley and Sons, Inc.

Grammatically speaking, words generally emphasized are nouns, verbs, and sometimes adjectives and adverbs.

Words that are of less importance in the sentence, words that are repeated, and words such as "a," "and," "the," are usually *subordinated* by using a lower tone and saying them faster.

Remember, you must not emphasize every word. To do so makes the selection boring. As an oral interpreter it is your job to determine the important aspects, to stress them, and to "throw away" the others.

In the beginning you may find it helpful to mark your script after you have carefully analyzed your selection. In script marking, use a soft leaded pencil that can be erased easily. Script marking includes diagonal lines / for pauses, underlining for words that need emphasis, and parentheses ( ) for passages to be subordinated. In the margin of your script you may also write words that remind you of the mood and climax you wish to achieve. The following shows a portion of a marked script:

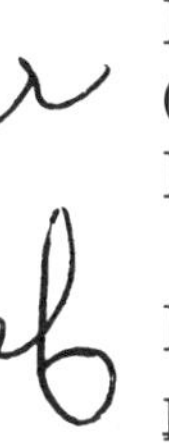

He hurried out to the mail box. / There was a stack of letters. (Quickly he sorted through them) and / there it was. / / Postmark / Rome. //

He felt suddenly a great weight lift from his shoulders. / The postmark said Rome.

ACTIVITY AND ITS PURPOSE

To help you develop skill in phrasing and emphasis you are to read orally a short cutting, possibly four or five paragraphs, from a story you like. Your purpose is to read the cutting so well that you tantalize your listeners into wanting to read the entire story themselves. Like the previews on television, you "tease a tale" for your audience.

HOW TO PREPARE

(1) Select a short story you like and that you feel the class would enjoy. It may be one that is full of suspense, humor, or description. The following are suggestions:

Top Man, by James Ullman
Miss Brill, by Katherine Mansfield
The Sniper, by Liam O'Flaherty
Learning One's Place, by Muga Gicaru
Why I Live At The P.O., by Eudora Welty
The Most Dangerous Game, by Richard Connell

The Deadly Detour At Zacatecas, by Jose Graham and Lew Baker
By The Waters of Babylon, by Stephen Vincent Benét

(2) Read the complete selection in order to determine what small portion you will prepare for oral reading.

(3) Choose a short excerpt (1 to 3 minutes) that occurs before the climax. It should consist of just a few paragraphs that are extremely interesting. Do not include the ending, as your purpose is to stimulate the audience to read the story for themselves at home in order to find out what happened. Type or neatly write the cutting and insert it in a small 5 1/2" X 8 1/2" notebook.

(4) Analyze your cutting as described in the previous chapter. Also go over your script carefully for phrasing and emphasis. If necessary, mark the script as discussed above.

(5) Fill out the activity sheet to this chapter. Be sure to do this, since you will not be allowed to read orally until the analysis is completed.

(6) Prepare a short (1 minute) introduction in which you announce the title and author and briefly summarize the past events that lead up to the portion you will read.

(7) Rehearse aloud both your introduction and your reading. Do this at least ten times or until you feel in command of the material. If possible, tape your reading and then listen to and criticize the replay.

HOW TO PRESENT

Hand your activity sheet to your teacher before going to the front to read. Pause and then give your introduction. Pause again before starting your selection. Read to communicate the meaning and the excitement in the material. Use vitality in your manner. If you show interest in your story, so will your listener.

Look at your audience frequently to help them remember that you are the intermediary, sharing with them the words of the author, suggesting the happening with your voice and body. After finishing, pause, quietly close your book, and return with poise to your desk.

ADDITIONAL ACTIVITIES

(1) Choose a short 3 to 4 minute folk tale, analyze and prepare it for reading aloud to the class. Examples: Paul Bunyan stories, Pecos Bill tales, "Little Red Riding Hood," "Goldilocks and the Three Bears."

(2) Choose a short (1 to 3 minute) humorous piece—perhaps something from the *Reader's Digest*—and prepare it to read orally to the class.

Chapter 46

Stir Up A Mood

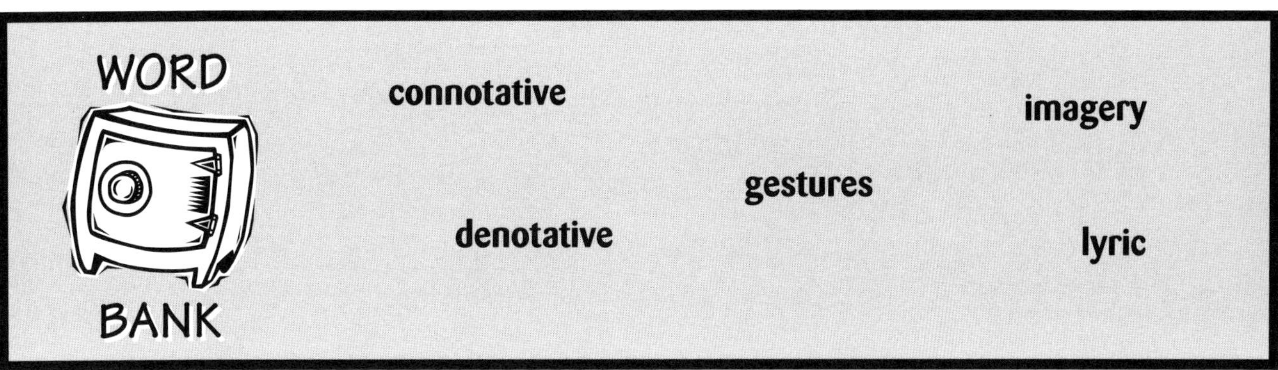

Watch for these valuable words wherever you see the word bank icon. 

BRAIN TEASERS

(1) Why must the oral reader be aware of the denotative and connotative value of words?
(2) As you read an image, what should occur in your mind and that of your listener?
(3) Why should you suggest rather than do the movement described in your reading?
(4) To what senses can images appeal?

PLATFORM NOTES

Writers paint pictures with words, pictures that can convey situations and moods as surely as do those drawn with oil, chalk, or watercolor. In fact, words used by gifted writers are magical. Choice of just the right word creates in the reader or listener a wealth of associations that widen experience.

That the author sometimes spends hours searching for an exact word to mirror his or her feelings and thoughts should indicate to you a need for respecting the terms employed.

Words have two types of meanings, the denotative and the connotative. *Denotative* is the literal, matter-of-fact meaning—one that you would find in a dictionary. For example, the denotative meaning of the word *chair* is "a seat with four legs and a back to be used by one person." *Connotative* means suggested or emotional meanings—words that convey whole stories and emotions within themselves. For example, suppose you are reading about a chair that has chipped paint, a wobbly leg, and a frayed cushion. If this is called an "old" chair, the word *old* suggests age with an aura of dilapidation about it. "Old" is something you disdain and discard. Its value is gone; throw it away. But suppose you are reading about that same chair, and the adjective *antique* is used. This word connotes value, rarity, something to be prized.

Do you see how meaning and feeling can be regulated through precise word choice? What are the different connotations attached to these words?

(1) old maid — spinster — career woman
(2) cheap — inexpensive
(3) house — home
(4) cooked dead steer — hot roast beef
(5) stench — smell — odor — fragrance
(6) cop — policeman — law enforcement officer
(7) face — countenance
(8) mommy — mom — mother

As an oral reader you need to study the words and learn to savor the richly endowed ones.

Authors also choose words according to how they sound. A repetition of the long vowel sounds can suggest sadness and slowness. For example:

"Alone, alone, all, all alone
Alone in a wide wide sea."
—Coleridge

"Roll on, thou deep and dark blue ocean, roll!"
— Byron

Repetition of short vowel sounds and consonants such as *l*, *t*, and *k* can suggest speed and gaiety.

"Lickity split the little ladies leapt."

In addition, words create *imagery*. Images are those word pictures that stimulate our various senses of sight, sound, taste, touch, smell, temperature, and movement. When you read an image, you should be able not only to sense it within yourself but also to call forth a response within your listener. For example, if you read about a "little yellow canary perched demurely on the twig, head back, tweeting its morning notes," in your imagination you must see that yellow bird, respond to its balancing act, and conjure in your mind the song. In that way your voice and body will respond truthfully to the images as you attempt to stimulate a similar picture, feeling, and sound in your listener's mind.

Learn to identify and be receptive to images. The following examples of imagery may be helpful:

Sight and temperature:

"All in a hot and copper sky,
The bloody Sun, at noon,
Right up above the mast did stand,
No bigger than the moon."

—Coleridge,
"The Rime of the Ancient Mariner"

Sound:

"I heard the distant rumbling of wagons over bridges . . . the baying of dogs, and sometimes again the lowing of some disconsolate cow in a distant barnyard."

—Thoreau, *Walden*

Smell, taste, and sound:

"Oranges and lemons,
Say the bells of St. Clement's,

Pancakes and fritters,
Say the bells of St. Peter's,

Two sticks and an apple,
Say the bells of White Chapel."

—English folk song

Movement:

"One by one they got up and stood, and went a-weaving around the ring so gentle and wavy and graceful, the men looking ever so tall and airy and straight, with their heads bobbing and skimming along."

—Mark Twain
Adventures of Huckleberry Finn

Touch:

"The rough male kiss of blankets."

—Rupert Brooke
"The Great Lover"

As you react to the imagery, you may use gestures. Just keep in mind that as an oral reader you are to *suggest* rather than actually represent or demonstrate. If you read that "He gave the telegram to Sheila," only a slight hand movement is necessary on your part. If you read that "She jumped three times," you will not actually jump, but with voice and body you will merely suggest the movement and feeling. Facial expression and muscle tension come into play here as you give the audience a hint that allows them to "fill in" with their minds. In all oral interpretation your aim is economic use of voice and body, unobtrusively assisting the imagination of the audience.

ACTIVITY AND ITS PURPOSE

You are to "stir up a mood" in your listener by reading aloud a 1 to 3 minute lyric poem that creates a definite emotion. Delve into the poem until you feel the emotion. Then use your suggestive vocal and physical powers to stimulate the audience into feeling the mood.

HOW TO PREPARE

(1) Choose a 1 to 3 minute poem that creates an emotion rather than tells a story. Most lyric poems fit this category. Following are suggestions:

"High Flight," by John G. Magee, Jr.
"Stars," by Sara Teasdale
"Telephone Conversation," by Wole Soyinka
"Chicago," by Carl Sandburg
"The Listeners," by Walter de la Mare
"Sea Fever," by John Masefield
"The Lake Isle of Innisfree," by W. B. Yates
"The World Is Too Much With Us," by William Wordsworth
"Spring Night," by Sara Teasdale
"On My Short-Sidedness," by Prem Chaya
"Lament," by Edna St. Vincent Millay
"The Man He Killed," by Thomas Hardy
"Stopping By Woods On A Snowy Evening," by Robert Frost
"The Negro Speaks Of Rivers," by Langston Hughes
"God's World," by Edna St. Vincent Millay
"Nancy Hanks," by Rosemary Benét
"The Four Little Foxes," by Lew Sarett
"The House On The Hill," by Edwin Arlington Robinson
"Forgive My Guilt," by Robert Tristram

(2) Read the whole poem for its total impression and for its effect on you.

(3) Type or copy the poem on $5^{1}/_{2}$" x $8^{1}/_{2}$" notebook paper so you can mark your script.

(4) Analyze your poem as described in Chapter 44. Pay particular attention to

word connotations, repetition of sounds, and imagery. Determine the poem's mood. Is it sad, solemn, reverent, bitter, defiant, calm, whimsical? If necessary mark your script for pauses, emphasis, climax, and moods.

(5) Fill out the activity sheet for this chapter. You will not be allowed to read to the class until this analysis is complete.

(6) Prepare a one minute introduction in which you announce the title and author and give any information necessary to help your listeners understand the poem.

(7) Rehearse aloud your introduction and poem. Pay close attention to the material. Taste the whole flavor of every line, savoring the emotive words. Truly create the images in your imagination. Let yourself sincerely be caught up in the emotion you communicate. You can have the whole audience hanging on every word, if you effectively stimulate their minds. Rehearse ten or more times until you feel that you are powerfully recreating the material and are establishing adequate eye contact.

HOW TO PRESENT

When you are called upon, hand both your activity sheet and the evaluation chart to your teacher. Take your manuscript and go to the front of the room. Pause before presenting your introduction. Remember to keep the introduction conversational and to look directly at the audience while giving it. Then pause and read the poem as rehearsed. Put your heart into it! Use an expressive voice and a responsive body that will suggest the feeling. Make the mood come alive. After the last word, pause, quietly close your book, and walk back to your desk.

ADDITIONAL ACTIVITIES

(1) Write an original poem from eight to fifteen lines in which you describe your first remembered experience as a small child. Your poem does not have to rhyme, but it must vividly create how you felt, what you heard and saw. Read aloud this poem to the class.

(2) Choose a theme such as death, happiness, the good old days, a child's world, Indian territory, pioneers of the west. Choose short selections around this theme and arrange them into an 8 to 10 minute program. Link selections together with brief extemporaneous comments. Present the program to the class.

(3) Choose two short mood poems and arrange special colored lighting to be beamed on you as you read them. Select colors and lighting positions to help sustain the mood of the material.

Chapter 47

Altogether In Parts

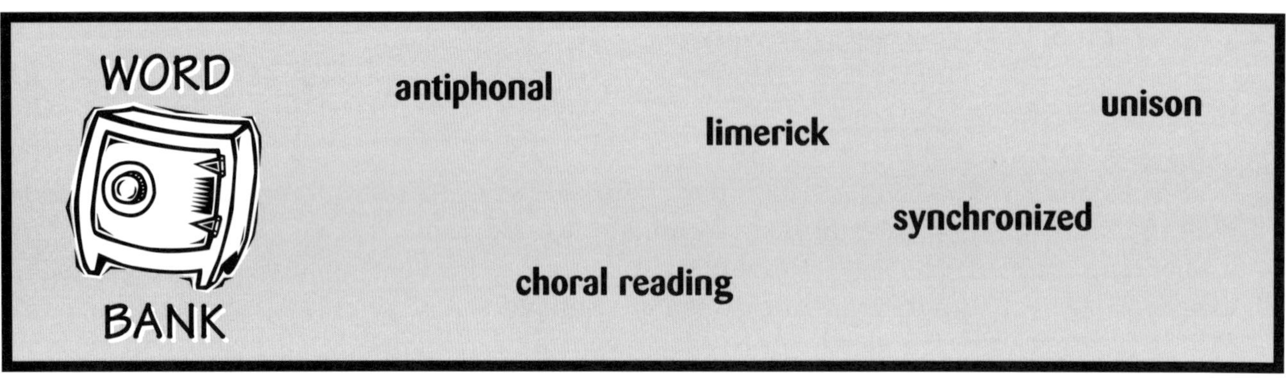

Watch for these valuable words wherever you see the word bank icon. 

BRAIN TEASERS

(1) What are the values of choral reading?
(2) How are voices grouped for choral reading?
(3) What four script patterns can you use in choral reading?
(4) Why must the group analyze each selection it is to read?
(5) What techniques must you master in rehearsal?
(6) How should you handle gesturing?

PLATFORM NOTES

Singing together in choral groups is fun and a widespread activity in most schools. But another type of group endeavor that is equally enjoyable, though less frequently found, is *choral reading* where groups under the direction of a leader read aloud rather than sing together.

Choral reading can help you in numerous ways. If you suffer from stage fright when you perform by yourself, your identification with a group where you are only a part of the whole can increase your self confidence. Participation in choral reading helps you improve your speech as you work for clear articulation, controlled breathing, and full use of vocal flexibility. You also learn group cooperation as you control your speaking voice to blend or harmonize with others for the desired group effect. Besides all of these values, choral reading is fun, igniting in you a love for literature and furthering your skills in oral interpretation.

GROUP DIVISION

Almost any size group can be used in choral reading, although an easily workable number is usually between fifteen and twenty. Participants are categorized according to the pitch and tone color or resonance of their speaking—not singing—voice. Usually each person reads a short selection, and the whole class decides in what category his or her voice belongs. A basic three part division includes:

(1) light voices for happy, whimsical, or delicate parts.

(2) medium voices for general material, description, and narration.

(3) dark voices for robust, tragic, and heavy material.

Some groups use a four part division that consists of:

(1) girls with light or medium voices.
(2) boys with light or medium voices.
(3) girls with dark voices.
(4) boys with dark voices.

The division chosen will depend on the nature of your whole group and on the material you are to read. Try to have about the same number of voices in each category.

PLACEMENT

As in a singing choir, participants in choral reading should be placed closely together—either standing or sitting. Your director should try the group in different positions until an acceptable one is found. Semicircles, regular and inverted "V" and "T" shapes are often used, as shown below:

Use of risers, platforms, or steps will help the performers to see the director easily and allow the audience to see each face. Also consider using different groupings for various selections, rehearsing the changes so that these are accomplished quickly and quietly.

MATERIAL

Poetry is used almost exclusively in choral reading. In fact, another name for choral reading is verse speaking choir. Any selection you read should have vivid imagery, contrasting moods, and intense climaxes. In particular choose poems with definite ear appeal, strong rhythm, and interesting melody. Material can be patterned in the following four different ways, depending on the selection and the group.

(1) *Choral refrain.* Single readers carry the main part with the whole group joining in the chorus or refrain. Examples of selections that lend themselves to this pattern are

> *Barbara Allen* — Traditional ballad
> *Blow Blow Thou Winter Wind,* by Shakespeare
> *Stolen Child,* by W. B. Yeats
> *The House That Jack Built* — Mother Goose Rhyme
> *Gunga Din,* by Rudyard Kipling
> (Marching songs and sea chants are good sources, too.)

Sample script:

Johnny At The Fair
—Folk Song

All Oh dear, what can the matter be!
Dear, dear, what can the matter be!
Oh, dear, what can the matter be
Johnny's so long at the fair!

Solo girl He promised to bring me a farthing to please me,
And then for a kiss, oh he said he would tease me.
He promised to buy me a bunch of blue ribbons
To tie up my bonnie brown hair.

All Oh dear, what can the matter be!
Dear, dear, what can the matter be!
Oh, dear, what can the matter be
Johnny's so long at the fair!

Solo girl He promised to buy me a basket of posies,
A garland of lilies, a garland of roses,
A little straw hat to set off the blue ribbons
That tie up my bonnie brown hair.

All Oh dear, what can the matter be!
Dear, dear, what can the matter be!
Oh, dear, what can the matter be
Johnny's so long at the fair!

Winter
—William Shakespeare

Voice 1 When icicles hang by the wall,
Voice 2 And Dick the shepherd blows his nail,
Voice 3 And Tom bears logs into the hall,
Voice 4 And milk comes frozen home in pail,
Voice 5 When blood is nipp'd, and ways be foul,
All Then nightly sings the staring owl,
To-who,
Tu-whit, to-who, a merry note,
All girls While greasy Joan doth keel the pot.

Voice 6 When all aloud the wind doth blow,
Voice 7 And coughing drowns the parson's saw,
Voice 8 And birds sit brooding in the snow,
Voice 9 And Martha's nose looks red and raw;
Voice 10 When roasted crabs hiss in the bowl,
All Then nightly sings the staring owl,
To-who,
Tu-whit, to-who, a merry note,
All While greasy Joan doth keel the pot.

(2) *Two part work.* Two groups alternate the reading of stanzas or lines. Selections for this antiphonal approach need a balancing of ideas, questions and answers, or appeals and responses. Examples:

Where Have All The Young Men Gone, — Traditional song
Lord Randall — Traditional ballad
The Camel's Hump, by Rudyard Kipling
Psalms 8, 24, 66, 90, 100, 121, 122 in the Bible
Molly Malone, (Cockles and Mussels song) — Folk song
Lament For The Alamo, by Arthur Guiterman

Sample script:

Whistle, Whistle, Old Wife
—Traditional Ballad

Boys Whistle, whistle, old wife and you will get a hen.
Girls "I wouldn't whistle," said the wife, "if you could give me ten."

Boys Whistle, whistle, old wife and you will get a coo.
Girls "I wouldn't whistle," said the wife," if you could give me two."

Boys Whistle, whistle, old wife and you will get a gown.
Girls "I wouldn't whistle," said the wife, "for the best one in town."

Boys Whistle, whistle, old wife and you will get a man.
Girls "Wheeple, whopple," said the wife, "I'll whistle if I can!"

The Beatitudes
—Matthew 5:3-11

Girls Blessed are the poor in spirit:
Boys for theirs is the kingdom of heaven.

Girls Blessed are they that mourn:
Boys for they shall be comforted.

Girls Blessed are the meek:
Boys for they shall inherit the earth.

Girls Blessed are they which do hunger and thirst after righteousness:
Boys for they shall be filled.

Girls Blessed are the merciful:
Boys for they shall obtain mercy.

Girls Blessed are the pure in heart:
Boys for they shall see God.

Girls Blessed are the peacemakers:
Boys for they shall be called the children of God.

Girls Blessed are they which are persecuted for righteousness' sake:
Boys for theirs is the kingdom of heaven.

All Blessed are ye, when men shall revile you, and persecute you,
and shall say all manner of evil against you falsely,
for my sake.

(3) *Unison.* The whole group reads together with precision and a singleness of purpose. Unison reading is difficult although rewarding. Examples:

Dreams, by Langston Hughes
Sea Fever, by John Masefield
Tarantella, by Hilaire Belloc
Deep Wet Moss, by Lew Sarett
Meeting At Night, by Robert Browning
Cradle Song, by Alfred Lord Tennyson
A Word, by Emily Dickinson
(Various Japanese haiku work well also)

(4) *Multiple part work*. This is a combination of all of the other patterns. It uses single speakers, small groups of three or four, large groups, and unison reading. Examples of selections:

They Closed Her Eyes, by Gustaro Adolfo Becquer
In Just Spring, by e. e. cummings
The Bells, by Edgar Allan Poe
I Hear America Singing, by Walt Whitman
Serves You Right, Beggar, by Hsu Chih-Mo
Jazz Fantasia, by Carl Sandburg
Danny Deever, by Rudyard Kipling
The Four Little Foxes, by Lew Sarett
We Real Cool, by Gwendolyn Brooks
The Squaw Dance, by Lew Sarett
Jabberwocky, by Lewis Carroll
Paul Revere's Ride, by Henry Wadsworth Longfellow
Barter, by Sara Teasdale
The Highwayman, by Alfred Noyes

Sample script:

The Brook
—Tennyson

Light voices	I slip,
Medium voices	I slide,
Dark voices	I gloom,
Medium voices	I glance,
	Among my skimming swallows;
Light voices	I make the netted sunbeam dance
	Against my sandy shallows
Dark voices	I murmur under moon and stars
	In brambly wildernesses;
Medium voices	I linger by my shingly bars,
Light voices	I loiter round by cresses;
Medium voices	And out again I curve and flow
	To join the brimming river,
Dark voices	For men may come
Dark & Medium voices	and men may go,
All	But I go on forever.

Salutation of the Dawn

—Kalidasa c1200 B.C.

One medium voice	Listen to the exhortation of the Dawn.
All	Look to this day!
Dark voices	For it is life, the very life of life.
Medium voices	In its brief course lie all the verities and realities of your existence:
Light voices	The bliss of growth,
Dark voices	The glory of action,
Medium voices	The splendor of beauty,
Light voices	For yesterday is but a dream
Light & Medium voices	and tomorrow is only a vision:
Dark voices	But today well lived makes every yesterday a dream of happiness,
Medium voices	And every tomorrow a vision of hope.
All	Look well, therefore, to this day.
Light voices	Such is the Salutation of the Dawn!

REHEARSAL PROCEDURE

Choral reading takes disciplined rehearsal. Under the direction of a leader who works much like a conductor of an orchestra, you and your group must become completely cohesive, thinking and responding as a unit.

Together you should analyze the meaning of each selection the group will read. Determine the words that need emphasis, determine where the pauses come, determine where the group must breathe as a unit.

Decide on the mood and volume of the piece indicated by the sounds of the words and the rhythm and music of the lines. Try to catch the natural swing of the poem. Does it dance, plod, march, swing, gallop? At first you may need to beat or tap out the rhythm until everyone feels it. Then in future rehearsals strive to incorporate this rhythmic flow without succumbing to the undesirable mechanical "singsong" effect that entraps many small children who "speak pieces" with a strict regularity of beat and a stop at the end of each line. As you analyze, mark your script. Underline for emphasis and mark a diagonal line / for pauses.

Throughout rehearsals your leader will "conduct" from the back of the room, getting you used to projecting into the audience. As the group becomes highly synchronized, your director will give you only a few signals, for you must learn to perform without a leader.

Many groups memorize their material, allowing constant eye contact between them and the audience. Groups who use scripts should keep them small and inconspicuous, without trying to hide them. Even with scripts you must be highly familiar with the material so you can establish sustained eye contact.

Much rehearsal is necessary to perfect a group to work as one. You must constantly be alert to come in on cue. Even when it is not your turn to read you must listen to and be aware of the other parts. Never desert the group with inattention between your speeches.

You must work on breath control so the group can sustain long passages without jerky gasps. Clear, precise articulation of words is needed if the audience is to understand.

Keep your voice and manner animated, spirited. Even in quiet, solemn pieces you must look alive, with good posture and muscle tone. Your group may wish to use some gestures. This is acceptable as long as the gestures show genuine inner response to an object or idea. Avoid using gestures to describe objects. Twenty pairs of arms stretching out with moving fingers to describe the pitter-patter of raindrops is a distracting and distasteful spectacle. You may rehearse gestures for precision of timing. Work always toward sincere expression, avoiding all artificiality.

ACTIVITY AND ITS PURPOSE

You are to participate in an 8 to 12 minute choral reading program directed by your teacher. Together with classmates you will rehearse the program until it is polished. It will take two or three weeks in class. Then give it as a performance for an assembly, a community program, or for a small invited audience.

HOW TO PREPARE

(1) Bring to class and read a short four line Mother Goose rhyme. The class and your teacher will listen and decide which division your voice best fits—light, medium, or dark.

(2) If the class is large, your teacher may divide it into two choral groups. He or she will direct each group for half of the class time. When the teacher is not directing your group, an appointed student will conduct. If possible, each group will rehearse in separate rooms. If not, use separate corners of one room.

(3) For warmups your teacher may have the groups say in unison limericks such as:

> There was a young man from Gorum,
> Who had some new pants and he wore 'em.
> He stooped and he laughed
> And he felt a big draft,
> And then he knew where he had tore 'em.
>
> —B. L. Averett

> As a beauty I am not a star,
> There are others more handsome by far.
> But my face I don't mind it
> For I am behind it
> It's the people in front get the jar!
>
> —Woodrow Wilson

Or he will lead the group in "rounds" that you will speak rather than sing. "Are You Sleeping (Frère Jacque)," "Row, Row, Row Your Boat," and "Three Blind Mice" work well.

(4) Your teacher will hand out scripts that have been compiled, or each class member may bring a selection and read it aloud for program consideration. In compiling a program work toward continuity of idea, contrast of moods, and material in good taste. If time is short, your teacher will divide the selections into parts. Otherwise, the class may do it as a whole. In using prepared scripts, you may need to change the suggested voice divisions to fit your group.

(5) As a class, analyze each selection as to meaning, mood, theme, climax, melody. The analysis process described in Chapter 44 is a workable guide. Determine phrasing, words to emphasize, passages to subordinate, images to enliven, rhythms to suggest, climax to achieve, and moods and volume to be sustained or contrasted. Mark your scripts after a decision has been reached. You will probably need several class sessions to complete this analysis.

(6) Your teacher will give you group positions to maintain in rehearsal and performance.

(7) With your director, repeatedly rehearse every selection. Each time you go over a poem, your director should announce your specific goal for that time and you should work toward it. When your teacher is busy with another group, cooperate with your student directors in a mature, professional manner, getting the job done.

(8) Determine some unification and suggestion of costume for the group. If the selections are generally optimistic and happy, pastel colors in boys' shirts

and girls' dresses may be used. For more somber material, white shirts and blouses, dark trousers and skirts are appropriate. Some groups dress in choir robes, some in formals for the girls and suits for the boys. Others perform in regular school clothing.

(9) Run a dress rehearsal and practice walking on and off the stage as well as going through the selections. If possible, use stage lighting.

HOW TO PRESENT

You will perform without your director who will start you by giving an unobtrusive signal from the auditorium. Perform as you rehearsed, striving towards genuine voice and body response to the material. Be sure you maintain good posture and muscle tone as you perform. Do your share well, for the group's success is dependent upon *each* member.

Your teacher will rate you according to the criteria listed on the activity sheet to this chapter. Your teacher will hand it out to you so that you will know what is expected of you.

ADDITIONAL ACTIVITIES

(1) Divide the class into groups with each group arranging, rehearsing, and presenting a thematic choral reading program. Each selection used should contribute to the theme. The following are theme suggestions: American heritage, modern life, sweet spring, terrible tales, woman's world, school days.

(2) As a group, use a holiday for a theme, and create, rehearse, and present a choral reading program around that event. Each student should contribute at least one poem that he or she has marked into parts.

(3) Invite other area schools to a choral speaking festival. Each school should perform a short program. Guest evaluators will discuss, though not rate, each contribution in a spirit of learning and having fun together—not on a competitive basis.

(4) Work up choral reading selections obtained from companies that specialize in contest material. For addresses see Appendix D.

Chapter 48

Theatre Of The Mind*

WORD BANK

"Close up" scene

prose

"point"

offstage focus

Readers Theatre

Watch for these valuable words wherever you see the word bank icon. 

BRAIN TEASERS

(1) What is meant by Readers Theatre?
(2) How does Readers Theatre differ from regular theatre?
(3) What two principles should guide your Readers Theatre program?
(4) What are the "five C's" in choosing program material?
(5) What must you do in adapting prose, drama, and poetry for Readers Theatre?
(6) What ways may you suggest exits and entrances?
(7) What are the three kinds of eye focus?
(8) How are readers positioned in Readers Theatre?
(9) What principle should guide your use of theatrical effects?

PLATFORM NOTES

Reader one: A lone reader sits in a satin pool of light.
Reader two: He looks into the imagination of his audience.
Both readers: He believes,
Reader two: And velvet images touch the silent air of the theatre.

* Term used by Leslie Coger in *Readers Theatre Handbook*, 3rd e. Scott, Foresman, 1982.

Reader one: A second reader appears,

Reader two: Then a third,

Reader one: And a fourth.

Both readers: All together they create

Reader one: the setting,

Reader two: touch life to sleeping characters,

Reader one: And the words on the page before them

Both readers: live again

Reader one: as when the author had first sought to create.

Reader two: Readers Theatre,

Reader one: Readers Theatre —

Reader two: a group activity in which the best of literature is communicated from the manuscript to an audience

Both readers: through the oral interpretation approach of vocal and physical suggestion —

Reader two: says one.

Reader one: But more

Reader two: more

Reader one: much more

Both readers: is Readers Theater!

Reader two: For the audience,

Reader one: For the reader,

Both readers: It is a shared experience!*

The above script defines Readers Theatre in Readers Theatre style. This art form is becoming widely popular around the nation. Schools, universities, community groups, and professional companies increasingly offer Readers Theatre performances — sometimes called Interpreters Theatre, Platform Theatre, Group Reading, Staged Reading, Chamber Theatre, Concert Theatre, or Concert Reading. Whatever the name, the results are exciting for both participant and spectator.

Readers Theatre is characterized by two or more oral readers who interpret a characterized script with the aim of stimulating the audience to experience imaginatively that literature. It is truly a theatre of the mind where the realities of the scene and characters are created and exist primarily in the imagination of the interpreter and the audience.

CHARACTERISTICS

Readers Theatre differs from regular theatre in several aspects. (1) Emphasis is on what the audience *hears* rather than on what it sees. It is the literature that has prime importance. Oral interpreters only suggest — subtly — the meaning, emotion, and action. Elaboration and completion occur in the minds of the audience. (2) Readers Theatre demands intensive audience participation. Since movement and action are limited and since scenery and costumes are only suggested, the audience must visualize these items for themselves, within their own imagination. (3) One reader may take many parts, rather than having but a single role as is characteristic in regular theatre. Boys may

* Written by Tim Bryson and used with his permission.

read women's roles and vice versa. A reader may be a character in one scene and a narrator in another scene, as long as the shift is clear to the audience and does not detract from the material. (4) Scripts are almost universally used or in evidence during the performance to remind the audience that the reader is an intermediary helping them to become actively involved in literature.

It should be evident then, that Readers Theatre is a discipline in itself, having its own art form. It should never be considered as a make-do or a substitute for regular theatre. Readers Theatre is a special creativity that emphasizes the written word!

It has many values. It allows the audience to enjoy many literary experiences. It allows the participants to continue to develop vocal and physical skills and to stimulate powers of creativity. Working in Readers Theatre helps you to understand all kinds of literature, since its material is all encompassing — short stories, plays, novels, poetry, radio scripts, letters, diaries, essays, newspaper columns, and magazine articles can effectively be used.

You can do Readers Theatre anywhere. Since you do not need scenery or costumes, you can take your program to an audience, instead of having the audience come to you. Readers Theatre can tour to classrooms, be presented in churches, be given in band shells, auction rings, city parks, or in a corner of the library. Medium sized rooms are better than large auditoriums, as Readers Theatre thrives in an "intimate" atmosphere.

There are only two basic principles of Readers Theatre that you must keep in mind as you develop a program.

(1) *Explore different ways to present the literature.* Remember, there is no one way to do Readers Theatre. Experiment to discover what is effective for a particular script with a particular cast. Use guidelines, yes, but let the material shape the method. Much of the fun comes from developing an original approach. Your only limitation is your imagination!

(2) *Stimulate the audience intellectually and emotionally.* Breathe life into the literature so that your listener's eyes sparkle and his or her imagination "fills in" the gaps. You accomplish this, of course, by understanding the material yourself and getting excited about it. All of the techniques of oral interpretation as described in Chapters 44-46 must also be used in Readers Theatre.

MATERIAL

Since very few prepared scripts are available for Readers Theatre, most groups adapt or compile their own material. Shows run from twenty minutes to no longer than an hour and thirty minutes, so material must be cut to fit the length. If you perform your program outside of regular class activity, be sure you obtain permission from the publisher to use the literature and that you pay any required royalty. To avoid royalty payment due the author is dishonest and is a punishable crime.

While all *kinds* of literature may be used, not all literature is effective in Readers Theatre. Make certain that the material you are considering meets the following criteria of "Five C's":

(1) *Compelling content* stirs your imagination and arrests your attention.

(2) *Conflict* includes both inner action (where the characters have a dynamic struggle within themselves) and outer action (where there is physical fighting from hair pulling to gang wars) .

(3) *Complete characters* seem alive and have many sides to their personalities.

(4) *Creative language* consists of word combinations that please the ear and rich images that stir the senses (for imagery see Chapter 46).

(5) *Cohesiveness* creates a sense of unity and wholeness, even within a cutting, preserving a series of events that lead up to a climax.

When you adapt *prose* (such as a short story or a novel) for Readers Theatre, determine what portions you must leave in to retain the story line and to give a few strong "close up" (well developed) scenes that show characters in particular events. The scenes that you cut out can be bridged by using a narrator. Try to keep speeches and narrations short, but if a long description is necessary, arouse interest by using a variety of voices to read the passages. Balance dramatic scenes with quiet ones; balance description with dialogue.

In adapting *drama*, it is sometimes necessary to combine characters and speeches or to cut out characters, as you focus on the main plot. You need not retain original scene or act structure. Some scenes you may leave out entirely, letting a narrator fill in the events. The narrator may also describe the setting, introduce the characters, and translate the visual elements into audible ones. However, it is wise to avoid using plays that rely heavily on visual elements (such as ghosts that perform tricks with objects) or that have many physical fights occurring on stage. Instead, pick a show where climactic action takes place off stage and can be reported in a speech, or pick shows that feature clever or intriguing dialogue.

In using *poetry*, "characterize" the lines—as you do in choral reading— with a variety of voices that enhance the material.

Keep in mind that a compiled script may include prose, poetry, and drama or any combination thereof. Below is a list of selections that some Readers Theatre groups have successfully adapted, cut, and used. Keep your mind alert for other possibilities as you read. Consider material in your literature books.

Novels
Animal Farm by George Orwell (also in a play script)
Alice in Wonderland by Lewis Carroll

Dandelion Wine by Ray Bradbury
Little World of Don Camillo by Guareschi Giovanni
Wait 'Til You Have Children by Erma Bombeck
Cheaper by the Dozen by Frank and Ernestine Gilbreth (also in a play script)

Short Stories
The Reluctant Dragon by Kenneth Graham (also in a play script)
A Christmas Carol by Charles Dickens (also in a play script)
The Devil and Daniel Webster by Stephen Vincent Benét (also in a play script)
A Christmas Memory by Truman Capote
The Lottery by Shirley Jackson
Thurber's Fables by James Thurber
The Split Cherry Tree by Jesse Stuart (also in a play script)
I'm a Fool by Sherwood Anderson (also in a play script)

Radio Scripts
My Client Curley by Norman Corwin
A Child is Born by Stephen Vincent Benét
The Lonesome Train by Millard Lampbell
The Fall of the City by Archibald MacLeish
Grandpa and the Statue by Arthur Miller

Also see the list of radio scripts, Additional Projects, Chapter 43.

One-Act Plays
Happy Journey to Trenton and Camden by Thornton Wilder
Everyman—anonymous
The Boor Anton Chekhov
The Long Christmas Dinner by Thornton Wilder
Rising of the Moon by Lady Gregory
Riders to the Sea by John M. Synge
Ugly Duckling by A. A. Milne
A Tenth of an Inch Makes the Difference by Rolf Forsberg

Three-Act Plays
A Raisin in the Sun by Lorraine Hansberry
I Remember Mama by John Van Druten
A Shayna Maidel by Barbara Lebow
Antigone by Sophocles
Our Town by Thornton Wilder

SCRIPTS

Scripts should be typewritten, double spaced and placed in stiff notebooks, uniform in size and color. If your group plans to use reading stands, $8^1/_2$" x 11" notebooks work well. If your group plans to use movement and grouping without stands, a smaller more easily held size such as $5^{1}/_{2}$" x $8^{1}/_{2}$" is better. If you hold scripts, handle them as you would in individual oral interpretation. Hold the script in one hand and put the other hand on top of the open book. From that position you can easily gesture with the free hand. If there are to be several pages between your scenes, paper clip these pages together to prevent needless and noisy page turning. Mark your entrances in large writing in the margin and make a warning sign several speeches before your entrance.

PLACEMENT

Readers Theatre may be staged in any number of ways. Some material lends itself to a static arrangement where interpreters read behind music stands placed in a small group, semicircle, diagonal or straight line. Other material demands readers to group into various areas, changing positions and locations as the scene changes or as character relationships alter. Motivated, fluid, and yet unobtrusive movement and blocking are needed in these instances. Economy and restraint should be your guidelines.

To provide for varied groupings and to allow the audience to see every face, your cast may wish to use wooden stools of various heights, or boxes, steps, platforms, ramps, a ladder. The following drawings indicate different placement arrangements:

ENTRANCES AND EXITS

There are numerous ways to handle entrances and exits. You may stand during your scene and sit for an exit. Sometimes you may walk on and off the playing area. You may turn your back for an exit and face the audience as you enter. You may lower your head or "freeze" in position to denote you have left. A spotlight beam turned on and off can begin and end a scene. Occasionally music and sound effects provide transitions.

Time your entrances carefully and move to suggest your character. When you "exit," be particular about your physical appearance "offstage." Since you are not out of sight, you must sit perfectly still to prevent a distraction from the scene in progress. Sit with a straight back. If you sit on a stool, place one foot on the floor and one on the stool's rung. These positions take discipline, so you should rehearse them from the beginning.

EYE FOCUS

Three kinds of eye focus are used in Readers Theatre. *Offstage* focus requires that readers look out into the middle of the auditorium with the lines of their vision intersecting slightly above the heads of the audience. As the reader describes actions and events, he or she should see them occurring at this focal point. Such a focus is desirable because it places the scene in the audience.

It is also a strong focus because the body is in full view and the voice can be projected straight out. Take care, though, that all readers place their scene in the same location and at the same eye level out front. At first it will seem strange to look and speak into the auditorium instead of turning and talking directly to the character beside you, but rehearsal will make you skilled at offstage focus. To assist you in early rehearsals, your director may have part of the cast work opposite you on the other side of the room so you can become accustomed to talking out front.

Onstage focus means that the readers look at each other, as actors do on stage. This technique can sometimes be employed when the cast is small and dialogue predominates the script. But use it sparingly, as it tends to take the scene out of the audience's mind and to place it on-stage.

A *combination* of off and on stage focus can be employed if the material is heightened by it and if the change does not call attention to itself. A narrator, however, should always use offstage focus and talk to and look directly at the audience as scenes are introduced.

THEATRICAL EFFECTS

Costumes, sound effects, special stage lighting, and scenery are not needed. Only a bare suggestion should ever be used. You can usually wear your own clothes, stimulating imagination with small costume details. For example, boys can roll up long sleeves and leave collars open for informal material. Vests or bow ties can indicate "bygone" days. White dresses with colored shoes and matching script covers may provide the costume suggestion for a feminine program. In one school's show the only hints of costume were hats that readers wore to indicate different periods in history. Often ensemble costume—when the whole cast dresses alike—is effective. The cast can all wear the same color, or they can all wear similar apparel. Keep jewelry at a minimum, as it is distracting. Also, all readers should specially style their hair so that it remains out of the eyes and off the face, thus allowing the audience to see the most expressive part of a reader's body.

The group can create its own sound—howling as the wind, chirping as birds, clapping as a group. Bells, tambourines, guitars, xylophones, harmonicas can all be used on stage by readers or by a special person if these sounds enhance the material or provide needed transitions.

Area spots that light the readers and not the audience are effective to have, but the only lighting necessary is general illumination of the interpreters.

Scenery is not needed. Most groups play in front of draped curtains or a lighted wall. Painted screens or scenery fragments may be used if they complement the literature.

If you decide to use any of these theatrical effects, remember, don't decrease audience pleasure by presenting too many tangibles that limit the use of your listener's imagination. Always keep this form a genuine "Theatre of the Mind."

REHEARSALS

The director prepares material and plans rehearsals as for a regular play (see Chapter 23). Major emphasis, of course, is on the aural. The director will constantly guide the readers to understand the material, to create believable characters, to "point" or emphasize important words, breathe life into the images, build to a climax, and provide for transitions.

ACTIVITY AND ITS PURPOSE

You and your classmates will participate in a 20 to 30 minute Readers Theatre program. Depending on class size, either one or two programs will be worked up. Plan to present the show to a special audience. This assignment will take about three or four weeks of class time.

HOW TO PREPARE

(1) Your teacher will provide you with scripts of a program.

(2) After tryouts the parts will be cast with every student having at least one role. Some readers may also assist with any lighting, staging, or publicity needed.

(3) Your teacher will conduct rehearsals, starting with analysis of the script, and then going to blocking, developing, and polishing sessions. If the class is doing two programs, your director will work with each group half of the class time while an appointed student will assist the other group.

(4) Have at least two dress rehearsals with a complete uninterrupted run-through. Use whatever lighting, costumes, and sound that you need. The whole cast should rehearse entering and leaving in full view of the audience.

HOW TO PRESENT

Before the program begins, an assigned and rehearsed student may explain to the audience the concept of Readers Theatre, or your teacher may wish to do this. Another way to introduce Readers Theatre to an audience who has never before seen this form is to start with a brief explanatory script written by a student, similar to the one that began this chapter.

If possible hand out programs at the door. Do the show as rehearsed, striving toward communication of the literature to the listener. You will be rated according to the criteria on the activity sheet your teacher will give you. Review it to see what will be expected of you.

ADDITIONAL ACTIVITIES

(1) Cut and adapt a short story from your literature book, a one-act play, or a radio script for Readers Theatre. Rehearse and present it in class.

(2) As a group choose a current problem or event that is in the news and find material to create a fifteen minute program around this event. Use newspaper stories and magazine articles as well as other types of literature. Connect the material with a narrative. The following are topic suggestions: illiteracy, crime, endangered species, child abuse.

(3) Create a 1 to 2 minute, two voice, "non-lit" script in which you use any nonliterary type of material such as magazine advertisements, street signs, graffiti, chemistry terms, recipes, or gardening pamphlets. Rehearse your script with a partner. Then practice his or her script. Attempt to put in as much motivated physical movement as possible. Present the programs to the class.

(4) Compile a Readers Theatre script comprised of poetry around a theme.

(5) Create a multimedia Readers Theatre program in which you use at least one medium other than the literature. For example, you may use projected slides behind the readers, an interpretative dancer who responds to the word, or music or sound effects incorporated in the script.

(6) Compile a children's program using Readers Theatre. Troupe it to the various grade schools, or present it on Saturday at the children's section of your town's library. Script example: "Animal Antics," a twenty minute program, could be comprised of "Thidwick the Big Hearted Moose" by Dr. Seuss and the animal poems "The New Baby Calf" by Edith Newling, "Puppy and I" by A. A. Milne, "The Mysterious Cat" by Vachel Lindsay, and "The House That Jack Built." Also, stories such as "Charlotte's Web" lend themselves well to Readers Theatre.

(7) Do a Readers Theatre presentation of a play in your literature book and

present it to the English classes in your school.

(8) Convert a radio play to Readers Theatre. For a selection of plays see Chapter 43, Additional Project number 7.

(9) Rehearse and present a Readers Theatre show from existing available scripts. See titles and sources in Appendixes I and J of Fran Tanner's *Readers Theatre Fundamentals*, 2nd ed. Clark Publishing, a division of Perfection Learning® Corporation, 1996. The list includes both professional and educational productions. There are also two Readers Theatre scripts with blocking suggestions and a photo essay in Appendix K of that book. Those titles are *My Client Curley* by Norman Corwin and *Justice Comes to Sharp Stick* by Dean Pettinger.

Chapter 49

Bending Ears

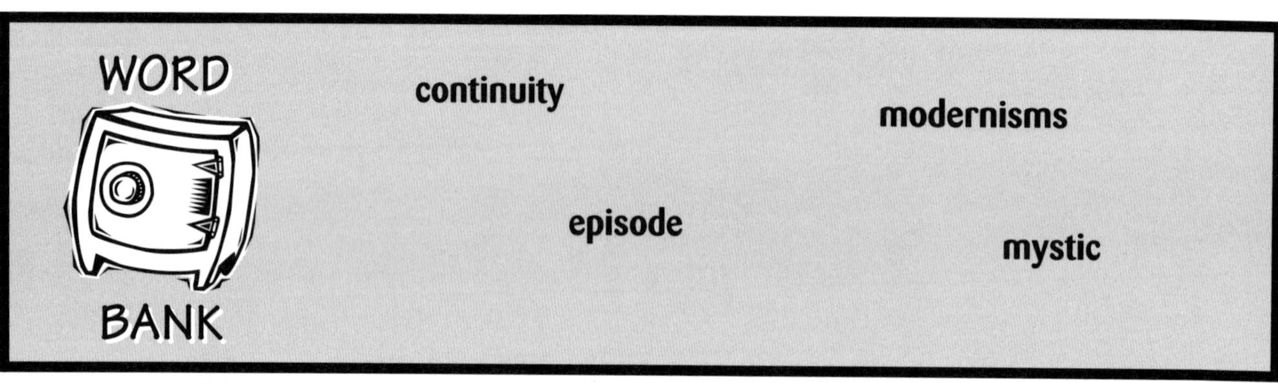

Watch for these valuable words wherever you see the word bank icon. 

BRAIN TEASERS

(1) How is the storyteller similar to the oral reader?
(2) How does the storyteller differ from the oral reader?
(3) What stories adapt well to retelling?
(4) Of what importance is vocabulary to the storyteller?
(5) What are the six ingredients necessary for effective story telling?

PLATFORM NOTES

Everyone likes to hear a story. Perhaps, as a child, you remember the magic of the words "once upon a time" that began a strange tale of witches and goblins, talking animals and fairy godmothers. But you needn't be a child to hear stories. You find a form of story telling everywhere—at the dinner table where the guest "bends" your ear as he or she relates an adventure, on a street corner where you tell a friend about a "funny thing that happened the other day," around a campfire where the glowing coals add believability to the tall tales, at a party where low lights set the mood for a spooky ghost story that tingles the spine.

Everyone is a storyteller, repeating adventures as soon as speech is learned. The difference among storytellers is in quality. Some people are so poor at telling stories that their listeners are bored. Others recreate tales so vividly that the listeners find the experience is exciting and stimulating.

It is this invigorating quality that makes story telling so rewarding. If you become effective at relating a tale, your audience, whether adults or children, will give you such a wholehearted response that you will have an exhilarating sensation of delight and accomplishment.

Also, story telling is a communication exercise that helps you develop vocal skills. And its informality assists you in controlling stage fright.

As you retell stories, your purpose is similar to that of the oral reader. You must imaginatively suggest the characters, moods, and situations so that they appear real in the minds of the audience. You differ from the oral reader, however, in that you commit to memory the outline of the written story and retell it in your own words.

Six ingredients provide the secret for retelling a story well.

(1) *Select a story that lends itself to retelling.* Your best choice is one with a tightly constructed plot that has an interesting beginning, a logical development of episodes, spirited conflict, and a definite climax that quickly brings out a brief, satisfying conclusion. To be memorable, your story should have a sense of earnestness about it, showing genuine emotions and respect for character.

(2) *Visualize every scene and character.* In your mind really "see" what is occurring until you feel you have actually lived that experience.

(3) *Use simple, powerful language consistent with the story's style.* Don't try to memorize the author's words. Use your own, except for a few phrases that you may need to retain, in order to create the "flavor" of the tale. Keep "once upon a time," for it adds a mystic touch. Keep a word like *ogre* which has a fuller meaning than if you changed it to "mean little person." Avoid such modernisms as "o.k.," or "cool," or "wow," for they destroy the far-off illusion. Because words are your major tools for building the story, use a rich vocabulary that arouses the imagination.

(4) *Breathe life into the tale.* Give it sparkle and spontaneity. Be enthused in your voice, in your body, in your eyes.

(5) *Create suspense through a varied rate.* It is boring to hear anything—music, speeches, lines of a play, stories—at the same dreary pace. Variety is necessary

to communicate thought and feeling. Some moments will be leisurely because the material calls for it, but as things begin to happen in the story, your tempo should increase and build toward the exciting climax.

(6) *Use a flexible voice.* Vocally distinguish between the various people, giants, animals, and monsters that appear frequently in stories. Use a wide range of pitch, quality, force, and rate (see Chapter 31). When you turn from character to narrator, keep your voice pleasant and medium pitched for easy listening. Always articulate clearly so the audience will catch every word.

ACTIVITY AND ITS PURPOSE

Here is your opportunity to learn the storyteller's skill. You are to relate in your words a 3 to 4 minute folk tale in such a colorful, delightful way that it stirs your listeners' imaginations and makes them "live" every word you utter.

If possible, your teacher will arrange to have a small group of children from the first, second, or third grades visit your class and become your audience, while your classmates sit on the sidelines, listening and observing. You will be rated according to the evaluation chart on the back of the activity sheet, so read the criteria for performance when your teacher gives it to you.

HOW TO PREPARE

(1) Choose a folk tale that merits telling and meets criteria described in the chapter. Be sure to select a story you sincerely like and one that will be appropriate for your audience, occasion, and time limits. The following are suggestions of good stories to tell. Consult the children's section of the library for copies.

Available in collections:

Bremen Town Musicians
Clever Manka
Elves and the Shoemaker
The Emperor's New Clothes
Epaminondas
The Lad Who Went to the North Wind
Master of All Masters
Rumpelstiltskin
The Ugly Duckling
What the Good Man Does Is Always Right
The Wonderful Pear Tree

Available in separate books:

Ask Mr. Bear by Marjorie Flack
The Five Chinese Brothers by Claire Bishop
Journey Cake, Ho! by Ruth Sawyer
Millions of Cats by Wanda Gag
Paddy's Christmas by Helen Monsell
Stone Soup by Marcia Brown
Story of Ferdinand by Munroe Leaf
Tale of Peter Rabbit by Beatrix Potter

(2) You may need to shorten the story if it is too long. Cut out unnecessary information while retaining the basic story line. Sometimes you can cut a whole scene and bridge it with a sentence transition. Sometimes you have to leave out minor characters. Be wise about your cutting. Make your story meet the time limits!

(3) Read the story silently for enjoyment. *Why* do you like the story? Be specific. Keep your answers in mind and incorporate those qualities into your telling.

(4) Read the story slowly once or twice to visualize each scene. In your mind see what happens. See what each character looks like. Are they brown bears or black bears? Do they wear clothes or are they content in their fur? Visualize the setting until you know exactly the rooms Goldilocks visits. Sense the emotions of the situation: Goldilocks' tiredness, or the Bears' surprise. Accomplish this visualization by using your powers of imagination, concentration, and sense recall.

(5) Close your book and silently think through the story. Usually the action divides itself into *(a) the problem*, *(b) the complication*, and *(c) the solution*. Attempt to see each of these developments as the plot unfolds.

(6) Outline the story's sequence of events on the activity sheet to this chapter.

(7) Now read the story aloud and listen to particular phrases of narration and dialogue that add color. Retain these to use with your own simple, direct language. Remember, do not memorize the words of the story. Fit your *own* words to the events.

Note: There are a few stories written by stylists such as Kipling and Dr. Seuss that must be memorized for retelling because the exact words are necessary for enjoyment. Most stories, however, do not fit this category.

(8) Rehearse the story aloud seven or eight times. Make it come alive. Use your voice to suggest character. For example, Papa Bear will be gruffer than Mama Bear who in turn will sound different from Baby Bear. Keep both vocal and bodily response simple and informal, yet full of vitality.

Polish the beginning of the tale, setting the mood and starting the plot immediately. Polish the end until it rings with enthusiasm and conviction. Lift out difficult sections of dialogue or emotional scenes and work on them until they come easily.

Build to the climax with a varied tempo. Learn to use the pause, a necessary tool to gain suspense or to allow an important fact to sink in before continuing to the next event. When you coordinate story and tempo, you will find the tale comes alive and smacks of fun!

(9) Overlearn your story. Think it through whenever you have a moment doing dishes at home or riding on the bus to school. If you live with it for a while it will be yours forever.

HOW TO PRESENT

Before telling your story, hand the activity sheet to your instructor. Gather the children around you in a circle where you can see each other. You may wish to sit on the floor with them, or you may pull a chair into the circle. Or stand up and seat the children on chairs. Your classmates will sit quietly and attentively around the room.

Introduce the tale to the children by relating it to something within their experience. Explain any unfamiliar words, to prevent the children from breaking into the story's continuity with questions. Maintain a relaxed, happy, informal atmosphere.

As you tell the story, be aware of your audience. If they don't seem to understand what you are saying, you may need to rephrase. Also, you may wish to let the children participate in the story with certain necessary sounds that contribute to the tale, such as the blowing of the North Wind, or the noise the Bremen Town musicians make.

ADDITIONAL ACTIVITIES

(1) Invite to your class an outstanding story teller from the community. You can learn much from hearing a gifted person present a tale. Listen and see if you can identify the factors that make the telling effective. Later, discuss these qualities in class.

(2) Plan a series of story telling hours for small children on Saturday or after school at the local library. Each class member should tell a story during the series.

the APPENDIXES

Appendix A

Warmups

BODY WARMUPS

Basic Routine for Relaxation

(a)

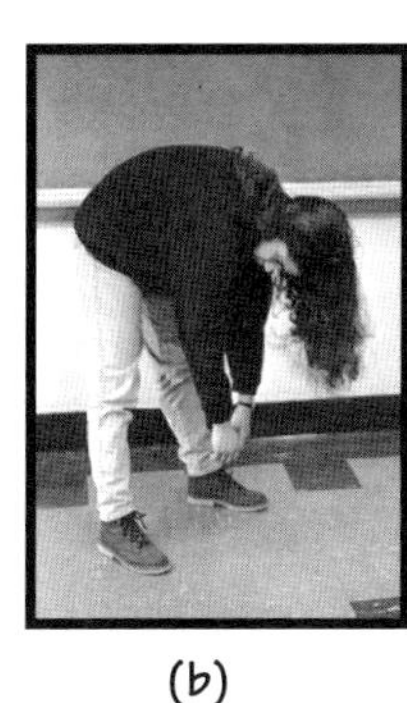
(b)

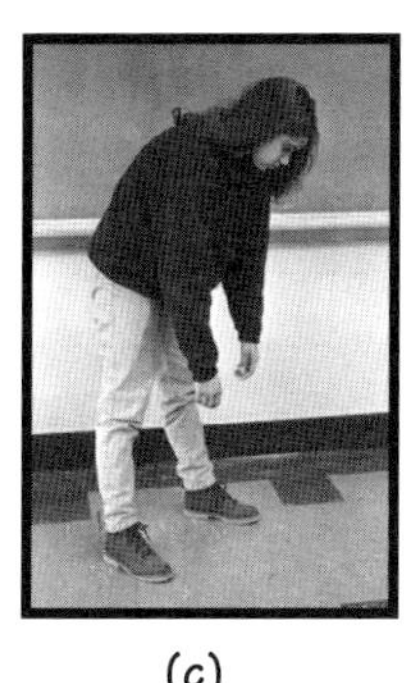
(c)

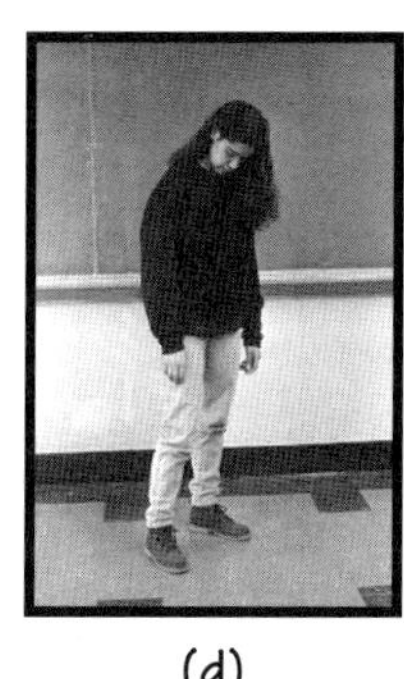
(d)

Rag Doll

(a) With feet apart in a comfortable balance, stretch up tall. (b) Then bend over by collapsing quickly and loosely from the waist with your relaxed arms and hands dangling to the floor. (c-d) Keep your arms, hands, and neck completely relaxed like a rag doll, slowly raise up, keeping relaxed. Repeat several times.

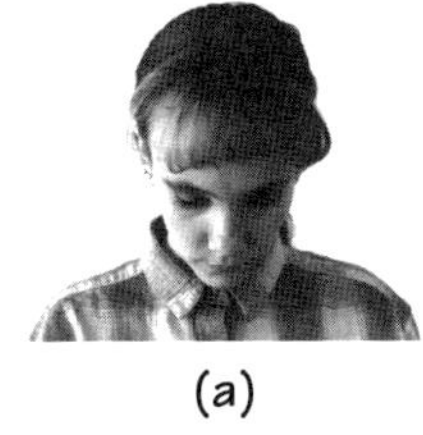
(a)

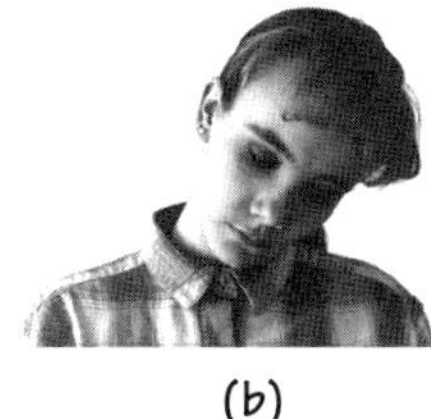
(b)

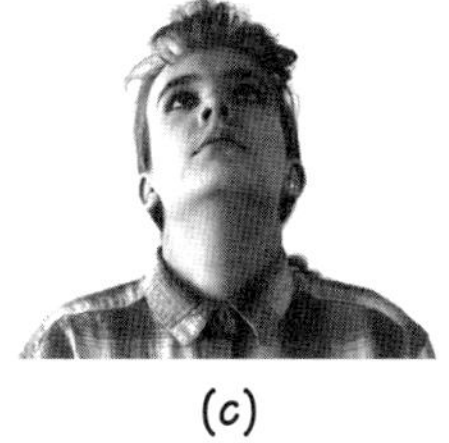
(c)

(d)

Head Roll

Immediately after the rag doll exercise while your neck is still relaxed with chin close to the chest (a) slowly rotate your head to the left (b), back (c), right (d), and down in front again (a). Reverse the rotation and repeat. Be sure to keep your neck relaxed, letting your head roll like a dead weight in a socket.

Arm Swing
Immediately after the head roll while arms are still relaxed, swing them in large circles one at a time.

Yawn
If you have done exercises one and two correctly, your face and neck muscles and vocal chords are completely relaxed. Slowly yawn, sounding an "ahhhhh" on exhalation from the yawn. The sound you make is a relaxed sound. You should strive for this relaxation and open quality of the throat whenever you speak.

Basic Routine for Stimulation

Rhythm Hop
With weight on left foot, hop once on it and at the same time point your right foot in front, extending your arms in front with hands clapping. Now simultaneously hop once on your left foot while placing the right foot way out to the right side and extending arms, shoulder height out to the sides. Again hop once on left foot and simultaneously bring right foot back to touch left foot, putting arms down at your sides. Change weight to right foot and repeat routine with left foot. Do rapidly and smoothly ten to twenty times. Eventually chant short nursery rhymes in rhythm while doing the exercise. (Try "Mary Had a Little Lamb.")

VOICE WARMUPS

Basic Routine for the Articulators

Smile Pucker
Smile with exaggeration, letting your teeth show and drawing the lips as tightly as possible, making your cheek muscles hurt. Say "eeeeeee." Then with exaggeration, pucker or protrude your lips, saying "ooooooooo." Repeat ten times each in quick succession (eeeeeee-ooooooooo). Repeat with "mee-moo," "tee-too," "bee-boo," "gee-goo," "lee-loo."

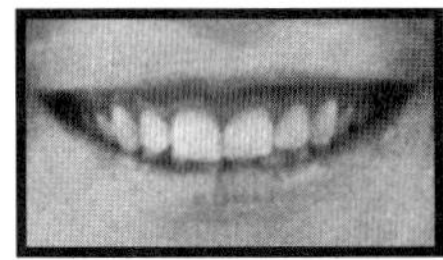

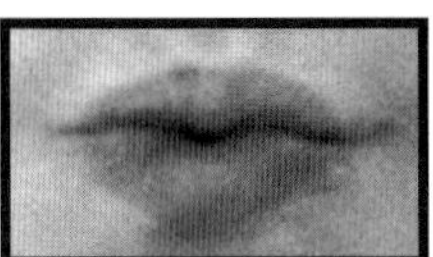

Open Wide
Open your mouth as wide as possible. Say "ahhhhh." Now close your mouth, saying "ooooo." Repeat "ahhhhh-ooooo" several times, being sure to open your mouth extremely wide.

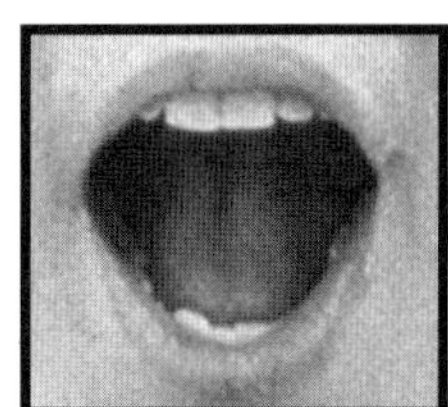

Tongue Tip
Stretch your tongue, trying to touch the tip of your nose. With your tongue, now try to touch your chin. Only one in 1000 can actually do either, so don't worry if you can't succeed. The stretch is the important thing. Repeat several times.

Tongue Stretch
Curl up your tongue and touch the soft palate at the back of your throat. Now push out your right cheek and then your left cheek as far as you can with your tongue. Repeat.

Tongue Twisters
Say quickly with exaggerated tongue, lip, and jaw movements several of the following tongue twisters. See Chapter 31 for others.

(a) Much whirling water makes the mill wheel work well.
(b) Odd birds always gobble green almonds in the autumn.
(c) She makes a proper cup of coffee in a copper coffee pot.
(d) Round and round the rugged rocks the ragged rascal ran.
(e) Shave a cedar shingle thin.
(f) Double bubble gum bubbles double.
(g) How much wood could a woodchuck chuck if a woodchuck could chuck wood?
(h) Sinful Caesar sipped his snifter, seized his knees and sneezed.

Appendix B

Housekeeping

CLASS CHAIRPERSON

To make speech presentations more efficient in class, your teacher may appoint a chairperson for the days when speeches are given. Each class member should rotate in this capacity, thus obtaining valuable experience. Your teacher will evaluate you on carrying out this task.

The following information in outline form will assist you in performing your chairperson's duties when introducing speakers.

I. The class chairperson has an important role:
   A. Arouse curiosity about the speaker and his or her subject.
   B. Help the audience respect the speaker.
   C. Introduce to the audience each speaker and the speech title.
II. The class chairperson should make adequate preparations.
   A. Look your best when presiding.
   B. Come quickly to class, being as early as possible.
   C. Arrange the speakers according to a varied program.
      1. You will get a 3" x 5" note card from each speaker stating name and speech title.
      2. You may arrange speakers in any order.
      3. You may give speakers their order preference, if they have one.
   D. Sit behind the chairperson's table.
      1. It should be in front of the audience but to the side.
      2. It should allow the speaker ample space in the center front of the room.
III. The class chairperson should address the audience properly.
   A. Rise calmly and walk to the center of the speaker's area.
   B. Pause until the audience grows quiet.
   C. Speak directly to the group.

1. Speak loudly enough to be heard.
2. Speak clearly.
    a. Open your mouth widely.
    b. Do not slur words or the speaker's name.
3. Speak with sincere enthusiasm.

D. Give brief, appropriate remarks.
    1. Only arouse interest.
    2. Do not give the speaker's speech.

E. After brief introductory remarks, present the speaker by saying something like this:
    1. "I am happy to present (name) who will speak to us on (title)."
    2. As you indicate the speaker by turning to him or her say "(name)."

F. After finishing the introduction, pause and return to your table.

G. When the speaker is finished, do not rise to introduce the next speaker until your instructor so indicates.

CLASS TIMEKEEPER

Strict adherence to time limits is necessary if a speech class is to run smoothly. It is unfair for one student to usurp the speech time of another or to lazily prepare a short speech when others have had to give long ones. True, mental discipline is required to stay within time limits. It is hard work to acquire information for a seven minute talk, or to condense a topic to two minutes. But part of the speaker's training is to learn to accept the responsibility of staying within the time limits. The speaker owes it to his audience, and in turn, the audience will be pleased. Have you ever had to sit through a speech announced to be thirty minutes long but that lasted for an hour? You were undoubtedly annoyed. Even if the speaker was excellent, such infringement on the time is discourteous. Let us repeat: It is the speaker's responsibility to find out what the time limit is and then abide by it! In class this makes for efficiency, and each speech assignment will be completed quickly before interest level has diminished.

Upon assigning a speech, your teacher will indicate a minimum and a maximum time such as two to three minutes. This means you must speak for at least two minutes but no longer than three. This gives you a one minute leeway. Sometimes your teacher may offer a two minute margin such as a speech lasting two to four or three to five minutes.

When you rehearse your speech at home, do so with a clock. Then you will definitely know your timing. The place to add or cut material is at home during rehearsal, not frantically in class. Of course there will be times during your class presentation when you will suddenly have to add or delete information because under pressure your speaking rate has been faster than that practiced, or you have given spur-of-the-moment material to adapt to your audience. When this occurs and you realize your timing is off, you must think quickly on your feet to adjust to the clock.

To make timing easier, you will have a timekeeper. Your teacher may appoint one or two students to alternate being timekeeper throughout the semester, or the job may rotate to all class members. If possible, the school should provide an easily read stopwatch and some 6" X 6" time cards, perhaps made by the art class.

When you are timekeeper be sure that you thoroughly understand how to read the stopwatch. Each student's grade will depend somewhat on how well he or she stays within the time limits, so take your timing job seriously and be honest and accurate about the reading.

After the speaker has set up the visual aids (if they are used) and begins to speak, you should immediately start the stopwatch. Carefully noting the time, raise time cards that correspond with the minutes used. For example, if the speech is to be three to four minutes, when the speaker has spoken for two minutes, show the two minute card. When three minutes have elapsed, show the three minute card. Hold cards up visibly but not distractingly. It is not necessary to wave or shake the card to gain the speaker's attention. Hold the card up until the next card is to be shown. It is the speaker's responsibility to notice the time cards, and if there is good eye contact with the audience, this task will be easy.

After the speaker sits down, your teacher will ask for the time total. When you announce it, this will be noted on the speaker's outline. You should then set the stopwatch back to zero, making ready for the next speaker.

Appendix C

Short Plays For Teenage Students

(For publishers' addresses see Appendix D)

SINGLE COPIES

Antic Spring. Robert Hall. Comedy. 3m 3w. Samuel French. Teenagers go on a pantomimed picnic.

Boris and the Briefcase. Anderson and Sweeney. Comedy. 3m 3w. Eldridge Publishing Company. Boris' family, who are busy getting ready for a costume party, won't believe him when he tells them he has found a briefcase with stolen government documents. Then a spy appears looking for the papers. Comedy results as Boris uses laughing gas to capture the spy. Another funny Boris play is *Boris and the Spaceman*.

Case of the Glass Slipper. Anne Coulter Martens. Comedy. 6m 4w and extras for the jury. Found in *Junior High School One-Act Comedies*. Dramatic Publishing Company. This is a mock trial of Sammy Shooster, who is accused of stealing Cinderella's glass slippers. A funny spoof.

Cleanest Town in the West. Earl Dias. Comedy. 6m 3w. In Dias' *One-Act Plays for Teen-Agers*. Plays, Inc. A humorous melodrama in which the sheriff of Red Gulch attempts to discover who robbed the stagecoach. Two strangers in town are the suspects. One quotes Keats, Chaucer, and Shakespeare. The other tries to order a whiskey, but in the "cleanest town in the west" soda pop is the only drink served. A clever parody of Westerns.

Dear Departed. Stanley Houghton. Comedy. 3m 3w. Samuel French. A family is quarreling over their dead father's possessions when he walks in, very much alive.

Father Says No. Donald Payton. Comedy. 4m 4w. Heuer Publishing Company. Fourteen-year-old Candy and her girlfriend are on diets to impress the boys. But Father won't let any of the boys date Candy. Grandma takes things into her own hands and invites three boys over while Father is gone. When Father returns unexpectedly, the fun begins.

Finders Keepers. George Kelly. Drama. 1m 2w. Samuel French. A woman refuses to return some money in a purse she found, even when the loser is known. But the tables are turned, and the lady learns a lesson in a unique way.

Free Bus to the Shopping Center. Joseph Baldwin. Fantasy-Drama. 3m 4w. Heuer Publishers. While on a free bus ride to a "shopping center," the characters disclose their personalities, their disappointments in life, and their hopes for a new chance in this place that seems to offer each of them a dream world. Is it really a shopping center or something else?

The Ghost Wore White. LeRoma Greth. Mystery. 2m 6w. Heuer Publishing Company. When the Conwells move into an old house they have inherited, they find it is inhabited by a ghost. Then they decide to set a trap for the ghost. And they catch it—or do they?

Goodbye to the Lazy K. Robert Finch. Comedy. 5m 1w. Chilton Company (Chilton Way, Radnor, PA 19089). The cowboy hero decides to leave his girl and go to the city where he hopes to become rich. Parting is difficult and his friends make matters worse. Song and dance mixed with comedy.

I'm a Fool. Christopher Sergel from Sherwood Anderson's story. Comedy. 4m 4w. Dramatic Publishing Company. To impress an attractive girl, a boy who works at a race track pretends he is a wealthy heir. The girl promises to write him, but unhappily her letters will go to the person he is impersonating.

In the Suds. Barnard and Rose Hewitt. Comedy. 1m 3w. Baker's Plays. A henpecked husband gains revenge upon his shrewish wife when she falls into a tub of suds and can't get out.

Landslide for Shakespeare. Earl Dias. Comedy. 4m 4w and extras. In Dias' *One-Act Plays for Teen-Agers*. Plays, Inc. For three weeks Horace has been the continuing winner on a televisison quiz show with the category of Shakespeare. Brain appears to be winning over brawn as far as the girls are concerned until Horace shows that both intellects and athletes have much to offer the school and community.

The Little Man Who Wasn't There. Earl Dias. Science-fiction comedy. 2m 5w. In Dias' *One-Act Plays for Teen-Agers*. Plays, Inc. Paul has a girlfriend problem until Mr. Siggzy, a man from another planet, comes to help him solve it. But since Mr. Siggzy can only be seen by two members of the family, complications arise with humorous results.

The Long Christmas Dinner. Thornton Wilder. Drama. 5m 7w. Samuel French. The story spans a family's history of Christmas dinners by showing the changing times and American life in general.

Miss Herkimer's Missile. John Murray. Comedy. 6m 3w and extras. Eldridge Publishing Company. When a missile from another planet lands in Miss Herkimer's petunias, the Army and reporters descend upon her. Then Mr. Mudd, an interesting little man from outer space, introduces himself to Miss Herkimer, and they hit it off well, since both are lonely and single. Mr. Mudd makes himself invisible to the others who think Miss Herkimer is seeing things. A surprise ending awaits the gathered throng.

Quiet Please. Howard Buermann. Comedy. 3m 4w. Dramatists Play Service. Two brothers who carry on a feud of silence find themselves having to be hospitable to an unexpected overnight guest. Humor results as the feud collapses only to be renewed as they argue over what started the original quarrel.

Run, Robber, Run. Anderson and Sweeney. Comedy. 4m 8w. Eldridge Publishing Company. Two would-be robbers discover they are not in the right place, but instead they are in an exclusive girl's school. Hiding their identity, they pose as two men the headmistress is expecting. Mistaken identity and a guest television star add to the merry complications. A funny show.

Selma Goes Psychic. Ruth Kelsey. Comedy. 3m 3w. Dramatic Publishing Company. Found in *Junior High School One-Act Comedies*. Selma has all of her friends believing she can foretell the future. When her brother decides to "cure" her by masquerading as a girl, humorous complications arise.

Shock of His Life. Donald Payton. Farce. 3m 3w. Heuer Publishing Company. Thirteen-year-old Wilbur jots down telephone messages from the butcher and the doctor. When his father returns from a physical examination, he reads the messages and thinks they apply to him: "Heart about gone—be over at 7:30." Rollicking humor develops as Dad thinks he is about to die. Other equally funny "Wilbur" shows that play well in middle schools include *Foxy Grandma, Wilbur's Wild Night, Sure As You're Born, Wilbur Minds the Baby, Wilbur Is a Genius, Love Hits Wilbur, Wilbur's Honey Bea, Say Uncle*.

The Shoemaker's Wife. David Thompson from Hans Sach's play. Comedy. 2m 1w. Baker's Plays. A husband tries to test his wife's love for him by pretending to be dead. But the wife catches on and gives him a merry scare.

Sparkin'. E. P. Conkle. Comedy. 1m 3w. Samuel French. A timid young man calls on an equally timid girl in a small rural town. He beats around the bush until Grandma steps in.

Split Cherry Tree. From Jesse Stuart's story dramatized by Polachek. Drama. 3m 1w. Dramatic Publishing Company. With gun in hand, a father barges into a country school at the turn of the century to fight with the teacher. Instead, he learns the value of educating his son.

The Still Alarm. George Kaufman. Comedy. 5m. Samuel French. There is a fire in a hotel, but the men are exceedingly unconcerned about it; and there the fun lies.

The Stolen Prince. Dan Totheroh. Comedy. 9m 3w (or all men or all women). Samuel French. A prince is stolen in infancy and raised by a poor couple. Brought before the Emperor for punishment, the young prince's true identity is discovered. Done in Chinese tradition. *The Lost Princess* is the sequel to this play.

A Thing of Beauty. Maurice Berger. Drama. 4m 2w. Pioneer Drama Service. A man carries a piece of driftwood into a park, where it is observed by numerous people whose reactions display their true character and make an enlightening comment on life.

Tommy in the Dark. Joseph Carlton. 5m 5w. Baker's Plays. Not only is fourteen-year-old Tommy's baby-sitting business thwarted by his father, but the FBI becomes interested in an advertisement Tommy prints to boost his business. In the end Tommy collects a reward, the FBI captures a spy, and Tommy's father hopes for some peace and quiet.

Two Crooks and a Lady. Eugene Pillot. Drama. 3m 3w. Samuel French. Two thieves are about to steal an old woman's jewels, but she is cleverly able to get them fighting between themselves.

Ugly Duckling. A. A. Milne. Comedy. 4m 3w. Samuel French. A prince and a princess are betrothed by their families, sight unseen. Each family in turn arranges a "stand in" until the wedding, because of their "plain" children. But the real prince and princess fall in love.

Wildcat Willie Gets the Woolies. Ann Coulter Martens. Comedy. 3m 4w. Dramatic Publishing Company. Willie, aged thirteen, expects his aunt to send him a red canoe for his birthday. Instead he receives itchy red woolen flannels, which he is made to wear when his aunt visits. A rollicking misunderstanding develops that includes pet fleas, an Indian Chief, and a bewildered aunt. This play is one of six humorous comedies especially suited for young teenagers. Other titles are *Wildcat Willie, Wildcat Willie Carves the Turkey, Wildcat Willie Gets Girl Trouble, The Search for Wildcat McGillicuddy, and Wildcat Willie Gets Brain Fever*.

Without Strings. Robert Porter. Fantasy. 1m 1w. Pioneer Drama Service. Two puppets come to life to discuss problems and create a short love story.

COLLECTIONS OF SHORT PLAYS

Each of the following collections contains several plays suitable for teenagers. Select judiciously for your students, school, and community:

Bland, Joellen. *Stage Plays From the Classics*. Rev. ed. Plays, Inc. 1994.

Hamlett, Christina. *Humorous Plays for Teen-Agers*. Rev. ed. Plays, Inc. 1994.

Kamerman, Sylvia. ed. *The Big Book of Christmas Plays*. Rev. ed. Plays, Inc. 1991.

__________. *The Big Book of Comedies*. Plays, Inc. 1989.

__________. ed. *The Big Book of Dramatized Classics*. Plays, Inc. 1993.

__________. ed. *The Big Book of Large Cast Plays*. Plays, Inc. 1994.

__________. ed. *The Big Book of Skits*. Plays, Inc. 1996.

__________. ed. *Christmas Play Favorites for Young People*. Plays, Inc. 1994.

__________. ed. *Holiday Plays Round the Year*. Plays, Inc. 1992.

__________. ed. *Patriotic and Historical Plays for Young People*. Plays, Inc. 1992.

__________. ed. *Plays of Great Achievers*. Plays, Inc. 1992.

Murray, John. *Modern Monologues for Young People*. Plays, Inc. 1991.

__________. *Mystery Plays for Young Actors*. Plays, Inc. 1989.

Nolan, Paul. *Folk Tale Plays Round the World*. Plays, Inc. 1991.

Appendix D

Addresses Of Play Publishers And Sources For Recordings, Magazines, And Theatre Supplies

(SEND FOR EACH COMPANY'S FREE CURRENT CATALOGUES)

PUBLISHERS

CONTEST MATERIAL

Contemporary Drama Service
389 Elkton Drive
Colorado Springs, Colorado 80907

Encore Performance
P.O. box 692
Orem, Utah 84057
(also carry plays and musicals for children, family and youth)

Hansen Drama Shop
718 East 3900 South
Salt Lake City, Utah 84107

PLAYS

Baker's Plays
P.O. Box 699222
Quincy, Massachusettes 02269-9222

David McKay Company
201 East 50th Street
New York, New York 10022

Contemporary Drama Service
389 Elkton Drive
Colorado Springs, Colorado 80907
(Specializes in skits and sketches)

Dramatic Publishing Company
P.O. box 129
Woodstock, Illinois 60098

Dramatists Play Service
440 Park Avenue South
New York, New York 10016

I.E. Clark Publishers
P.O. Box 246
Shulenberg, Texas 78956
(Specializes in young adult theatre)

Pioneer Drama Service
P.O. Box 4267
Englewood, Colorado 80155

Play for Young Audiences
P.O. Box 4267
Englewood, Colorado 80155

Players Press
P.O. box 1132
Studio City, California 91614

Plays, Inc.
120 Boylston Street
Boston, Massachusetts 02116
(Specializes in play collections and radio scripts)

Samuel French
45 West 25th Street
New York, New York 10010

The Drama Book Shop
250 W. 40th Street
New York, New York 10018

RECORDINGS

Listening Library
P.O. Box L
Old Greenwich, Connecticut 06870
(Recordings, cassettes, tapes for classroom use)

Valentino, Inc.
500 Executive Boulevard
Elmsford, New York 10523
(Sound effects and mood music)

SPEECH AND DRAMA MAGAZINES

Plays
120 Boylston Street
Boston, Massachusetts 02116
(Designed for all levels through senior high with much material especially written for young teenagers. Several non-royalty plays published each month.)

The Communication Teacher
Speech Communication Assoc.
5105 Backlick Road, Suite E
Annandale, Virginia 22003
(Designed for all levels of education)

Dramatics Magazine
2343 Auburn Avenue
Cincinnati, OH 45219

THEATRE SUPPLIES

(FOR A MORE COMPLETE LIST OF SUPPLIERS LOCATED IN EACH STATE, CONSULT *THEATRE CRAFTS DIRECTORY*.)

Theatre Supply Houses

(These companies handle almost every item you will need for staging school plays—lights, makeup, stage hardware, fabrics, tools, celastic, special effects. Send for their informative catalogues.)

Alcone Company
Paramount Theatrical Supplies
5-49 49th Avenue
Long Island City, New York 11101

Norcosto
P.O. Box 22597
Minneapolis, Minnesota 55422

Olesen Company
1535 Ivar Avenue
Hollywood, California 90028

Theatre House
P.O. Box 2090
Covington, Kentucky 41012-2090

The following suppliers are specialists in the listed commodity. Upon request most of these companies will send free catalogues to teachers.

Costumes

Broadway Costumes
1100 West Cermak Road
Chicago, Illinois 60608

Costume Armour
P.O. Box 85, Mill Street
Cornwall, New York 12518

Dodger Costumes
21-07 41st Avenue
Long Island City, New York 11101

Rubies Costume
1 Rubie Plaza
Richmond Hill, New York 11418

The Costumer
1020-1030 Barrett St.
Schenectady, New York 12305

FABRIC FOR THE THEATRE

(For costumes, drapes, scenery)

Dazian Fabrics
423 West 55th Street
New York, New York 10019

Rose Brand Theatrical Fabrics
75 Ninth Avenue
New York, New York 10011

LIGHTING

Grand Stage Lighting
630 West Lake Street
Chicago, Illinois 60606-1465

Strand Century Lighting
18111 South Santa Fe Avenue
Rancho Dominguez, California 90221

The Great American Market
826 N. Cole Avenue
Hollywood, California 90038

LIGHTING GELATINS AND PLASTICS

(For colored lighting)

Lee Filters
2237 North Hollywood Way
Burbank, California 91506

Rosco Laboratories
52 Harbor View
Stanford, Connecticut 06902

MAKEUP

Ben Nye Makeup
11571 Santa Monica Blvd.
Los Angeles, California 90025

Bob Kelly Cosmetics
151 West 46th Street
New York, New York 10036

Stein Cosmetic Company
430 Broome Street
New York, New York 10013

SCENE PAINT

Gothic Color
P.O. Box 189
Glen Cove, New York 11542

Rosco Laboratories
52 Harbor View
Stanford, Connecticut

STAGE HARDWARE

J.R. Clancy, Inc.
7041 Interstate Island Road
Syracuse, New York 13209

Mutual Hardware
5-45 49th Avenue
Long Island City, New York 11101

Appendix E

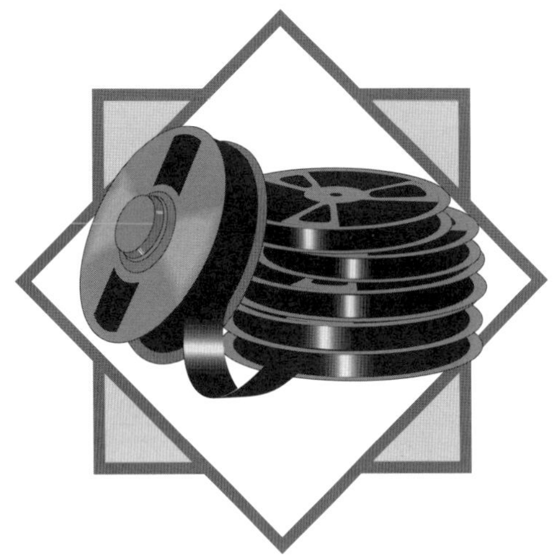

Videos, Films, And Filmstrips For Classroom Study

Many state universities offer rental videos and films on drama. For a list of teaching videos and films, see —

R.R. Bowker's *Educational Film Locater*.
A consortium of university film centers.
Excellent.

The Video Source Book.
National Video Clearing House.
Lists thousands of available videos.
Excellent.

The following companies rent professional films of plays:

Contemporary Films
24 Southwood Lawn Road
London N6 55F

Arthur Cantor Inc.
One West 72nd Street, Suite 66
New York, New York 10023

Audio Brandon Films
8400 Brookfield Avenue
Brookfield, Illinois 60513

The following companies offer videos on most aspects of speech communication, and theatre arts:

Coronet MTI Film & Video
4350 Equity Drive
Columbus, OH 43228

DVC, Inc.
7301 East 46th Street
Indianapolis, Indiana 46226

Educational Video Network
1401 19th Street
Huntsville, Texas 77340

Films for the Humanities
P.O. Box 2053
Princeton, New Jersey 08543

Insight Media
2162 Broadway
New York, New York 10024

Learning Seed
330 Telser Road
Lake Zurich, Illinois 60047

Olesen Company
1535 Ivar Avenue
Hollywood, California 90028

Theatre Arts Video Library
174 Andrew Avenue
Leucadia, California 92024

Appendix F

Book Lists for Students, Teachers, and School Libraries

THEATRE BOOKS

Acting

Barton, Robert. *Acting: Onstage and Off*. Wadsworth Publishing Co., 2002.

Crawford, Jerry, and Joan Snyder *Acting: In Person And In Style.* 5th ed. McGraw-Hill, 1994.

Delgado, Ramon. *Acting With Both Sides of Your Brain*. Holt, Rinehart and Winston, 1986.

Franklin, Miriam, and James Dixon. *Rehearsal: The Principles and Practices of Acting for the Stage*. 6th ed. Prentice-Hall, 1983.

Hagen, Uta, with Haskel Frankel. *Respect for Acting*. John Wiley & Sons, Inc., 1973.

McGaw, Charles. *Acting Is Believing*. 7th ed. Wadsworth Publishing Co., 1995.

Tanner, Fran. *Basic Drama Projects*. 7th ed. Perfection Learning, 2002.

Costumes

Arnold, Janet. *Patterns of Fashion*. 3rd ed. Drama Book Specialists, 1977.

Ingham, Rosemary, and Elizabeth Covey. *The Costumer's Handbook*. Prentice-Hall, 1980. Very practical.

Prisk, Berneice. *Stage Costume Handbook*. Greenwood, 1979.

Directing

Cohen, Robert, and John Harrop. *Creative Play Direction*. 2nd ed. Prentice-Hall, 1984.

Dean, Alexander, and Lawrence Carra. *Fundamentals of Play Directing*. 5th ed. Holt, Rinehart and Winston, 1989.

Kirk, John and Ralph Bellas. *The Art of Directing.* Ad Hoc Productions, 1990.

Sievers, David W. *Directing for the Theatre*. 3rd ed. WBC/McGraw-Hill, 1974.

History

Barranger, Milly. *Theatre Past and Present*. Wadsworth, 1984. Excellent presentation.

Brockett, Oscar. *History of the Theatre*. 8th ed. Allyn and Bacon, 1998. Thorough.

Improvisational Acting

Barker, Clive. *Theatre Games*. Methuen Drama, 1988.

Frost, Anthony, and Ralph Yarrow. *Improvisation in Drama*. Palgrave Macmillan, 1990.

Hodgson, John, and Ernst Richards. *Improvisation*. Grove, 1987.

Polsky, Milton. *Let's Improvise*. University Press of America, 1989.

Spolin, Viola. *Theatre Games for the Classroom*. Northwestern University Press, 1986. Good approach to improvisations.

Lighting

Gillette, Michael. *Designing With Light.* 3rd ed. McGraw-Hill, 1997.

Parker, Oren, and Harvey Smith. *Scene Design and Stage Lighting.* 7th ed. International Thompson Publishing, 1996. Thorough and easy to understand.

Pilbrow, Richard. *Stage Lighting*. Applause Theatre Books, 1990.

Makeup

Baygan, Lee. *Makeup for Theatre, Film, and Television*. Drama Books, 1992.

Buchman, Herman. *Stage Makeup*. 2nd ed. Watson-Guptill, 1989.

Corson, Richard. *Stage Makeup*. 9th ed. Allyn & Bacon, 2000. Excellent material and illustrations.

Movement

King, Nancy. *Movement Approach to Acting*. Prentice-Hall, 1981.

Sabatine, Jean, with David Hodge. *The Actor's Image: Movement Training for Stage and Screen*. Simon & Schuster, 1983.

Play Production

Gillette, Michael. *Theatrical Design and Production*. 4th ed. McGraw-Hill, 1999.

Stern, Lawrence. *Stage Management*. 7th ed. Allyn & Bacon, 2001.

Kelly, Thomas. *A Backstage Guide To Stage Management*. Back Stage Books, 1999.

Plays

Coleman, Wim. *Nine Muses: Modern Plays from Classic Myths.* 1st ed. Perfection Learning Corporation, 2001.

PLC editors. *Drama for Reading & Performance: Collections One and Two*. 1st ed. Perfection Learning Corporation, 2001.

PLC editors. *Page to Stage: Plays from Classic Literature*. 1st ed. Perfection Learning Corporation, 2002.

Scenery

Buerki, F. A. *Stagecraft for Non Professionals*. 4th ed. University of Wisconsin Press, 1982.

Gillette, Arnold, and Michael Gillette. *Stage Scenery, Its Construction and Rigging*. 4th ed. Harper and Row, 1989.

Sporre, Dennis, and Robert Burroughs. *Scene Design in Theatre*. Prentice-Hall, 1990.

SPEECH BOOKS

Debate

Barnes, R. Eric. *Philosophy in Practice: Understanding Value Debate*. 1st ed. Perfection Learning, 1996.

Davis, Bill. *Fool For Forensics.* 1st ed. Perfection Learning, 1997.

Freeley, Austin. *Argumentation and Debate*. 10th ed. Wadsworth, 1999.

Hensley, Dana, and Diana Carlin. *Mastering Competitive Debate*. 6th ed. Perfection Learning, 2001.

Wiese, Jeffrey. *Lincoln—Douglas Debate*. 2nd ed. Perfection Learning, 2000.

Discussion

Brilhart, John. *Effective Group Discussion.* 7th ed. Wadsworth, 1990.

Beebe, Steven and John Masterson. *Communicationg In Small Groups.* 7th ed. Allyn & Bacon, 2002.

Jensen, Arthur and Joseph Chilberg. *Small Group Communication.* Wadsworth, 1991.

GENERAL SPEECH

Bradley, Bert. *Fundamentals of Speech Communication*. 5th ed. William Brown, 1988.

Carlile, Clark and Dana Hensley. *38 Basic Speech Experiences*. 10th ed. Perfection Learning, 1999. Projects for giving all types of speeches.

DeVito, Joseph. *Elements of Public Speaking.* Back Stage Books, 1996.

Gronbeck, Bruce, *et al. Principles and Types of Speech Communication*. Addison Wesley Publishing Co., 1998.

Radio and Television

Armer, Alan. *Directing Television and Film*. 2nd ed. Wadsworth, 1991.

Burrows, Thomas, *et al. Television Production*. 4th ed. William Brown, 1988.

Hyde, Stuart. *Television and Radio Announcing*. 5th ed. Houghton-Mifflin, 1986.

O'Donnell, Lewis, *et al. Modern Radio Productions*. 3rd ed. Wadsworth, 1993.

Voice and Articulation

Crannel, Kenneth. *Voice and Articulation.* 4th ed. Wadsworth, 1999.

Eisenson, Jon. *Voice and Diction*. 7th ed. Allyn & Bacon, 1996.

King, Roibert, and Eleanor DiMichael. *Voice and Diction Handbook*. Warland, 1991.

Seidler, Ann, and Doris Bianchi. *Voice and Diction Fitness*. Harper Collins, 1989.

INTERPRETATION BOOKS

Choral Reading

Provenmire, E. Kingsley. *Choral Speaking and the Verse Choir*. A. S. Barnes, 1975.

Oral Interpretatlon

Gamble, Teri, and Michael Gamble. *Literature Alive*. 2nd ed. National Textbook Company, 1994.

Lee, Charlotte, and Timothy Gura. *Oral Interpretation*. 10th ed. Houghton-Mifflin, 2001.

Yordon, Judy. *Roles in Interpretation*. 5th ed. McGraw-Hill, 2001.

Readers Theatre

Coger, Leslie, and Melvin White. *Readers Theatre Handbook*. 3rd ed. Scott, Foresman, 1982.

Tanner, Fran. *Readers Theatre Fundamentals*. 2nd ed. Perfection Learning, 1996.

Storytelling

Baker, Augusta. *Storytelling: Art and Technique*. Bunker-Greenwood, 1996.

Sawyer, Ruth. *The Way of the Storyteller*. Rev. ed. Penguin, 1977.

the INDEX

H

I

J

K

L

M

N

S

T

Illustration and Photo credits:

(This page constitutes a continuation of the copyright page.)

Illustration credits *(All illustrations Copyright © 1996 Perfection Learning)*

Artist: **Michèle M. Jackson**
Observation Puzzle, p.16
Knock Knock, p.57
Puppet stage illustrations, p.64
Shhh...Listen, p.141
Mixed Bag, p.199
A Telling Time, p.250
Altogether In Parts, p.260
Theatre Of The Mind, p.270
Readers Theatre placement illustrations, p.275
Bending Ears, p.280

Artist: **Forest A. Newlin**
Hand signals, p.236

Artist: **Diana Persell**
Distinguish the Difference, p.24
Evolving Emotions, p.75

Artist: **Janis Swanson**
Many Meanings, p.72
Stir Up A Mood, p.255

Photo credits *(All photos Copyright © 1996 Perfection Learning)*

Photgraphers: **Michael Meakins**
Andrew Wroth

Models: Highland Park H.S. of Topeka, KS
Special thanks to H.P.H.S. teachers **Ms. Rebecca Olivas** and **Mr. Gregg Ratzloff**
Students: **Lisa Ables, Felicha Albright, Anna Arasmith, Kevin Brown, Sarah Corley, Angela Davis, Scott Escalante, Jessica Lozada, Gerald Meakins, Michael Meakins, Amy Ogle, Sam Olliso, Steve Pillay, Cecil Simpson, Dustin Thompson.**

Proofing

Beverly Axmann, Paul Douglas Billings, Brenda Catt

Clip Art

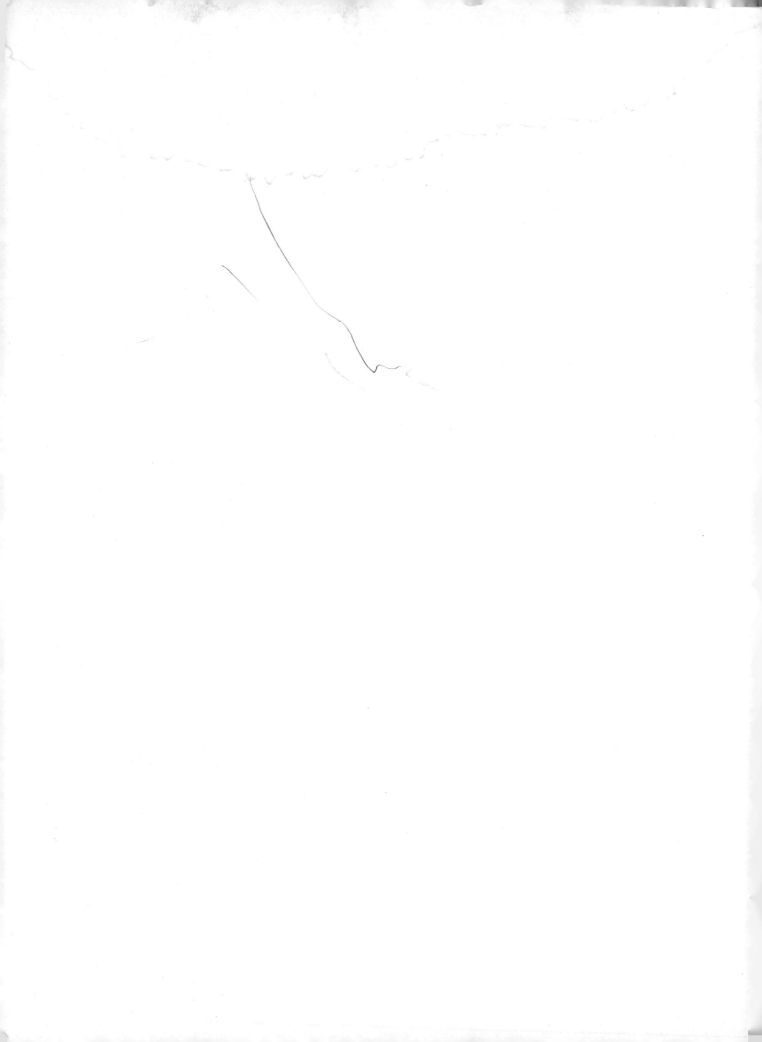